About The Book By The Editor

I have been in the Pastorate for 50 years and have put together a research library of several thousand books that have helped me in my efforts to "rightly divide the truth." At this point in my life I need to begin to pare down my library. I have several shelves in my library that contain books that have been very helpful to me throughout my ministry. One of my favorite books was written by Dr. Stephen Swihart. The original title was *The Victor Bible Sourcebook* which was published in 1977. I contacted the publisher and they said they no longer owned the rights to the book. I wrote to the author and asked if I could publish the book. He wrote back saying, "you may do as you wish with my book." Because it was such a help to me as a young man I am publishing the book under the title **The Bible Source Book**.

About The Author

Steve Swihart graduated from Ashland Theological Seminary with a Master of Divinity and a Doctor of Ministry degree. For twenty years he served as a pastor, and for nine years was both a graduate dean and a Bible professor. For the past fifteen years, Steve has worked from his home as a writer, mentor and guest speaker.

The Bible Sourcebook

By Stephen D. Swihart, D.Min.
Edited by David L. Brown, Ph.D.

Unless otherwise noted, Scripture quotations are from the:

King James Version of the Bible

(Editor's note: There are a few places other versions are quoted. Please refer to your King James Bible.)

This book is reprinted by permission of the author and the editor. Please see the previous pages.

ISBN: 978-1-7344467-7-7

No part of this work may be reproduced without the expressed consent of the publisher except for brief quotes, whether by electronic, photocopying, recording, or information storage and retrieval systems.

Published by
The Old Paths Publications
www.theoldpathspublications.com
TOP@theoldpathspublications.com
April 2020

Contents

Part 1 How to Use the Bible   7
1. Personal Qualifications   9
2. The Importance of Tools   12
3. Various Methods of Bible Study   16
4. A Reading Plan   20
5. Where to Turn in Your Bible   27
6. The Roman Road   29
7. Buying a New Bible   31

Part 2 Basic Bible Doctrine   33
8. The Scriptures   35
9. God   58
10. Jesus Christ   70
11. The Holy Spirit   91
12. Man   99
13. Sin   111
14. Salvation   114
15. Christian Growth and Maturity   124
16. Prayer, Faith, and Fasting   135
17. The Church   152
18. Angels   161
19. Prophecy   176

Part 3 Glossary and Concordance   199
20. Concise Bible Dictionary   200
21. An Abbreviated Topical Concordance   224

Part 1

How to Use the Bible

1 | Personal Qualifications

Since the Bible is not an open book to everyone, not all readers, as intelligent as they may be, really understand it. To some people the Scriptures are mere words, but to others these words burst with life. What accounts for the difference?

Upward Qualifications

Conversion: To begin, the Bible is unique because we cannot really understand its contents until we first know its Author, God. Only through a personal acknowledgment of our sinful state and an absolute reliance upon Jesus Christ's work on Calvary can we be in a position to genuinely understand this divine message. Conversion is necessary in order to read the Bible with profit.

Spirituality: Even believers often have difficulty reading the Scriptures fruitfully. Why is this so, seeing they have been converted? The answer is really quite simple. The words of God are not like the words of men. Men's words can be understood with a man's mind, but God's words require a spiritual mind in order to grasp them. That is, a believer must read with a deep sensitivity to the voice of the Spirit (John 16:13; 1 John 2:20, 27). The believer must be on intimate talking terms with God Himself before he can expect to hear His voice and understand as he reads the Word of God.

Maturity: There are two types of words in the Scriptures—milk words (1 Peter 1:23) and meat words (Heb. 5:11—6:2). The milk words are readily understood; the meat words, however, require a level of spiritual development on the part of the believer. Not every verse of the Bible and not every book of the Bible is as simple as every other verse or book, as in any study. In math, for instance, addition and subtraction are not difficult; but calculus is another story. It takes time to be able to understand and use calculus. In like manner, only growth and maturity will bring an understanding and enjoyment of certain portions of God's Word.

Outward Qualifications

God always measures our *rightness* with Him by our *rightness* with people. In other words, in order to grasp the Bible's intended meaning, we must have right relationships—both vertically and horizontally. No Christian can rightly divide God's Word who harbors sin in his heart toward his fellow man—saved or lost. The sins of resentment, bitterness, unforgiveness, impatience, negativism, temper, unfaithfulness, and insubordination automatically close the door to reading God's Book (see Matt. 5:23-24).

Inward Qualifications

In a real sense both the "upward" and "outward" qualifications may be said to be inward qualifications. But we have another specific matter in view—namely the proper attitude for effective Bible reading and study. It is imperative that we approach God's Word with right motives.

Wrong Motives: Some persons search the Scriptures in a quest for knowledge, information, and facts. They zealously pursue intellectual data. Others delve into God's Word because it is expected of them to do so. They merely plunge into the Bible out of obligation or guilt or pressure. Still others look to God's Word because of a Sunday School lesson they must teach or a sermon they must preach. These are all wrong motives.

Right Motives: A true searching of the Scriptures has a very personal base: *obedience to God.* The psalmist gives us the right manner for approaching the Scriptures. "Thy Word have I hid in my heart, that I might not sin against Thee" (119:11).

Ezra, too, gives us an illustration of a right way to approach God's Word. "Ezra had prepared his heart [this constitutes the upward and outward qualifications] to seek the law of the Lord, and to do it [this is the inward qualification], and to teach in Israel statutes and ordinances" (Ezra 7:10). Note carefully that Ezra prepared his heart to *practice* God's Word, not to teach it (as is so often done today). Right motives beget right priorities—obedience to God's Word always precedes teaching God's will.

Joshua, too, knew this lesson in correct motives. Notice:

> Only be strong and very courageous; be careful to do according to all the law which Moses My servant commanded you; do not turn from it to the right or to the left, so that you may have success wherever you go. This book of the law shall not depart from your mouth, but you shall meditate on it day and night, so that you may be careful to do according to all that is written in it; for then you will make your way prosperous, and then you will have success (Joshua 1:7-8, NASB).

Joshua was not to seek prosperity. He was to meditate upon and obey God's words. Prosperity and success would follow, but only after the motives were properly aligned. How desperately this lesson needs to be learned by many of our so-called teachers today!

2 | The Importance of Tools

Everyone needs tools. A housewife needs them for cleaning and a plumber needs tools for his trade. A student's tools are his books. Successful Bible reading and study require certain basic aids and the person who doesn't use them will have great difficulty in anchoring himself in the foundational truths or in scaling the utmost heights.

The Dictionary: Here is a simple truth, but one which so many seem to miss—*You can't understand God's message if you don't know the meaning of the words He uses!* For instance, these words appear in the King James Bible:
    Abaddon, Ablution, Adjure, Anathema, Apothecary, Appertained, Artificer, Asp, Asswage, Austere, Averse, Aul, Axletrees, Bastards, Beeves, Bulwarks, Buttocks, Cankered, Carbuncles, Chafed, Chalcedony, Chamois, Chastise, Chide, Churl, Cieled, Circumspect, Clave, Clemency, Comeliness, and Cormorant.

Can you define all of them? If you can't, then you are normal. You need a dictionary, but not just any dictionary will do. Put simply, you need a *Bible dictionary*. The one in chapter 20 of this book will do for the milk reader, but in a very short time you will want (and need) a more substantial volume. Recommended: *The New Bible Dictionary*, J. D. Douglas, ed. (Eerdmans, 1962) and *The Zondervan Pictorial Bible Dictionary*, M. Tenney, ed. (Zondervan, 1969).

The Concordance: There are two types of concordances—the *alphabetical* concordance and the *topical* concordance. The former will list *words* and tell you their location in the Bible. The latter will list Bible *concepts* and tell you their scriptural address. Both are indispensable tools for the Bible reader. We have included a 343-word topical concordance in this volume. Eventually, however, you should consider more complete publications, for example, *The New Compact Topical Bible* (Zondervan, 1972), or *The New Topical Textbook* (Revell, 1970). For an alphabetical concordance, you will want either *Strong's Exhaustive Concordance* (Abingdon, 1958) or *Young's Analytical Concordance* (Eerdmans, 1955).

Basic Study Aids: Solomon said "Of making many books there is no end" (Eccl. 12:12). This can be very helpful, but it can also be rather confusing. Which books ought *you* to buy? Below is a topical index of recommended books for Christians. Good Christian literature is an eternal investment.

STUDY
Search the Scriptures (InterVarsity, rev. ed.); *How to Search the Scriptures,* Lloyd Perry and R. Culver (Baker, 1967); *Effective Bible Study,* H. Vos (Zondervan, 1956).

BASIC DOCTRINES
Bible Doctrines, Mark Cambron (Zondervan, 1954); *Lectures in Systematic Theology,* H. C. Thiessen (Eerdmans, 1949); *Summary of Christian Doctrine,* L. Berkhof (Eerdmans, 1939).

BIBLE HELPS
Strong's Exhaustive Concordance (Abingdon, 1958); *The New Compact Topical Bible,* Gary C. Wharton, ed. (Zondervan, 1972); *Treasury of Scripture Knowledge* (Revell, 1973); *The New Compact Bible Dictionary,* T. A. Bryant, editor (Zondervan, 1967).

CHRISTIAN GROWTH
Godliness Through Discipline, J. E. Adams (Presbyterian & Re-

formed); *Calvary Road,* Roy Hession (Christian Literature Crusade, 1964); *The Spiritual Man,* W. Nee (Christian Fellowship Publishers); *Sit, Walk, Stand* and *The Normal Christian Worker,* W. Nee (Christian Literature Crusade).

CHURCH HISTORY

A History of the Christian Church, W. Walker (Charles Scribner's Sons, 1970); *History of Christian Education,* C. B. Eavey (Moody Press, 1964); *The New International Dictionary of the Christian Church,* J. D. Douglas, ed. (Zondervan); *Who Was Who In Church History,* E. Moyer (A Pivot Family Reader).

CHURCH RENEWAL

Sharpening the Focus of the Church, Gene Getz (Moody Press, 1974); *Call to Discipleship,* Juan C. Ortiz (Logos); *Disciple,* J. C. Ortiz (Creation House); *Christ in Session,* Bob Mumford (Box 22341, Ft. Lauderdale, Florida 33315); *Making Disciples,* Charles Simpson (New Wine Magazine, P.O. Box 22888, Ft. Lauderdale, Fla. 33315).

COUNSELING

Competent to Counsel, J. E. Adams (Presbyterian and Reformed); *The Christian Counselor's Manual,* J. E. Adams (Baker, 1974); *Encyclopedia of Psychological Problems,* C. M. Narramore (Zondervan, 1966).

FAMILY LIFE

Christian Living in the Home, J. E. Adams (Presbyterian and Reformed); *The Christian Family,* L. Christenson (Bethany, 1970); *Dare to Discipline,* J. Dobson (Regal, 1972); *Heaven Help the Home,* Howard G. Hendricks (Victor Books, 1973); *How to Make Your Marriage Exciting,* Charles & Frances Hunter (Regal, 1972); *A Handbook to Marriage,* T. Bovet (Doubleday, 1969); *The Family That Makes It* (Victor Books, 1971).

NEW TESTAMENT COMMENTARY SERIES

Everyman's Bible Commentary (Moody Press; may be purchased individually); *Tyndale New Testament Commentaries* (Tyndale; purchased individually); *New Testament Commentary Series,* W. Hendriksen (incomplete—Baker, purchased individually); *The New International Commentary on the New Testament* (incomplete—purchased individually).

NEW TESTAMENT GREEK: BIBLE-BOOK STUDIES IN ENGLISH
Word Studies in the Greek New Testament, K. S. Wuest (Eerdmans); *Word Pictures in the New Testament,* A. T. Robertson (Broadman, 1943); *Word Studies in the New Testament,* M. Vincent (Eerdmans, 1957).

OLD TESTAMENT COMMENTARIES
Old Testament Commentaries, C. F. Keil & F. Delitzsch (Eerdmans, 1971); *Barnes' Notes on the Old Tesament,* A. Barnes (Baker).

ORIGINAL LANGUAGE WORD STUDIES IN ENGLISH
An Expository Dictionary of New Testament Words, W. E. Vine (Revell); *The New Bible Dictionary,* J. D. Douglas, ed. (Eerdmans, 1962); *Synonyms of the Old Testament,* R. B. Girdlestone (Eerdmans, 1948); *New Testament Words,* W. Barclay (Westminster, 1974).

BIBLE SURVEYS
The Bible—Book by Book, G. C. Luck (Moody Press, 1955); *Explore the Book,* J. S. Baxter (Zondervan); *Eerdman's Handbook to the Bible,* David Alexander and Patricia Alexander (Eerdmans, 1973); *Unger's Bible Handbook,* M. F. Unger (Moody Press, 1966); *Halley's Bible Handbook,* H. H. Halley (Zondervan, 1959).

3 | Various Methods of Bible Study

Hearing

A vital source of Bible knowledge is hearing God's Word proclaimed from the pulpit and in Sunday School. Daily instruction during the week is available from several sources, for instance, television, radio, records, tapes, conventions, conferences, seminars, evening classes, and community Bible studies. Make the most of such opportunities to be hearers daily.

Reading

The next resource for fruitful Bible study is reading the Scriptures. How dreadfully weak are believers at reading! God requires more of Christians than being spoon-fed by teachers. We must learn to feed ourselves! There is no shortcut method for reaping God's harvest. You must *hear* (passive participation in God's Word), and you must *read* (active participation in God's Word). Here are four profitable suggestions for your Bible reading:

1. *Use a translation you can understand,* and one you can trust for accuracy. The following Bibles are well-qualified: *New American Standard Bible, The Amplified Bible,* and *New International Version.*

2. *Be systematic.* Don't jump around in your reading. Be deliberate. Read through a book or a series of books.

3. *Take notes.* Jot down discoveries as you read along, and then file them topically in a larger file system.

4. *Be consistent.* Read the Bible daily, even if it is only for a few minutes.

Study

There is a difference, obviously, between merely reading the Bible and studying it. In reading the Scriptures, we remove the surface gems, but in studying we drill for the deeper nuggets. Christians ought to be familiar with both experiences. There are several ways you can study your Bible:

Surveying the Bible: This is not a book-by-book survey of the Scriptures. It is much more. When the whole Bible is surveyed, the intent is to discover main themes and key structures which permeate the whole Bible. For example, the unifying principle of the covenants, the administrative dealings of God in dispensations, and the sacrificial motifs of salvation through Jesus Christ are foundational to a proper grasp of the scriptural message. In other words, in studying the Word of God it is wise to start with the telescopic (the all-embracing, the general, the simple) and work your way down to the microscopic (the specific and complex). Several good books along this vein are: *The Divine Covenants* by A. W. Pink (Baker, 1973); *The Unfolding Drama of Redemption* by W. Scroggie (Zondervan, 1970); *The Structure of Biblical Authority* by M. Kline (Eerdmans, 1972); and *The Books and the Parchments* by F. F. Bruce (Revell, rev. ed.).

Surveying Bible Books: The purpose here is to learn each book's central message, its various supporting themes, its natural divisions, its author, its recipients, its date, etc. In brief, the *who, what, where, when, why,* and *how* are learned in this form of study. In penetrating a book, we also need to find personal applications: doctrines to learn, errors to avoid, obligations to perform, examples to follow, promises to experience, and prayers to repeat. Some good Bible surveys are listed in chapter 2.

Biblical Theology: This is the study of a topic as it is revealed progressively throughout the Scriptures. For example, the theme of sacrifices has its origins in Genesis 3:21. The culmination of this theme appears in the book of Revelation. Between these two points is a mounting record of data. Tracing this theme is the specialized study of biblical theology. Another term for this discipline is *contextual studies,* which is a study of a topic in its specific historical and theological context so that we discover God's will for a specific point in time. Several profitable books in this area are: *The Theology of the Older Testament* by J. B. Payne (Zondervan, 1962) and *A Theology of the New Testament* by G. E. Ladd (Eerdmans, 1974).

Systematic Theology: While biblical theology works historically or progressively, systematic theology works topically and panoramically. In the former method the emphasis is placed on how a doctrine evolves. In the latter, the focus is placed on the whole teaching of Scripture as it logically presents itself. If you turned to Part II: Basic Bible Doctrines, you would find a clear example of systematic theology. For instance, under the heading "Holy Spirit" are seven major divisions. These seven points express the major truths regarding the person and work of the Holy Spirit throughout the Bible. For recommended reading, see chapter 2, under the heading: "Basic Doctrines."

Memorizing
The only way to hide God's Word in your heart is to memorize it. Jesus memorized the Scriptures (Matt. 4:1-10); how much more must we do so (Col. 3:16).

Meditating
How to fulfill the biblical injunction to renew their minds often perplexes Christians, but the answer comes in meditating on the Word of God (Rom. 12:1-2; Eph. 4:17-24; Col. 3:10). Andrew Murray brilliantly described meditation as "Holding the Word of God in your heart until it has affected every phase of your life." We must meditate, but first we must put something into our minds to

meditate upon! Therefore, let us hear God's Word; let us read God's Word; let us study God's Word; let us memorize God's Word; and let us meditate on it. Only in this process do the Scriptures become genuinely profitable to us!

4 | A Reading Plan

The order in which this schedule lists the books is not how they occur in the Bible. It is a chronological arrangement. The poetic and prophetic books of the Old Testament are inserted in the historical books at about the point in the narrative where they are thought to have been written. In the same way, the epistles of the New Testament are inserted in the narrative of the book of Acts. While there is some difference of opinion as to details, the chronological arrangement used here is acceptable to many leading conservative Bible scholars.

JANUARY

1/Genesis 1—2
2/Genesis 3—5
3/Genesis 6—9
4/Genesis 10—11
5/Genesis 12—15
6/Genesis 16—19
7/Genesis 20—22
8/Genesis 23—26
9/Genesis 27—29
10/Genesis 30—32
11/Genesis 33—36
12/Genesis 37—39
13/Genesis 40—42
14/Genesis 43—46
15/Genesis 47—50
16/Job 1—4
17/Job 5—7
18/Job 8—10
19/Job 11—13
20/Job 14—17
21/Job 18—20
22/Job 21—24
23/Job 25—27
24/Job 28—31
25/Job 32—34
26/Job 35—37

27/Job 38—42
28/Exodus 1—4
29/Exodus 5—7

30/Exodus 8—10
31/Exodus 11—13

FEBRUARY
1/Exodus 14—17
2/Exodus 18—20
3/Exodus 21—24
4/Exodus 25—27
5/Exodus 28—31
6/Exodus 32—34
7/Exodus 35—37
8/Exodus 38—40
9/Leviticus 1—4
10/Leviticus 5—7
11/Leviticus 8—10
12/Leviticus 11—13
13/Leviticus 14—16
14/Leviticus 17—19
15/Leviticus 20—23
16/Leviticus 24—27
17/Numbers 1—3
18/Numbers 4—6
19/Numbers 7—10
20/Numbers 11—14
21/Numbers 15—17
22/Numbers 18—20
23/Numbers 21—24
24/Numbers 25—27
25/Numbers 28—30
26/Numbers 31—33
27/Numbers 34—36
28/Deuteronomy 1—3

MARCH
1/Deuteronomy 4—6
2/Deuteronomy 7—9
3/Deuteronomy 10—12
4/Deuteronomy 13—16
5/Deuteronomy 17—19
6/Deuteronomy 20—22
7/Deuteronomy 23—25
8/Deuteronomy 26—28
9/Deuteronomy 29—31
10/Deuteronomy 32—34
11/Joshua 1—3
12/Joshua 4—6
13/Joshua 7—9
14/Joshua 10—12
15/Joshua 13—15
16/Joshua 16—18
17/Joshua 19—21
18/Joshua 22—24
19/Judges 1—4
20/Judges 5—8
21/Judges 9—12
22/Judges 13—15
23/Judges 16—18
24/Judges 19—21
25/Ruth 1—4
26/1 Samuel 1—3
27/1 Samuel 4—7
28/1 Samuel 8—10
29/1 Samuel 11—13
30/1 Samuel 14—16
31/1 Samuel 17—20

APRIL

1/1 Samuel 21—24
2/1 Samuel 25—28
3/1 Samuel 29—31
4/2 Samuel 1—4
5/2 Samuel 5—8
6/2 Samuel 9—12
7/2 Samuel 13—15
8/2 Samuel 16—18
9/2 Samuel 19—21
10/2 Samuel 22—24
11/Psalms 1—3
12/Psalms 4—6
13/Psalms 7—9
14/Psalms 10—12
15/Psalms 13—15
16/Psalms 16—18
17/Psalms 19—21
18/Psalms 22—24
19/Psalms 25—27
20/Psalms 28—30
21/Psalms 31—33
22/Psalms 34—36
23/Psalms 37—39
24/Psalms 40—42
25/Psalms 43—45
26/Psalms 46—48
27/Psalms 49—51
28/Psalms 52—54
29/Psalms 55—57
30/Psalms 58—60

MAY

1/Psalms 61—63
2/Psalms 64—66
3/Psalms 67—69
4/Psalms 70—72
5/Psalms 73—75
6/Psalms 76—78
7/Psalms 79—81
8/Psalms 82—84
9/Psalms 85—87
10/Psalms 88—90
11/Psalms 91—93
12/Psalms 94—96
13/Psalms 97—99
14/Psalms 100—102
15/Psalms 103—105
16/Psalms 106—108
17/Psalms 109—111
18/Psalms 112—114
19/Psalms 115—118
20/Psalm 119
21/Psalms 120—123
22/Psalms 124—126
23/Psalms 127—129
24/Psalms 130—132
25/Psalms 133—135
26/Psalms 136—138
27/Psalms 139—141
28/Psalms 142—144
29/Psalms 145—147
30/Psalms 148—150
31/1 Kings 1—4

JUNE
1/Proverbs 1—3
2/Proverbs 4—7
3/Proverbs 8—11
4/Proverbs 12—14
5/Proverbs 15—18
6/Proverbs 19—21
7/Proverbs 22—24
8/Proverbs 25—28
9/Proverbs 29—31
10/Ecclesiastes 1—3
11/Ecclesiastes 4—6
12/Ecclesiastes 7—9
13/Ecclesiastes 10—12
14/Songs 1—4
15/Songs 5—8
16/1 Kings 5—7
17/1 Kings 8—10
18/1 Kings 11—13
19/1 Kings 14—16
20/1 Kings 17—19
21/1 Kings 20—22
22/2 Kings 1—3
23/2 Kings 4—6
24/2 Kings 7—10
25/2 Kings 11—14:20
26/Joel 1—3
27/2 Kings 14:21-25
    Jonah 1—4
28/2 Kings 14:26-29
    Amos 1—3
29/Amos 4—6
30/Amos 7—9

JULY
1/2 Kings 15—17
2/Hosea 1—4
3/Hosea 5—7
4/Hosea 8—10
5/Hosea 11—14
6/2 Kings 18—19
7/Isaiah 1—3
8/Isaiah 4—6
9/Isaiah 7—9
10/Isaiah 10—12
11/Isaiah 13—15
12/Isaiah 16—18
13/Isaiah 19—21
14/Isaiah 22—24
15/Isaiah 25—27
16/Isaiah 28—30
17/Isaiah 31—33
18/Isaiah 34—36
19/Isaiah 37—39
20/Isaiah 40—42
21/Isaiah 43—45
22/Isaiah 46—48
23/Isaiah 49—51
24/Isaiah 52—54
25/Isaiah 55—57
26/Isaiah 58—60
27/Isaiah 61—63
28/Isaiah 64—66
29/Micah 1—4
30/Micah 5—7
31/Nahum 1—3

AUGUST

1/2 Kings 20—21
2/Zephaniah 1—3
3/Habakkuk 1—3
4/2 Kings 22—25
5/Obadiah
 Jeremiah 1—2
6/Jeremiah 3—5
7/Jeremiah 6—8
8/Jeremiah 9—12
9/Jeremiah 13—16
10/Jeremiah 17—20
11/Jeremiah 21—23
12/Jeremiah 24—26
13/Jeremiah 27—29
14/Jeremiah 30—32
15/Jeremiah 33—36
16/Jeremiah 37—39
17/Jeremiah 40—42
18/Jeremiah 43—46
19/Jeremiah 47—49
20/Jeremiah 50—52
21/Lamentations 1—5
22/1 Chronicles 1—3
23/1 Chronicles 4—6
24/1 Chronicles 7—9
25/1 Chronicles 10—13
26/1 Chronicles 14—16
27/1 Chronicles 17—19
28/1 Chronicles 20—23
29/1 Chronicles 24—26
30/1 Chronicles 27—29
31/2 Chronicles 1—3

SEPTEMBER

1/2 Chronicles 4—6
2/2 Chronicles 7—9
3/2 Chronicles 10—13
4/2 Chronicles 14—16
5/2 Chronicles 17—19
6/2 Chronicles 20—22
7/2 Chronicles 23—25
8/2 Chronicles 26—29
9/2 Chronicles 30—32
10/2 Chronicles 33—36
11/Ezekiel 1—3
12/Ezekiel 4—7
13/Ezekiel 8—11
14/Ezekiel 12—14
15/Ezekiel 15—18
16/Ezekiel 19—21
17/Ezekiel 22—24
18/Ezekiel 25—27
19/Ezekiel 28—30
20/Ezekiel 31—33
21/Ezekiel 34—36
22/Ezekiel 37—39
23/Ezekiel 40—42
24/Ezekiel 43—45
25/Ezekiel 46—48
26/Daniel 1—3
27/Daniel 4—6
28/Daniel 7—9
29/Daniel 10—12
30/Esther 1—3

A READING PLAN / 25

OCTOBER
1/Esther 4—7
2/Esther 8—10
3/Ezra 1—4
4/Haggai 1—2
   Zechariah 1—2
5/Zechariah 3—6
6/Zechariah 7—10
7/Zechariah 11—14
8/Ezra 5—7
9/Ezra 8—10
10/Nehemiah 1—3
11/Nehemiah 4—6
12/Nehemiah 7—9
13/Nehemiah 10—13
14/Malachi 1—4
15/Matthew 1—4
16/Matthew 5—7
17/Matthew 8—11
18/Matthew 12—15
19/Matthew 16—19
20/Matthew 20—22
21/Matthew 23—25
22/Matthew 26—28
23/Mark 1—3
24/Mark 4—6
25/Mark 7—10
26/Mark 11—13
27/Mark 14—16
28/Luke 1—3
29/Luke 4—6
30/Luke 7—9
31/Luke 10—13

NOVEMBER
1/Luke 14—17
2/Luke 18—21
3/Luke 22—24
4/John 1—3
5/John 4—6
6/John 7—10
7/John 11—13
8/John 14—17
9/John 18—21
10/Acts 1—2
11/Acts 3—5
12/Acts 6—9
13/Acts 10—12
14/Acts 13—14
15/James 1—2
16/James 3—5
17/Galatians 1—3
18/Galatians 4—6
19/Acts 15—18:11
20/1 Thessalonians 1—5
21/2 Thessalonians 1—3
   Acts 18:12—19:10
22/1 Corinthians 1—4
23/1 Corinthians 5—8
24/1 Corinthians 9—12
25/1 Corinthians 13—16
26/Acts 19:11—20:1
   2 Corinthians 1—3
27/2 Corinthians 4—6
28/2 Corinthians 7—9
29/2 Corinthians 10—13
30/Acts 20:2
   Romans 1—4

DECEMBER

1/Romans 5—8
2/Romans 9—11
3/Romans 12—16
4/Acts 20:3—22:30
5/Acts 23—25
6/Acts 26—28
7/Ephesians 1—3
8/Ephesians 4—6
9/Philippians 1—4
10/Colossians 1—4
11/Hebrews 1—4
12/Hebrews 5—7
13/Hebrews 8—10
14/Hebrews 11—13
15/Philemon, 1 Peter 1—2
16/1 Peter 3—5
17/2 Peter 1—3
18/1 Timothy 1—3
19/1 Timothy 4—6
20/Titus 1—3
21/2 Timothy 1—4
22/1 John 1—2
23/1 John 3—5
24/2 John, 3 John, Jude
25/Revelation 1—3
26/Revelation 4—6
27/Revelation 7—9
28/Revelation 10—12
29/Revelation 13—15
30/Revelation 16—18
31/Revelation 19—22

This schedule was arranged by Leslie B. Flynn in the tract *Through The Bible in a Year* (American Tract Society, PO Box 214986, Sacramento, Calif.).

5 | Where to Turn in Your Bible

When:
Afraid	Ps. 34:4; Matt. 10:28; 2 Tim. I:7
Anxious	Ps. 46; Matt. 6: 19-34; Phil. 4:6-8
Backsliding	Ps. 51; 1 John 1:4-10
Bereaved	Matt. 5:4; 2 Cor. 1:3-4; 5:1-8
Defeated	Rom. 8:31-39; 2 Cor. 2:14; 4:8-18
Depressed	Pss. 34; 139; Rom. 8; 1 Cor. 10:1-13
Disaster threatens	Pss. 91; 118:5-6; Luke 8:22-25
Discouraged	Pss. 23; 42:6-11; Matt. 5: 1-12, 19-34
Doubting	Matt. 8:26; 21:22; Heb. 11; James 1
Facing a crisis	Ps. 121; Matt. 6: 19-34; Heb. 4: 16
Friends fail	Ps. 41:9-13; Luke 17:3-4; Rom. 12: 14
Lonely	Ps. 23; Heb. 12:1-2; 13:1--6
Peace is needed	John 14: 1-4; 16:33; Phil. 4:6-9
Protection is needed	Pss. 27:1-6; 91; Rom. 8:28-39
Sorrowful	Ps. 51; John 14; 2 Cor. 1:3-4
Tempted	Ps. 1; 1 Cor. 10: 12-14; James 4:7
Traveling	Ps. 127
Troubled	Pss. 16; 31; John 14:1-6, 13-14, 27
Weary	Ps. 90; Matt. 11:28-30; 1 Cor. 15
Worried	Matt. 6: 19-34; I Peter 5:6-8

Where to Turn in Your Bible for:

Angelic protection	Ps. 91:11; Matt. 18:10; Heb. 1:14
Assurance of salvation	Rom. 8:16; 1 John 5:13
Baptism in Spirit	Matt. 3:11; Luke 24:49; Acts 1:5, 8
Beatitudes	Matt. 5:1-12; Luke 6:20-49
Crucifixion of Christ	Matt. 27:27-50; Mark 15:16-41
Forgiveness of sins	Ps. 51; 1 John 1:4—2:2
Fruit of the Spirit	Gal. 5:22-23; John 15:1-8, 16
Guidance	Prov. 3:5-6; Isa. 58:11
Healing	Ex. 15:26; 3 John 2; James 5:14-16
Lord's prayer	Matt. 6:9-13; Luke 11:1-4; John 17
Love chapter	1 Cor. 13
Maturity from trials	Rom. 5:3-5; James 1:2-4
Rapture	1 Cor. 15:51-57; 1 Thes. 4:13-18
Rest of soul	Matt. 11:28-30; Heb. 3:7—4:8
Sermon on the mount	Matt. 5—7; Luke 6:20-49
Shepherd's psalm	Ps. 23
Sound mind	Luke 21:12-15; 2 Tim. 1:7; James 1:5
Temptation deliverance	1 Cor. 10:13; 2 Peter 2:9
Ten Commandments	Ex. 20
Victory over all things	2 Cor. 2:14; Rom. 8:31-39

6 | The Roman Road

One of the greatest joys in life is introducing someone to Jesus Christ and to salvation. Many never experience this joy because they don't know how to begin.

Can you lead someone through the appropriate Scriptures of salvation? If you cannot, then you need an aid such as THE ROMAN ROAD. To use this tool effectively you will need three items: a small piece of colored tape, a pen, and the Bible you plan to use.

Turn in your Bible to the Book of Romans, chapter three and verse twenty-three (3:23). Now, take the piece of tape and affix it to the outer edge of the page so that it neatly folds over onto the other side of the page. This marker will always tell you where to start on THE ROMAN ROAD.

Next, take your pen and circle the number "23" in Romans, chapter 3. This additional accent makes it easy to begin your salvation journey through Romans.

Somewhere beside verse 23 write "5:12." This indicates that once you have shared the information contained in this verse with a prospective Christian you are ready to go to the next verse—5:12. Here, circle the number "12" and write "6:23." Turn there (6:23), circle again, and write "5:8." Turn to 5:8, circle and write "10:9-10." Turn to 10:9-10, circle, and write "10:13." This is the final verse, and now you have God's road map of salvation in the Book of Romans!

See how simple it can be! Why not begin by sharing it with a Christian friend. This experience will increase your understanding and build your confidence. Then use THE ROMAN ROAD to point your lost friends to Christ, to salvation, and to heaven itself!

7 | Buying a New Bible

There are so many different Bibles being printed today. Which one is the best? It is best to use the King James Bible because 98% of all the underlying Hebrew and Greek manuscripts support this translation. They are from what is called *The Traditional Text Group*. Most modern versions of the Bible are from the *Eclectic Text Group* of which there are less than 50 manuscripts or portions. In most modern versions there are 17 complete verses that are missing and hundreds of partial verses and words missing.

Some Suggestions for selecting a King James Bible.

FIRST, do not let anyone talk you into a paraphrase Bible. This really is NOT a Bible at all. It does not translate the words from the underlying text but is like a mini commentary. A paraphrase of the Scriptures may be easily read, but it may also take from or add to the Scriptures.

SECOND, there are a wide variety of King James Bibles available. There are some that only have text, some that have cross references, some have a basic concordance in the back, and there are study Bibles that are filled with explanatory notes. You will have to decide which one best fits you.

THIRD recognize the fact that the Bible you select will never completely satisfy all your study needs. You may wisely invest in several different Bibles and some basic Bible tools, such as a Strong's Concordance, and a Bible Handbook.

FOURTH, remember, whichever Bible you finally decide on, it is only as helpful to you as the amount of time you spend reading, studying, meditating and memorizing it. 2 Timothy 2:15 *"Study to shew thyself approved unto God, a workman that needeth not to be ashamed, rightly dividing the word of truth."*

Part 2

Basic Bible Doctrines

8 | The Scriptures

This Book contains the mind of God, the state of man, the way of salvation, the doom of sinners, and the happiness of believers. Its doctrines are holy, its precepts are binding; its histories are true, and its decisions are immutable. Read it to be wise, believe it to be safe, practice it to be holy.

It contains light to direct you, food to support you, and comfort to cheer you. It is the traveler's map, the pilgrim's staff, the pilot's compass, the soldier's sword, and the Christian's character.

Here paradise is restored, heaven opened, and the gates of hell disclosed. Christ is its grand subject, our good its design, and the glory of God its end. It should fill the memory, rule the heart, and guide the feet.

Read it slowly, frequently, prayerfully. It is a mine of wealth, a paradise of glory, and a river of pleasure. Follow its precepts and it will lead you to Calvary, to the empty tomb, to a resurrected life in Christ, yes, to glory itself, for eternity.

—Unknown

The Writing of the Scriptures

Writing Materials: Writing requires materials on which to write. This sounds simple *today,* but 4,000 years ago writing was rather difficult. Materials used from the time of Moses up until the time of Christ were:

1. Clay tablets—engraved with a sharp instrument and then dried for a permanent record (Jer. 17:13; Ezek. 4:1).

2. Papyrus—a plant which grew in the shallow lakes and rivers of Egypt and Syria. Large shipments of papyrus were sent to the Syrian port of Byblos. It is believed that the Greek word for "books" (*biblos*) comes from this port. The English word "paper" is derived from the Greek term papyrus.

3. Other writing materials included stones, wax tablets (a piece of flat wood covered with a coat of wax), ostraca (unglazed pottery), and vellum (calf skin).

Writing Instruments: These were no less difficult to use than the materials themselves. A company like Bic or Parker could have rendered great assistance to our forefathers.

1. Metal stylus—used to write on clay and wax tablets.

2. Pen—a pointed reed about 6 to 16 inches long for writing on papyrus, parchment, and vellum. The ink consisted of a compound of charcoal, gum, and water.

Books: The form and shape of books were also quite different from what we know today.

1. Rolls or Scrolls—sheets of papyrus glued together and then wound around a stick. The average scroll was between 20 and 35 feet in length, though one is known to be 144 feet long. Writing was usually only on one side.

2. Codex—papyrus sheets were eventually assembled in leaf form (like modern books) with both sides written on. This occurred about the 3rd century A.D.

Language of the Original Scriptures: One of the hurdles which is important for an accurate understanding of the Scriptures is a study of the languages in which they were originally written.

1. Hebrew—most of the Old Testament
2. Greek—most of the New Testament
3. Aramaic—Gen. 31:47 ("Jegar-sahadutha"), Ezra 4:8—

6:18; 7:12-26; Jer. 10:11; Dan. 2:4-7:28; Mark 5:41; 7:34; 15:34 (,"abba"-cf. Rom. 8:15; Gal. 4:6); John 19:13; 1 Cor. 16:22 Original Hebrew Manuscripts: For over 3,000 years-from the time of Moses to the invention of printing-the Hebrew text was copied with exacting care.
1. Masoretes-Originally, the Hebrew text was composed only of consonants. In the fifth to the tenth centuries, the Masoretes (rabbis of Tiberias and Babylon) devoted themselves to copying the best available Hebrew manuscripts and devising a vowel system to perpetuate a correct pronunciation of the words.
2. Dates of Texts-The oldest known Hebrew text dates back to around the 9th century A.D. It was preserved owing to the Jewish custom of burying out-of-use texts.
3. Septuagint- The Septuagint is a very loose Greek translation of the Old Testament. There are no historical references to it before the time of Christ except for the bogus "Letter of Aristeas." What is call the Septuagint today was is a blend of 3 different codices which were written three centuries after the time of Christ.
4. Dead Sea Scrolls-A most significant discovery of Hebrew texts occurred in 1947 (and following). The greatest discovery was the uncovering of the entire text of Isaiah. It was dated as a 2nd century B.C. writing and conformed perfectly to our present Isaiah texts!

Original Greek Manuscripts:
1. Whole Texts- We possess more than 6000 partial manuscripts of the entire Greek New Testament. Ninety-eight percent plus of these texts are from the Traditional Text line from which our King James Bible was translated from. Here are some texts that modern Bible translators have used:

    a. Sinaitic Codex—It is alleged that this N.T. manuscript was written at the beginning of the 4th century, but serious questions about the date have surfaced in the 21st Century (see *Neither Oldest Nor Best* by David H. Sorenson; www.northstarministries.com)

    b. Vatican Codex- This New Testament Manuscript alleged to be from the 4th Century is of little value. I wrote in my book *The Indestructible Book: Examining The History of The English Bible* - I question the 'great witness' value of this manuscript. There is evidence that Vaticanus was overwritten letter by letter in the 10th or 11th century, with accents and breathing [marks] added along with corrections from the 8th, 10th and 15th centuries. All this activity makes precise paleographic analysis impossible. (The Editor)

c. Alexandrian Codex-(5th century) comprises almost all the Old Testament (in Greek) and the New Testament. This codex contains many non-canonical books. The text of the Septuagint (Old Testament) codices is in too chaotic a condition to permit of a sure judgment on the textual value of the great manuscript. I remind you that numerous paleographers believe that whoever prepared the text could not even read Greek.

2. Oldest Fragments

   a. John Ryland MS-(A.D. 130) is the oldest New Testament fragment. It is a section from the Gospel of John.

   b. Chester Beatty Papyri-(A.D. 200) contains papyrus codices which cover major portions of the New Testament.

   c. Bodmer Papyrus //-(A.D. 150-200) contains most of John.

The English Bible: The first complete translation of the whole Bible into (Middle) English was made by John Wycliffe (1380-1382). It took 10 month to write out this manuscript Bible.

The first book ever printed was the Bible, between the years 1450 and 1455, at Mintz, Germany, by Gutenberg, the inventor of moveable type.

The first New Testament printed in English was by William Tyndale, A.D. 1525-1526.

The first Bible printed in English was that of Miles Coverdale, A.D. 1535.

The chapter divisions commonly used today were developed by Stephen Langton, an Archbishop of Canterbury. Langton put the modern chapter divisions into place in around A.D. 1227.

These Old Testament chapters were divided into verses, as we now have them by Rabbi Nathan. Parisian printer Robert Stephanus is responsible for the verse divisions that first appeared in the Geneva New Testament in 1557 and the whole Geneva Bible in 1560.

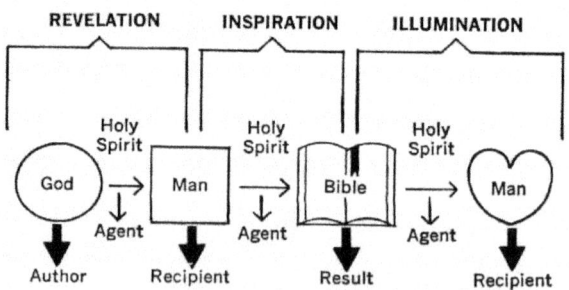

Diagram of Revelation, Inspiration, and Illumination

Revelation, Inspiration, and Illumination

Revelation: The term "revelation" means "to uncover, to unveil and to reveal." So biblical revelation is the uncovering or revealing of God through the Scriptures.

Inspiration: This word is a compound of two Greek words meaning *God* and *to breathe.* The resultant definition, therefore, is *God breathed* or *inspiration.* Orthodox Christians believe that though man penned the Scriptures (2 Peter 1:21), it was God who moved them to write His desired message.

1. Proofs for Divine Inspiration of the Old Testament
    a. The expressions, "Thus saith the Lord," "Hear the word of the Lord," and similar phrases, occur 3,808 times in the Old Testament.
    b. The New Testament endorses the validity of the Old Testament by quoting it 278 times and alluding to it another 613 times. These quotations account for about 10% of the New Testament text.
    c. Jesus affirmed the inspiration of the Old Testament (Matt. 5:18; Luke 16:17; John 10:35). One tenth of Jesus' words were taken from the Old Testament.
    d. New Testament writers affirm the inspiration of the Old Testament (2 Tim. 3:16; James 1:18, 21-25; 2:8; 1 Peter 1:10-12, 16, 23-25; 2:2-3; 2 Peter 2:4-8, 15-16; 3:2, 5, 15-16).

2. Proofs for Divine Inspiration of the New Testament
    a. Jesus spoke God's words (Matt. 7:24; 24:35; Mark 2:10; Luke 5:1; John 5:34; 6:68; 8:26, 28; 12:48-50; 14:10; 17:8, 14, 17).
    b. Jesus promised inspiration to New Testament authors (Luke 21:15; John 14:26; 15:26-27; 16:12-15).
    c. Paul claimed to speak God's words (Acts 22:14-15; Rom. 16:25-26; 1 Cor. 2:13, 16; 7:10; Eph. 3:3-5, 8; Titus 1:2-3).
    d. Peter taught that Paul's writings were on a parity with other Scripture (2 Peter 3:15-16).

e. Peter spoke God's words (1 Peter 1:23, 25; 4:11).
f. John spoke God's words (Rev. 1:1-2, 11, 19; 2:1—3:22; 22:6).

Illumination: The Greek term for "illumination" comes from the word for "light" and means "enlightenment." A proper understanding of the Scriptures requires a divine illumination or insight (Prov. 14:6; Matt. 13:11; 16:17, 23; John 3:3; 6:44-45, 65; Rom. 8:5-8; 1 Cor. 2:14; 1 John 2:20, 27; 5:20).

The Names of Scripture
The Scripture—Mark 12:10; 15:28; Luke 4:21
The Scriptures—Matt. 21:42; 22:29; Rom. 15:4
The Holy Scriptures—Rom. 1:2; 2 Tim. 3:15
The Oracles of God—Acts 7:38; Rom. 3:2; Heb. 5:12; 1 Peter 4:11
The Law of Moses, the Prophets, and the Psalms—Luke 24:44
The Word of God—Mark 7:13; Rom. 9:6; 1 Tim. 4:5
The Word of Christ—Col. 3:15
The Sword of the Spirit—Eph. 6:17
The Word of Life—Phil. 2:16
The Word of Truth—Prov. 22:21; 2 Tim. 2:15; James 1:18
The Writing of Truth—Dan. 10:21
The Word of the Gospel—Acts 15:7; Rom. 1:16
The Message of Truth—Eph. 1:13
The Word of the Lord—1 Thes. 4:15
The Word of Reconciliation—2 Cor. 5:19
The Covenants, the Law, and the Promises—Rom. 9:4; Eph. 2:12
The Book—Ps. 40:7; Heb. 10:7
The Old and New Testaments—Luke 22:20; 1 Cor. 11:25; Heb. 9:15; 12:24
Testimonies—Ps. 119:2, 14, 22, 24, 31, 36
Precepts—Pss. 19:8; 119:40
Commandments—Ps. 119:6, 10, 19, 21
Statutes—Ps. 119:5, 8, 12, 16
The Law—Matt. 12:5; Luke 16:16; John 7:19

What the Scriptures Are Likened To
Mirror—James 1:23
Hammer—Jer. 23:29
Fire—Jer. 5:14; 23:29
Seed—Matt. 13:38; 1 Peter 1:23
Water—Eph. 5:26
Lamp—Ps. 119:105
Solid food—Heb. 5:11-12
Milk—1 Cor. 3:1-3; 1 Peter 2:2
Honey—Pss. 19:10; 119:103
Rain—Isa. 55:10-11
Snow—Isa. 55:10-11
Sword—Heb. 4:12; Eph. 6:17
Light—Ps. 119:105; 2 Peter 1:19

The Nature of Scripture
Settled forever—Ps. 119:89
Stands forever—Isa. 40:8
Shall never pass away—Matt. 24:35; Mark 13:31
Living—Heb. 4:12; 1 Peter 1:23
Not imprisoned—2 Tim. 2:9
Refined—2 Sam. 22:31; Prov. 30:5; Ps. 12:6
Powerful—Jer. 23:29
Sharp—Heb. 4:12
Cannot be broken—John 10:35
True and Righteous—Pss. 19:9; 111:7-8; James 1:18
Wonderful—Ps. 119:129
Perfect—Ps. 19:7

Why the Scriptures Were Written
To reveal Christ—Matt. 5:17; 26:24, 54; John 5:39; 1 Peter 1:10-12; Rev. 19:10
To generate faith—Rom. 10:17
To bring salvation—John 5:24; 20:31; Rom. 1:2, 16; 2 Tim. 3:15; James 1:21
To edify believers—Acts 20:32; 1 Tim. 4:6
To give comfort—Ps. 119:50, 52, 76; 1 Thes. 4:18

To produce full joy—Ps. 19:8; 1 John 1:4
To bring sanctification—John 17:17
To produce hope—Pss. 119:116; 130:5; Rom. 15:4
To supply guidance—Ps. 119:105; 1 Cor. 10:11
To yield a blessing—Luke 11:28; Rev. 1:3
To revive a soul—Ps. 119:50
To give prosperity and success—Josh. 1:8-9; Ps. 1:1-3
To restore the soul—Ps. 19:11
To make wise the simple—Pss. 19:7; 119:98-99, 104, 130
To produce purity—John 15:3; Eph. 5:26; 1 Peter 1:22
To provide assurance of salvation—1 John 5:13
To keep one from sin—1 John 2:1
To serve as the standard for faith—John 12:48; Gal. 1:4-8

Fitting Responses to the Scriptures
Awe them—Ps. 119:161
Treasure them more than food—Job 23:12
Love them—Ps. 119:97, 113, 140, 163
Obey them—Ps. 119:67, 112, 134; Matt. 7:24-25; James 1:25
Hide them in the heart—Ps. 119:11
Delight in them—Pss. 1:2; 119:24, 35, 77, 143, 174
Long after them at all times—Ps. 119:20
Rejoice in them—Ps. 119:14
Give thanks for them at midnight—Ps. 119:62
Meditate upon them—Pss. 1:2; 119:15, 23, 48, 78, 97, 99, 148
Praise God for them—Pss. 56:4, 10; 119:164
Study them—Isa. 34:16; John 5:39; 2 Tim. 2:15
Share them—Acts 4:29, 31; 8:4, 25; 2 Cor. 2:17; 1 Thes. 1:8
Desire them more than gold—Ps. 119:72, 127
Wear them—Ex. 13:9; Deut. 6:8; 11:18
Display them—Deut. 6:9; 11:20; 27:2-3, 8; Josh. 8:32

Arrangement and Dates of the Scriptures
Some Bibles place the date of each book on the first page of that book, along with an introduction. But many Bibles omit this historical data. Therefore, we have provided it here. You may wish to put these dates in your own Bible.

Old Testament

Pentateuch
   Genesis—c. 1445 B.C.
   Exodus—c. 1444 B.C.
   Leviticus—c. 1443 B.C.
   Numbers—c. 1443-1405 B.C.
   Deuteronomy—c. 1405 B.C.

Conquest and Monarchy
   Joshua—c. 1375 B.C.
   Judges—c. 1375-1075 B.C.
   Ruth—during the Judges
   1 Samuel—c. 1000 B.C.
   2 Samuel—c. 960 B.C.
   1 Kings—c. 6th century B.C.
   2 Kings—c. 6th century B.C.
   1 Chronicles—c. 5th century B.C.
   2 Chronicles—c. 5th century B.C.

Post-Exilic Events
   Ezra—c. 535-457 B.C.
   Nehemiah—c. 445-433 B.C.
   Esther—c. 483-474 B.C.

Poetry
   Job—c. 1800 B.C.
   Psalms—from 1440 to 580 B.C.
   Proverbs—c. 950 B.C.
   Ecclesiastes—c. 935 B.C.
   Song of Solomon—c. 960 B.C.

Prophets
   Isaiah—c. 739-700 B.C.
   Jeremiah—c. 627-560 B.C.
   Lamentations—c. 586 B.C.
   Ezekiel—c. 593-571 B.C.

Daniel—c. 606-534 B.C.
Hosea—c. 760-725 B.C.
Joel—c. 838 B.C.
Amos—c. 760 B.C.
Obadiah—c. 845 B.C.
Jonah—c. 782 B.C.
Micah—c. 735 B.C.
Nahum—c. 650 B.C.
Habakkuk—c. 609-599 B.C.
Zephaniah—c. 640 B.C.
Haggai—c. 520 B.C.
Zechariah—c. 520 B.C.
Malachi—c. 5th century B.C.

New Testament

Biography
Matthew—c. A.D. 60
Mark—c. A.D. 60
Luke—c. A.D. 60
John—c. A.D. 60

History
Acts—c. A.D. 64

Letters
Romans—c. A.D. 58
1 Corinthians—c. A.D. 56
2 Corinthians—c. A.D. 57
Galatians—c. A.D. 56
Ephesians—c. A.D. 62
Philippians—c. A.D. 62
Colossians—c. A.D. 62
1 Thessalonians—c. A.D. 52
2 Thessalonians—c. A.D. 52
1 Timothy—c. A.D. 64
2 Timothy—c. A.D. 66

Titus—c. A.D. 64
Philemon—c. A. D. 62
Hebrews—before A.D. 70
James—c. A.D. 60
1 Peter—c. A.D. 63
2 Peter—c. A.D. 68
1 John—c. A.D. 85-90
2 John—c. A.D. 85-90
3 John—c. A.D. 85-90
Jude—c. A.D. 65-80

Prophecy
Revelation—c. A.D. 90-96

Basic Bible Outlines

Have you ever been up in a plane and looked down at the ground, or have you ever looked out from the window of a tall building? What an amazing view. You can see things in a way never dreamed possible. In a swift glance your eye can capture miles of detailed territory. In outlining the Scriptures we come across the same effect. We are able to see the whole of God's Word (in capsule form) in its symmetrical, historical, literary, and topical formations.

Trinitarian Perspective
1. Father—Old Testament
  2. Son—Gospels
    3. Holy Spirit—Acts and Letters
  2. Son—Revelation
1. Father—Eternity (see 1 Cor. 15:24)

Christological Perspective
1. Christ in the Old Testament: Preparation
2. Christ in the Gospels: Manifestation
3. Christ in the Acts: Propagation
4. Christ in the Letters: Explanation
5. Christ in the Revelation: Consummation

Progressive Perspective
1. Old Testament: Revelation
2. New Testament: Realization
   a) Gospels and Acts: Experience (History)
   b) Letters: Expression (Doctrine)
   c) Revelation: Expectation (Prophecy)

Human Perspective
1. Old Testament: The account of a nation—Israel
2. New Testament: The account of a man—Jesus Christ

Literary Perspective
1. Historical: The Rise and Fall of Israel (Gen.—2 Chron.)
2. Poetical·   The Literature of Israel's Golden Age (Job—Song
3. Prophetical: The Literature of Israel's Dark Age (Isa.—Mal.)
4. Biography: The Life of Christ (Gospels)
5. Documentary: The Witness of Christians (Acts)
6. Letters: The Discourse among Christians (Rom.—Jude)
7. Revelation: The Hope of Christians (Rev.)

Salvation Perspective
1. In the Old Testament: Salvation Prepared
2. In the Gospels: Salvation Effected
3. In the Acts: Salvation Propagated
4. In the Letters: Salvation Explained
5. In the Revelation: Salvation Fulfilled

Lamb Perspective
1. Lamb for a Man: Genesis
2. Lamb for a Family: Exodus
3. Lamb for a Nation: Leviticus—Malachi
4. Lamb for a World: Matthew—Jude
5. Lamb for a Universe: Revelation

THE SCRIPTURES / 47

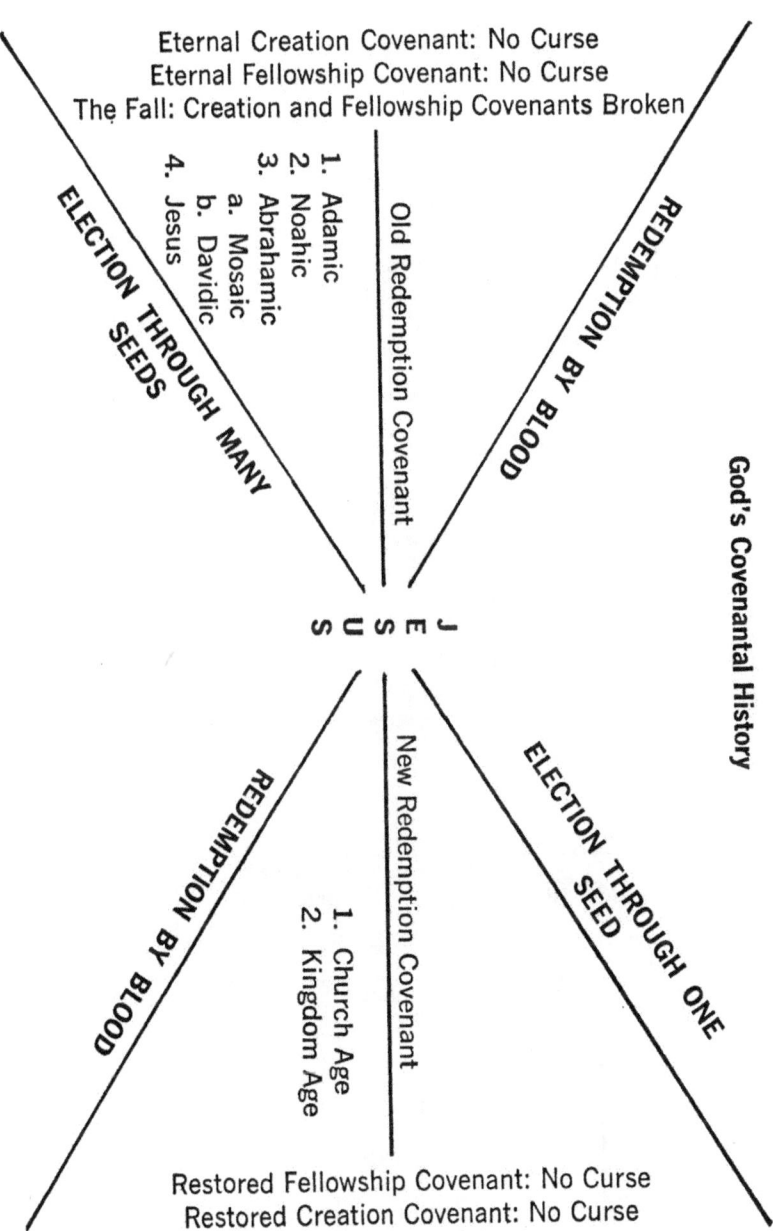

The Sixty-six Books of the Bible

39 Old Testament Books				
Historic 17		Poetic 5	Prophetic 17	
Torah—5	The Land—12	Poetry & Wisdom	Major—5	Minor—12
Gen. Exod. Lev. Num. Deut.	Josh. Judg. Ruth 1-2 Sam. 1-2 Kings 1-2 Chron. Ezra Neh. Esther	Job Psalms Proverbs Ecclesiastes Song	Isaiah Jeremiah Lamen. Ezekiel Daniel	Hosea Joel Amos Obadiah Jonah Micah Nahum Habakkuk Zephaniah Haggai Zechariah Malachi

27 New Testament Books				
Biographical 4	Historical 1	Apostolic 21		Prophetic 1
Christ	Church	Paul—14	General—7	
Matthew Mark Luke John	Acts	Romans 1-2 Cor. Gal. Eph. Phil. Col. 1-2 Thes. 1-2 Tim. Titus Philemon	James 1-2 Peter 1-3 John Jude Hebrews	Revelation

The Covenantal Perspective of Scripture

(See *Trinitarian Perspective* on p. 45 for an explanation of the outline numbers—1, 2, and 3.)

1. *Creation Covenant: Heaven and Earth are Void of Curse.*
2. *God's Direct Fellowship Covenant with Man.*
   a. Responsibility: Gen. 1:26-29; 2:15-17 (Do not eat).
   b. Failure: Gen. 3:1-6 (They ate).
   c. Judgment: Gen. 3:7-19 (Death: spiritual and physical; curse upon serpent, woman, man, and ground).
3. *God's Old Redemption Covenant Through Chosen Seeds* (Gen. 3:15; 9:27; 12:2-3; 17:7-8, 19; 26:1-4; 28:10-15; Gal. 3:1-29).
   a. Adamic Race: Gen. 3:21 (Conscience)
      (1) Responsibility: Gen. 4:7 (Do good, blood sacrifices)
      (2) Failure: Gen. 4:7-8; 6:1-6 (Wickedness)
      (3) Judgment: Gen. 6:7, 13, 17; 7:7—8:14 (Flood)
   b. Noah: Gen. 6:18; 8:20-22; 9:1-17 (Human Government)
      (1) Responsibility: Gen. 9:1-7 (Scatter, multiply)
      (2) Failure: Gen. 11:1-4 (Did not scatter)
      (3) Judgment: Gen. 11:5-9 (Confusion of languages)
   c. Patriarchs, Moses, and David: Gen. 12:1-3; 13:14-17; 15:1-21; 17:1-19; 26:1-4; 28:10-15; 32:24-32; 49:8-12; Ex. 19:5ff.; 2 Sam. 7:4-17 (Promise)
      (1) Responsibility: Ex. 19:5-6 (Faithfulness)
      (2) Failure: 2 Kings 17:7-23 (Disobedience)
      (3) Judgment: Deut. 28:63-65 (Dispersion)
   d. Jesus: Mark 1:15 (Earthly Kingdom)
      (1) Responsibility: Mark 1:14-15 (Repent and believe)
      (2) Failure: Matt. 27:1-25; Acts 2:22-23 (Messiah rejected)
      (3) Judgment: Rom. 11:1-25 (Israel cut off)

3. *God's New Redemptive Covenant Through Chosen Seed* (Gal. 3:1-29)
     a. Jesus: Acts 15:15-19 (Church and Heavenly Kingdom)
        (1) Responsibility: Acts 2:38; 16:31 (Repent and believe)
        (2) Failure: 2 Thes. 2:1-12 (Apostasy)
        (3) Judgment: Rev. 6—19 (Tribulation)
     b. Jesus: (Earthly Kingdom)
        (1) Responsibility: Zech. 14:16-21 (Worship Jesus as King)
        (2) Failure: Rev. 20:7-9 (Rebellion)
        (3) Judgment: Rev. 20:9 (Fire from heaven)

 2. *God's Direct Fellowship Covenant with Man* (Rev. 21:3-8; 22:3-5)

 1. *Creation Covenant: Heaven and Earth are Void of Curse* (Isa. 65:17; 66:22; 2 Peter 3:10-13; Rev. 21:1-2).

The Canon of Scripture [1]

The word "canon" comes from a term meaning "reed." The "reed" was a measuring rod and eventually it came to be used in the sense of "standard" and as that which represented an official "list" or "index." Hence, the canon of Scripture is generally understood to mean "the officially accepted list of books in the Christian faith."

Although the Christian heritage accepts only a select number of books as canonical, the word *canon* encompasses more in its meaning than a formal "index." The term also means "that which is authoritative or binding at the present moment." The canon of Scripture, in the specific sense, is that portion of Scripture which sets certain Divine controls upon man within a definite time period.

Canonization took place at the very instant God declared His will. Whenever God spoke there was revelation, and when this

---

1. For a full discussion along this line see *The Structure of Biblical Authority* by Meredith G. Kline, William B. Eerdmans Publishing Company, Grand Rapids, Michigan, 1972.

revelation became written, it was officially both inspiration and canon. God's words needed no human stamp of approval or endorsement to be authoritative.

The Extent of Canon: In the general sense, canon refers to the official listing of accepted books that constitute the Bible. In the specific sense, canon refers to that portion of Scripture which is *presently binding* upon the believer.

In the general sense, all Scripture is inspired and profitable for teaching, for reproof, for correction, and for training in righteousness (2 Tim. 3:16-17). No portion of Scripture is valueless for growth in *the faith,* but at the same time, not every passage is authoritative in its demands.

Polity Norms: In the narrow sense, only certain portions of Scripture are to be presently obeyed. God's laws change, and when they do, the canon is either amended or abolished. For example, all the laws for offering a sacrifice hold no authority with the believer today, though such former regulations are profitable as a faith norm. Polity or governmental norms, however, shift with God's covenants and time, whereas, the faith norms are always applicable. Therefore, in the specific sense, there are canons (plural) of Scripture because the rule of conduct (polity norms) change with progressive revelation and inspiration.

Individual Book Themes

Genesis:	Beginnings
Exodus:	Redemption through Blood
Leviticus:	Holiness through Sacrifice
Numbers:	Wilderness Trials
Deuteronomy:	Preparations for Entering the Promised Land
Joshua:	Possessing the Inheritance
Judges:	Judges for Repentant Israel
Ruth:	Kinsman-Redeemer
1 Samuel:	The Monarchy Begins
2 Samuel:	David—Israel's Greatest King

1 Kings:	The Monarchy is Divided
2 Kings:	The Fall of Israel and Judah
1 Chronicles:	David—Israel's Greatest King
2 Chronicles:	The House of God and Judah's Fall
Ezra:	Returning to Jerusalem
Nehemiah:	Rebuilding Jerusalem
Esther:	A Threat to the Diaspora
Job:	The Mystery of Why the Righteous Suffer
Psalms:	Praise
Proverbs:	Wisdom through Instruction
Ecclesiastes:	A Sermon on Vanity
Song of Solomon:	A Love Affair
Isaiah:	Salvation through God's Servant
Jeremiah:	Judgment of Israel's Monarchy
Lamentations:	Sorrow over Jerusalem
Ezekiel:	Consummation of Israel's Monarchy
Daniel:	The Times of the Gentiles
Hosea:	God's Covenantal Love
Joel:	The Day of the Lord
Amos:	God Judges Sin and Promises a Blessing
Obadiah:	Retribution for Edom
Jonah:	Jonah's Reluctance and Nineveh's Repentance
Micah:	God Judges Sin and Promises a Blessing
Nahum:	Judgment upon Nineveh
Habakkuk:	The Just Shall Live by Faith
Zephaniah:	The Day of the Lord
Haggai:	Mandate to Rebuild the Temple: Rebuke
Zechariah:	Mandate to Finish the Temple: Exhortation
Malachi:	Rebuke for Lukewarm Worship
Matthew:	Jesus is the Promised and Rejected Messiah
Mark:	Jesus is the Perfect Servant of God
Luke:	Jesus is the Perfect Man and Saviour
John:	Jesus is the Saviour of the World
Acts:	The Works of Jesus through the Church

Romans:	Three Peoples: Gentiles, Jews, and the Church
1 Corinthians:	Answering Questions and Correcting Problems
2 Corinthians:	Paul's Ministry
Galatians:	A Defense for Christian Liberty
Ephesians:	The Believer's Position, Walk, and Warfare
Philippians:	Rejoicing in Christ
Colossians:	The Preeminence of Jesus Christ
1 Thessalonians:	The Second Coming of Christ
2 Thessalonians:	The Second Coming of Christ
1 Timothy:	Proper Order in the Church
2 Timothy:	Exhortations to Pastors
Titus:	The Character of the Saint
Philemon:	Paul's Entreaty for Onesimus
Hebrews:	Jesus: Our Great Saviour and Priest
James:	Faith and Works are Inseparable
1 Peter:	Encouragement for Perils From Without
2 Peter:	Exhortations for Perils From Within
1 John:	Fellowship with God and One Another
2 John:	Exhortations to Love and to Beware
3 John:	Compliments and Exhortations Regarding Conduct
Jude:	Contending for the Faith
Revelation:	The Unveiling of Jesus Christ and Last Things

Notable Sayings About the Scriptures

George Washington. "Above all, the pure light of revelation has had an influence on mankind, and increased the blessings of society. It is impossible to rightly govern the world without God and the Bible."

Thomas Jefferson. "I have always said that a studious perusal of the sacred volume will make better citizens, better fathers, and better husbands."

John Adams. "The Bible contains more philosophy than all the libraries that I have ever seen; and such parts as I cannot reconcile with my little philosophy, I postpone for future investigation."

John Quincy Adams. "The first and almost the only book deserving of universal attention is the Bible. I speak as a man of the world."

Zachary Taylor. "It was for the love of the truths of this great and good Book that our fathers abandoned their native shores for the wilderness."

Abraham Lincoln. "I am profitably engaged in reading the Bible. Take all of this Book that you can by reason and the balance by faith, and you will live and die a better man. It is the best Book which God has given to man."

W. E. Gladstone. "I have known ninety-five of the world's great men in my time, and of these eighty-seven were followers of the Bible."

Ulysses S. Grant. "To the influence of this Book we are indebted for the progress made in civilization, and to this we must look as our guide in the future."

Queen Victoria. "England has become great and happy by the knowledge of the true God through Jesus Christ . . . This is the secret of England's greatness."

Theodore Roosevelt. "Almost every man who has by his lifework added to the sum of human achievement . . . has based his lifework largely upon the teachings of the Bible."

Woodrow Wilson. "A man has deprived himself of the best there is in the world who has deprived himself of this" (a knowledge of the Bible).

Herbert Hoover. "There is no other book so various as the Bible, nor one so full of concentrated wisdom. Whether it be of law, business, morals, etc. . . . He who seeks for guidance . . . may look inside its covers and find illumination."

Franklin D. Roosevelt. "The young must be taught, and they must be taught truly if spring waters of democracy are to be kept untainted. The influence of the Scriptures in the early days of the Republic is plainly revealed in the writing and thinking of the men who made the nation possible. . . . They found in the Scriptures that which shaped their course and determined their action."

John Bacon. "What I was as an artist seemed to me of some importance while I lived; what I really was, as a believer in Christ Jesus, is the only thing of importance to me now."

Napoleon Bonaparte. "The Bible is more than a book; it is a living being with an action, a power which invades everything that opposes its extension."

Mark Twain. "It is hard to make a choice of the most beautiful passage in a Book which is gemmed with beautiful passages as the Bible."

Alexander Hamilton. "I have carefully examined the evidences of the Christian religion, and if I were sitting as a juror upon its authenticity I would unhesitatingly give my verdict in its favor."

"We the undersigned, Students of the Natural Sciences, desire to express our sincere regret that researchers into scientific truth are perverted by some in our own times into occasion for casting doubt upon the truth and authenticity of the Holy Scriptures. We conceive that it is impossible for the Word of God written in the book of nature, and God's Word written in Holy Scripture, to contradict one another." Signed by *eight hundred scientists of Great Britain,* recorded in the Bodleian Library, which is located in Oxford, England.

Thomas Huxley. "The Bible has been the Magna Charta of the poor and the oppressed. The human race is not in a position to dispense with it."

Patrick Henry. "The Bible is worth all other books which have ever been printed."

Horace Greeley. "It is impossible to enslave mentally or socially a Bible-reading people. The principles of the Bible are the groundwork of human freedom."

Robert E. Lee. "In all my perplexities and distresses, the Bible has never failed to give me light and strength."

Lord Tennyson. "Bible reading is an education in itself."

Immanuel Kant. "The existence of the Bible, as a book for the people, is the greatest benefit which the human race has ever experienced. Every attempt to belittle it is a crime against society."

Charles Dickens. "The New Testament is the very best Book that ever was or ever will be known in the world."

Sir Isaac Newton. "There are more sure marks of authenticity in the Bible than in any profane history."

THE SCRIPTURES / 57

A clearer picture here: www.thegloriousgospel.ca/antioch-vs-alexandria

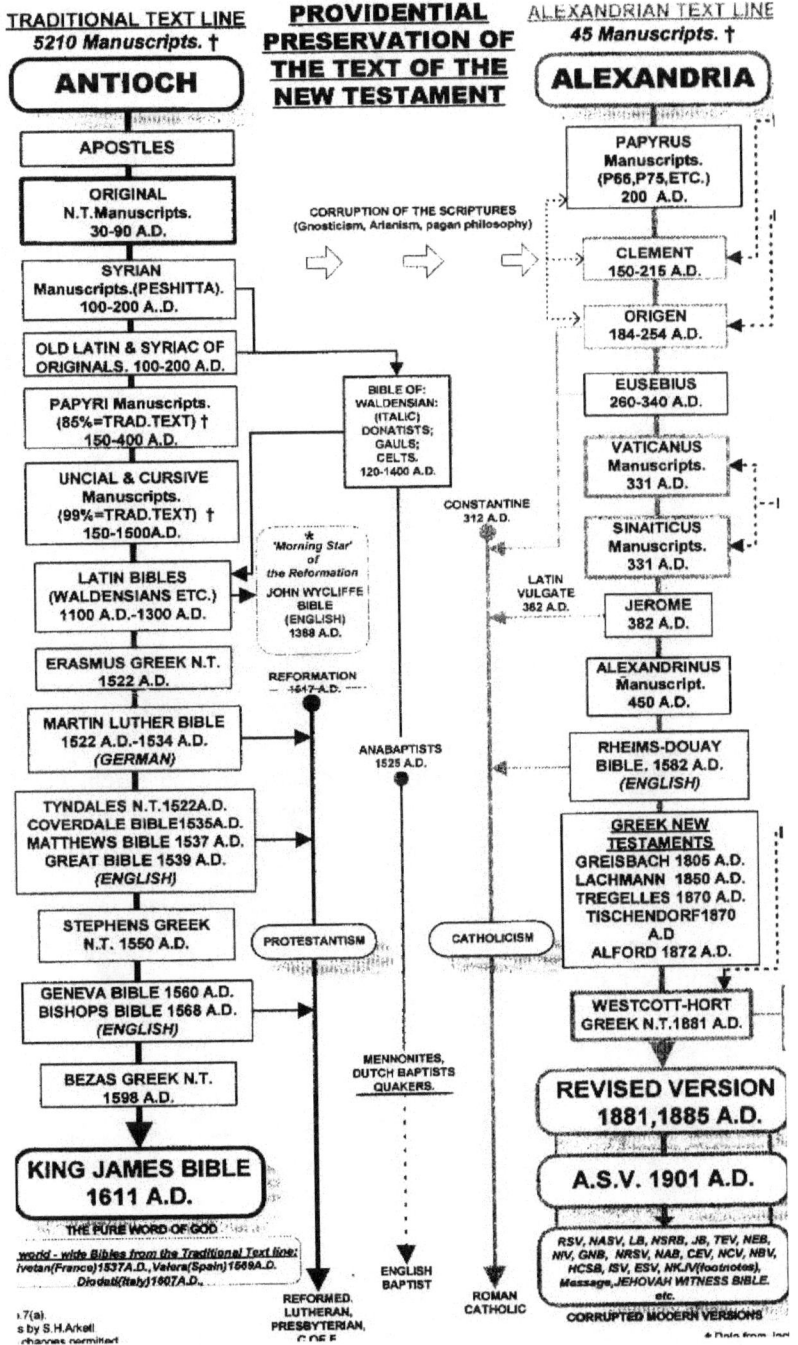

9 | God

What were we made for? To know God. What aim should we set for ourselves in life? To know God. What is the 'eternal life' that Jesus gives? Knowledge of. God. What is the best thing in life, bringing more joy, delight, and contentment, than anything else? Knowledge of God.   From *Knowing God* by J. I. Packer

The Identity of God
Here are 27 ways in which the Bible describes God:

Existence: The Bible assumes the existence of God (Gen. 1:1). It is the very foundation of all knowledge and wisdom (Prov. 1:7; 9:10). Only "fools" deny His existence (Pss. 14:1; 92:6).

Incomprehensibility: The chasm that utterly divides the infinite God from finite man is of such immensity that no human intellect could ever span the gulf (Job 26:14; 36:3-6; 37:5; 38:1—42:6; Isa. 40:12-18, 25; 55:8-9; Jer. 23:18; Rom. 11:33-36; 1 Cor. 2:4-5, 16).

God is wholly above man's most profound formulations and speculations. Besides His existence, power, and glory (which are revealed in nature, conscience, and history), God is completely unknowable apart from a special revelation (Matt. 11:27; John 1:18; 6:46; 1 Cor. 2:11, 14; 2 Cor. 4:3-4; 1 Tim. 6:16).

Monotheistic: The unanimous verdict of Scripture is that there is only one God—the God of Abraham, Isaac, and Jacob; the God and Father of our Lord Jesus Christ (Deut. 4:35; 32:39; John 5:44; 1 Cor. 8:4).

Trinity: While there is but one God (monotheism), there is a definite triune nature within this oneness. The concept of "oneness" does not imply a rigid singularity. Frequently the word "one" denotes a compound or plural unity—as in the cases of marriage (Gen. 2:24; Mal. 2:15; 1 Cor. 6:16), language (Gen. 11:6), of those who minister (1 Cor. 3:6-8), and of a believer's relationship to God (John 17:11, 22-23; Gal. 3:28). Therefore, oneness, with reference to God, describes the unity and commonness that is shared in the Godhead itself.

The plurality in the oneness of God is readily evidenced in the very term "God" (usually *Elohim*). In the Hebrew this is a *plural noun.* The English Scriptures make this point plain in such passages as Genesis 1:26; 3:22; 11:7; Isaiah 6:3, 8; where God, speaking of Himself, uses the expression *us.*

The triune nature of the Godhead is often expressed in Scriptures (Isa. 42:1; 48:16; Matt. 3:16; 12:18; 28:19; Luke 3:22; John 3:34-35; 14:16-17; 15:26; Acts 1:2, 4-5; 10:36-38; Rom. 1:3-4; 1 Cor. 12:3-6; 1 John 5:6-7).

Further proof can be found in the names that are used for each member of the Godhead. All three are specifically called *Lord* (Father: Matt. 22:37; Son: John 20:28; and Spirit: 2 Cor. 3:17-18) and *God* (Father: 1 Cor. 8:6; Son: Isa. 9:6; John 20:28; Titus 2:13; Heb. 1:8; 2 Peter 1:1; Spirit: Acts 5:3-4).

Spirit: God is spirit (John 4:24); that is, He is spiritual in substance and invisible to the human eye (Luke 24:39). God has no flesh and bones; therefore, He is not confined to space.

Omnipresent: The heavens and the earth cannot contain God (1 Kings 8:27; 2 Chron. 2:6), yet He fills them both (Ps. 139:7-10;

Acts 17:27-28). While God is at every place, He is not present in the same degree or manner everywhere. His special or more conscious presence can be detected in only certain locations, such as in heaven (Matt. 6:9) or in the life of a believer (John 14:16-18, 20, 23).

Invisible: No man, at any time, has seen God in His unveiled glory (Deut. 4:15-18; John 1:18). To view God in His most brilliant glory would mean certain death (Ex. 33:18-23); yet men have viewed God in His veiled glory and lived (Gen. 16:7-10, 13; Ex. 3:6; 24:9-10; Isa. 6:1). In a future day, however, all the redeemed will behold God in His full and matchless splendor (Ps. 17:15; Matt. 5:8; Heb. 12:14; Rev. 22:4).

Eternal: God has no beginning and He will have no end. He is the eternal *I am* (Ex. 3:14). He always was, always is, and always will be (Gen. 21:33; 1 Chron. 16:36; Pss. 90:1-4; 145:13; Isa. 40:28; 41:4; Dan. 4:34; Rom. 1:20; Eph. 3:21; 1 Tim. 1:17; 2 Peter 3:8; Rev. 4:8-9).

Omniscient: Because God is eternal, there is no increase in His knowledge. God is never shocked by any act from the realm of creation, for all things lie before Him—past, present, and future (Gen. 41:25-32; 1 Sam. 23:10-12; Ps. 139:15-16; Isa. 41:26; 42:9; 44:7; 46:10; Jer. 1:5; Dan. 2:28-45; Matt. 6:8, 32; 24:36; Acts 2:23; 3:18; 4:28; 15:18; Rom. 8:29; 11:2; Gal. 1:15-16; 2 Tim. 1:9; 1 Peter 1:2, 20).

The scope of God's knowledge is absolutely infinite. His eyes run throughout the whole earth, seeing everything (2 Chron. 16:9; Heb. 4:13). Every act of man is fully done in God's penetrating sight (2 Kings 19:27). He even knows the thoughts and intents of the heart (Gen. 6:5; Ps. 7:9; Prov. 15:11; Acts 1:24; 15:8; 1 Thes. 2:4). The condition of His people is ever before Him (Ex. 3:7; Deut. 2:7). Even the hairs of every head are numbered (Matt. 10:30). Within nature, sparrows cannot fall without Him (Matt. 10:29), and He has counted and named every star (Ps. 147:4-5).

Wise: Divine wisdom might be expressed as the process whereby God takes all His knowledge and applies it to His every act so that the result will always be perfect in accomplishing its goal (Rom. 11:33; 14:7-8; Eph. 1:4-6, 11-12; Col. 1:16). This infinite ability to appropriately apply knowledge is most clearly evidenced in Creation (Ps. 19:1-7; Prov. 8), in providence (Ps. 33:10-11; Rom. 8:28), and in salvation (Rom. 9:11; 1 Cor. 1:18, 24; 2:7; Eph. 3:10).

True: It is impossible to think of knowledge and wisdom apart from truth. Repeatedly, the Scriptures proclaim that God is truth and that beside Him all else is deception, perversion, and vanity (Ex. 34:6; Num. 23:19; Isa. 65:16; John 17:3; Titus 1:2; Heb. 6:18; 1 John 5:20-21).

Independent: The eternal nature of God demands His self-existence or independence. That is, God is absolutely autonomous. His existence is free of all things. He has no needs to sustain His endurance (Acts 17:25). To the contrary, everything depends upon Him (Rom. 11:36; Col. 1:16).

Immutable: If God is eternal and independent, then He must also be immutable—changeless, unalterable, indestructible, and immovable in His nature and attributes. Thus, God cannot become better or worse. He is always the same—perfect (Num. 23:19-20; 1 Sam. 15:29; 2 Sam. 22:31; Ps. 33:11; Mal. 3:6; Matt. 5:48; Acts 4:28; Titus 1:2; James 1:17).

Faithful: It naturally follows that since God is immutable, He is equally faithful, dependable, and consistent. God demonstrates His faithfulness in keeping His promises (Deut. 7:9; Heb. 10:23), in not allowing His own to be tempted above what they are able (Ps. 89:20-26; 1 Cor. 10:13; 1 Peter 4:19), in abiding with His people even when they are unfaithful to Him (1 Sam. 12:20-22; 1 Cor. 1:8-9; 1 Thes. 5:23-24; 2 Tim. 2:13), in forgiving us when we confess our sins (1 John 1:9), and in answering prayer (Ps. 143:1-2).

Sovereign: To say that God is sovereign is to declare that God is on His most high throne, designing, creating, directing, executing, regulating, and permitting every event that occurs in heaven and on earth, according to His own good pleasure and without any restraining influences. Sovereignty affirms God's absolute authority to govern the full course of creation (including nations and men) in any manner that best fits His eternally wise, holy, and loving counsels.

Nothing is untouched by the sovereign will of the Lord. What He wills, He performs or controls or permits. No accidents are even possible in the face of the omniscient, omnipresent, and sovereign God. God is said to be sovereign over the following:

Angelic activity—Acts 8:26; Heb. 1:14

Birth of animals—Ps. 104:30

Birth of man—Gen. 15:5; 22:17; Jud. 13:3-5; 1 Sam. 1:5-6, 19; Zech. 12:1

Blessings—Gen. 22:17; 2 Chron. 15:2; 31:10; Jer. 29:11-14

Concealing matters—Prov. 25:2

Confusion—1 Sam. 5:9, 11; 2 Kings 19:7; Neh. 4:15; Isa. 19:14; 22:5

Creation—Ex. 8:22; Josh. 3:11; Ps. 24:1-10

Curses—Jud. 9:57; 2 Kings 2:24; 5:27; 2 Chron. 15:2; Prov. 3:33

Death of animals—Ps. 104:29

Death of man—Deut. 32:39; 1 Sam. 2:27-36; 5:9-12; 6:19

Decisions of man—2 Sam. 17:14

Deliverance from affliction—Ps. 34:19

Departing from men—2 Chron. 24:20; Isa. 8:17-18; Ezek. 7:22

Distress—2 Chron. 15:6; Eccl. 7:14; Amos 3:6

Divine guidance—1 Sam. 8:7-9, 22; 9:15, 17; 10:22; 23:2, 4; 1 Chron. 17:4

Ears being closed—2 Chron. 25:20

Choosing—Isa. 41:9; Jer. 1:5; Ezek. 20:5-6; Hag. 2:23; Rom. 9:8-14

Evil spirits—1 Sam. 16:14-15, 23; 1 Kings 22:19-21; 2 Chron. 18:18-22

False Prophets—Deut. 13:1-5
Famine of food—2 Sam. 21:1; 2 Kings 8:1; Ps. 105:16; Jer. 14:1-11
Famine of God's Word—Amos 8:11-12
Fear—Deut. 2:25; Josh. 2:9-11; 5:1; 2 Kings 7:6-7; 17:25
Forgiveness/Redemption—Pss. 103:3, 12; 130:8; Ezek. 18:22; Acts 2:23, 39
Hardening hearts—Ex. 4:21; 7:3; 9:12; 10:20, 27; Josh. 11:20; Rom. 9:18
Hate—Ps. 105:25
Healing—Deut. 32:39; 1 Sam. 2:6; 2 Kings 5:14; Prov. 3:6-8; 20:12
Helping people—1 Chron. 15:26; 18:6, 13; Ezra 5:5; Ps. 3:5; 68:6, 19
History—Pss. 44:3; 86:9; Jer. 40:2-4; Acts 14:16-17; 17:24-30
Hornets—Deut. 7:20-24
Joy—Neh. 12:43; Eccl. 5:19; John 15:11
Justice—Prov. 29:26
Kings, who rule—1 Sam. 16:1-7; 1 Kings 16:2; Dan. 2:21-22; 4:17, 24-35
Knowledge—Dan. 1:17
Life—Num. 16:22; 27:16; Deut. 32:39; 2 Kings 4:34; Prov. 10:27; Isa. 42:5
Man's exaltation—Josh. 3:7; 4:14; Jud. 3:9-10; 2 Sam. 5:10; 8:6, 14
Man's speech—1 Sam. 3:19
Man's will—Gen. 15:5; Num. 27:16; Deut. 10:14, 17; 32:39; 1 Sam. 2:6-9; 2 Chron. 21:16; 30:12; 36:22-23; Ezra 1:1, 5; Neh. 2:12; 7:5; Job 12:9-10, 16-17; 14:5; 31:15; 33:9-12, 15-17; 37:23; Prov. 16:1, 3, 9, 33; 19:21; 20:24; 21:1; Ecc. 9:1; Isa. 8:4-10; 9:11-12; 10:5-16; 13:17; 19:2-10; 44:18, 28; 45:1-6; Jer. 20:4; 24:7; 51:11; Dan. 2:21; 5:23; Matt. 11:25-27; 20:15; Luke 22:42; John 6:44, 65; 7:6, 30; 19:11; Acts 1:16; 4:25-28; Rom. 9; 15:32; 1 Cor. 12:11; Phil. 2:13; 2 Tim. 1:9; 1 John 5:20; Rev. 17:17
Miracles—Ex. 4:5-9; John 2:23; 4:48; 11:41-44

Mercy—Rom. 9:15, 18
Poverty—1 Sam. 2:7; Prov. 22:2
Prayer, answers to—Pss. 3:4; 69:33; 145:18; Prov. 15:29; Jer. 7:16; 29:13
Promises—2 Sam. 7:5-16
Prosperity—1 Sam. 18:14; 2 Chron. 27:6; Ps. 34:10
Punishment/Judgment—2 Sam. 12:10-12; 24:12; 1 Kings 11:12; 13:2-9
Reigning supreme in all things—Ex. 15:18; 2 Kings 10:30; Pss. 22:8; 82:8; 103:19; 115:3; 135:6-7; Prov. 16:4; Ecc. 11:9; Isa. 6:5; 7:1-9; 14:24, 27; 19:12; 33:22; 40:15-18, 22, 25; 43:13; 45:7; Jer. 18:1-12; Dan. 4:26, 35; 5:18; 11:36; Obad. 21; John 19:11; Rom. 9:16
Remembrances—Isa. 26:14; 65:17
Revealing His will—1 Sam. 3:4, 6, 8, 10; 1 Chron. 17:10; Isa. 29:10
Safety—1 Sam. 2:9; 23:14; 1 Kings 18:10; Ezra 8:21-23; Pss. 3:3; 66:9
Satan—Job 1:7-12; 2:2-6; Zech. 3:1-5
Sickness—Deut. 7:15; 32:39; 1 Sam. 5:6-12; Ps. 106:15; Micah 6:13
Spirit's gifts—1 Sam. 19:20-24; 2 Chron. 1:11-12; Acts 11:28; 1 Cor. 12:11
Spirit's presence—1 Sam. 16:13; Ezek. 2:2; 3:12, 24-27; 9:3; Acts 1:4
Spirit's voice—John 16:13-14; Acts 8:29; 13:1-4
Spiritual insight—Deut. 29:4; Matt. 11:25; Luke 10:21
Sun's movement—Josh. 10:12-13; 2 Kings 20:11
Testing—Pss. 11:5; 17:3; Prov. 3:12; 17:3; Ecc. 3:18
War—Deut. 2:30-36; 3:2-4, 22; 4:38-39; 7:2; 9:3; Josh. 8:1; 10:8-11, 32, 42; 1 Kings 11:14; 12:24; Isa. 13:4; 22:8; Dan. 1:1-2; Joel 3:2; Heb. 1:6-7; Rev. 13; 17
Wealth—Deut. 8:18; 11:12-17; 1 Sam. 2:7; 2 Chron. 32:29; Prov. 22:2
Weather—1 Sam. 12:18; 1 Kings 17:1; Pss. 135:6-7; 147:8-18; Isa. 29:6
Wicked people—Prov. 16:4; Rom. 9:22

Omnipotent: Within the person of God lies all power to perform what He wills. His power is limitless; it has no bounds. There is nothing too difficult for Him (Ex. 9:16; 15:6-7; Pss. 29:3-9; 105:26-41; 111:6; Matt. 19:26; Mark 10:27; Rev. 19:1).

Love: On four occasions the Scriptures declare that "God is . . ." He is "spirit" (John 4:24), "a consuming fire" (Heb. 12:29), "light" (1 John 1:5) and "love" (1 John 4:16). Respectively, these descriptions depict God's substance, holiness, perfection and goodness. It would be impossible to place any one of these aspects above the other. God's personality cannot be divided into primary and secondary classes. (See Deut. 4:37; 7:8, 13; 10:15; 23:5; John 3:35; Rom. 5:8; 8:37; Heb. 12:6.)

Good: "No one is good," said Jesus, "except God alone" (Mark 10:18; Luke 18:19). This goodness of God is threefold: (1) Perfect goodness—indicating that there is nothing evil or perverted in the character of God (1 Chron. 16:34; Pss. 25:8; 86:5; 106:1; Acts 14:17); (2) Benevolent goodness—indicating that God shows mercy to the righteous as well as the unrighteous (Matt. 5:45; Luke 6:35; Acts 14:17); and (3) Character goodness—indicating that God is the source of all virtue and morality (Gal. 5:22-23; James 1:17; 2 Peter 1:3-9).

Kind/Loving-kindness: God has an affectionate attachment for His people (to Joseph—Gen. 39:21; to Israel—Num. 14:19; to David—2 Sam. 7:15; etc.). It is most frequently associated with God's goodness to faithfully discharge His providential care (Ex. 15:13; Pss. 6:4; 31:17) and to provide repentance and forgiveness for sins (Ps. 51:1; Rom. 2:4; 11:22; Eph. 2:7; Titus 3:4).

Merciful/Compassionate: To those in misery and need, God displays His love through a tender, personal and eternal interest (1 Chron. 16:34, 41; 2 Chron. 5:13; 7:3, 6, 14; Ezra 3:11; Pss. 89:1-2; 136:1-26). For this reason He is addressed as "the Father of mercies and God of all comfort" (2 Cor. 1:3).

Long-suffering: God's enduring patience, with those who deserve His punishment, is called long-suffering. God withholds His judgments, as it were, until the last possible moment (Jer. 11:7; Micah 7:8; Matt. 23:37; Luke 13:6-9, 34; 2 Peter 3:9, 15).

Gracious: God is free in His goodness to those who have neither earned nor merited, in any manner, its bestowal. God receives nothing from man so as to prompt His giving. God gives out of love, not out of obligation or necessity. At best, man deserves only God's wrath (Rom. 3:10-20), but He stretches forth His hand and offers an escape for those under a just condemnation. This is grace (Deut. 7:7-8; 9:5; Isa. 42:1—43:8; Acts 14:3; 18:27; Rom. 3:24; 4:16; 2 Thes. 2:16; Titus 2:11; 3:4-7).

Holiness: The rich term *holiness,* in both the Hebrew and Greek, expresses the idea of "being set apart." This separateness involves two realms: physical and moral. In the physical or geographic realm, God is set apart from all other so-called "gods" (Ex. 12:12; 15:11; 20:3). Further, God is set apart from all Creation; that is, as the Creator, He stands infinitely and overpoweringly above the Creation (Rom. 1:18-25). Also, God is set apart unto His redeemed. Even as the redeemed are separated unto Him (Lev. 11:44; 1 Peter 1:15), so too, God is separated unto them as their Redeemer, Creator, King, and Lord (Isa. 43:14-15; 49:7; 54:5). In the moral realm, God is set apart from all that is evil (Job 34:10; Hab. 1:12; 1 John 1:5).

Righteous/Just: Because God is holy, He demands holiness of His Creation. Therefore, all unholiness must be punished. It is God's righteousness or justice (same word in the original) that demands a "just" recompense for violating His moral government. Thus, God is the Judge of the universe (Gen. 16:5; Jud. 11:27; 1 Chron. 16:33; Pss. 11:4-5; 26:1-2; Acts 17:31; 1 Cor. 5:13; Heb. 10:30-31).

Of God's retribution, the following may be said:

1. The judgment is impartial—Deut. 10:17; Job 13:6-12; Ps. 75:7.

2. The Judge is righteous; that is, He is the Standard by which judgment will be made—Gen. 4:7; 18:25; Ps. 62:12; Acts 10:34-35.
3. The guilty will not go unpunished—Ex. 20:7; Neh. 1:3.
4. The Judge cannot be bribed—Deut. 10:17.
5. The unrighteous are judged both temporally (Lev. 26:14-39; Deut. 28:15-68) and eternally (Matt. 13:30; 25:31-46).
6. The righteous are rewarded both temporally (Matt. 5:4-7; 19:29; Mark 10:30) and eternally (Matt. 5:8; 16:27; 1 Cor. 3:10-15).
7. The eternal judgment will be according to opportunity given and works done—Gen. 4:7; 1 Sam. 26:23; Prov. 12:14; 24:11-12; Isa. 3:10-11; 59:18; Jer. 17:10; 32:19; Hos. 4:9; 12:2; Zech. 1:6; Luke 12:47-48; 13:6-9; John 3:19-20; Rom. 2:5-12; Gal. 6:7; Rev. 2:23; 20:12-13.

Jealous: The jealousy of God is a key principle in the protection of His people. Because God is holy and righteous, He is jealous that His impeccable rules not be broken. He zealously seeks to maintain the loyalty of His redeemed and thereby reflect the worthiness and integrity of His holy nature (Ex. 20:5, 7; 34:14; Joel 2:18).

Blessed: The blessedness of God refers to His inexpressible perfection—the sum of all His identifying parts. When the Scriptures state, "Blessed be the Lord," the idea is this: "Let God be adored and worshiped and praised." Originally, the word "blessed" meant to bow the knees, but it came to be used commonly in the sense of "to worship, adore, and praise." Therefore, to bless God is to exalt Him above all (Ex. 18:10; Ruth 4:14; 2 Chron. 2:12; Dan. 3:28; Luke 1:68; 19:38; John 12:13; 1 Peter 1:3).

Glorious: The term "glory" and the phrase "glory of the Lord" speak of the visible presence of God. Wherever God is manifested, there is His glory. Objectively, this expression has reference to the magnificent appearance, radiating splendor, and beautiful luster of His figure. God's semblance is matchless in glory and brilliance

(Ex. 33:18-23; Rev. 1:12-17). Subjectively, the term depicts the solid recognition that He is completely worthy to receive all honor, respect, and exaltation (1 Chron. 16:29; Ps. 24:8-10; Phil. 1:11; 4:20; 1 Tim. 1:17; 1 Peter 5:11).

The Names of God (Primary)

God (Hebrew—*El, Elohim, Elyon;* Greek—*Theos*). The basic idea behind the first two Hebrew terms is strength and might. For instance, *Elohim* appears 34 times as the powerful Creator in Genesis chapter one. The third Hebrew word suggests elevation, making God the high and exalted One who is worthy of all reverence and worship (Gen. 14:18-22). The Greek word, *Theos,* is used in the New Testament to correspond to these three Hebrew words. There is no additional significance in the term.

Lord (Hebrew—*Adon, Adonai;* Greek—*Kurios*). The two Hebrew words come from a root meaning "to judge or rule." Therefore, this name, "Lord," depicts God as the Almighty Ruler, before whom everything and everyone must bow. The word also provides the comforting assurance that the Lord is no tyrant but a provider and protector (Gen. 15:1-2). The Greek equivalent means "power, master and ruler." Its core concept is that of authority. Thus, the Lord has the right to reign supreme in all man's affairs.

LORD (Hebrew—*Yahweh*). This is the most frequently used (5,500 times) and sacred name of God. Some of the Jews, either due to superstition or piety, refused to even speak this awesome name. In reading the Scriptures they would usually read *Adonai* in its place. The meaning of the term appears in Exodus 3:14, *I am that I am.* That is, "I shall be to you what I was for your fathers before you." The idea of God's eternal, convenantal faithfulness to Israel is the predominant thrust behind the word. It is invariably used in contexts of salvation (Joel 2:32; cf. Rom. 10:13).

The Names of God (Compound forms)
El-Shaddai: Almighty Blesser (Gen. 17:1; 28:3; 43:14).

Yahweh-Tsidkeenu: Yahweh our Righteousness (Jer. 23:6).
Yahweh-Nissi: Yahweh our Banner (Ex. 17:15).
Yahweh-Jireh: Yahweh will Provide (Gen. 22:14).
Yahweh-Tsebaboth: Yahweh of Hosts/Armies (Isa. 47:4).
Yahweh-Hoseenu: Yahweh our Maker/Life Maker (Ps. 95:6).
Yahweh-Ropheca: Yahweh our Physical (Ex. 15:26).
Yahweh-Shalom: Yahweh our Peace/Well Being (Jud. 6:24).

NOTE: In the Semitic world, proper and personal names were frequently selected to depict the character or characteristics inherent within that person or object. Hence, God is named after His nature, and significantly, His nature is to be the solution to man's every problem. Each name of God suggests His all-sufficiency for man's needs. Thus, for each need of man, God has a corresponding name of resolution.

10 | Jesus Christ

Heretical Views

During the first 70 years of the Church (c. A.D. 30-100) there were tremendous advances—both geographically (Col. 1:23) and theologically (Eph. 3:1-5). Like a giant fireworks display, the apostles and prophets gave witness to the Word of God. By the turn of the century, however, these two offices were completed (Eph. 2:20), and the lights which once shown brilliantly were now largely gone. The foundation had been laid. Now remained the exacting work of building upon it. This would be no easy task. With persecutions from the outside, and heretics on the inside, the Church began to act as one massive (though weakly organized) body. Its main mission was to define its doctrines and to defend its positions.

The center of controversy was often focused upon the person and work of Jesus Christ. Here is a partial sketch of the heresies which the Church was forced to confront and defeat.

1. *Ebionites:* This group handed the church its first challenges (c. A.D. 100-150). These were mostly "Christian" Jews who sought to maintain the Old Testament system of law above grace. This naturally led to an improper evaluation of the work of Christ to deliver the believer from the death of the law. Further, it led men to view Christ as a mere men and to deny His deity.

2. *Gnostics:* This body (c. A.D. 100-160) claimed to possess special, mystical, and supernatural knowledge which only its ini-

tiates were taught. Salvation came through the enlightened intellect. Although there were various brands of Gnosticism, they all subscribed to the notion that matter was evil. This means that Christ could not have been a real man with a genuine body; neither could He have died or been resurrected.

3. *Marcion:* He was an influential member of the congregation at Rome (c. A.D. 139) who rejected the whole Old Testament, including its God, and accepted only Paul's writings (excluding the Pastoral letters). He, like the Gnostics, denied the Incarnation. In A.D. 144 he was excommunicated.

4. *Monarchians:* In the 2nd and 3rd centuries a certain theological movement sought to promote the unity of the Godhead without promoting a trinity. In other words, they supported the view of three Gods in unity, rather than the orthodox position of one God with three personal modes of expression. The followers of Monarchianism held to one of two primary doctrines:

Dynamic Monarchianism or *Adoptionism* is the view that Jesus, as a man who lived a blameless life, *became* the Son of God by adoption at his baptism. It wasn't until the resurrection that he actually became deified.

Modalistic Monarchianism, the other option, contended that Christ was but the temporary form of the manifestation of the one true God. Hence, God the Father became God the Son, and God the Son became God the Spirit.

5. *Arians:* The Arians were followers of Arius, who denied the eternality of Jesus Christ. This heresy was officially refuted at the Council of Nicea in A.D. 325. The most Arian-like group today is the Jehovah's Witness body, which denies the eternality of the Son of God and the Trinity.

6. *Apollinarians:* The Apollinarians denied the absolute humanity of Christ. It was impossible for them to conceive of Jesus as being both God and man at the same moment. They held the position that Christ's body and soul were human but that His spirit or mind was eternal.

7. *Nestorians:* This group had the same problem as the Apollinarians, though they attempted to solve the dilemma differently. They contended that while Jesus was human, He was indwelt with

deity, much as a believer is indwelt with the Holy Spirit. The Nestorians were ultimately banished since this position left the full deity of Christ in jeopardy.

8. *Eutychians:* The followers of Eutyches went to the opposite extreme. They held the view that Christ's body was unlike man's body. They believed that it was divine and not human. *Christian Science* parallels this heresy.

9. *Unitarians:* This group rejects the doctrines of the Trinity and the deity of Christ. Unitarians believe in the goodness of man, and criticize such doctrines as the Fall, the Atonement, and eternal damnation. With its roots in Monarchianism and Arianism, Unitarians found some acceptance in Spain until A.D. 799. It was revived again in the 1500s and continued to spread until today, with its traditionally acknowledged center at Harvard Divinity School in Boston.

The Creeds

The church didn't, in its earliest stages, systematize its doctrines into neat formulas. But when confronted with intellectual inquiries and intellectual assaults, it began to organize and categorize what it believed to be basic Christian truths.

In various councils (the gathering of churchmen to discuss and find unity in all the doctrines for the entire universal church, the first being held in A.D. 325—the Nicene Council; see also Acts 15) the doctrines of the church emerged with greater and greater clarity, until approximately A.D. 450, when the final Nicene Creed and the Chalcedonian Creed were settled, establishing the position of the Orthodox church.

1. *The Nicene Creed* reads: "We believe in . . . one Lord Jesus Christ, the Son of God, begotten of the Father, Only-begotten, that is, of the substance of the Father, God of God, Light of Light, true God of true God, begotten not made, of one substance with the Father, through whom all things were made . . ."

2. *The Chalcedonian Creed* reads: "Therefore, following the holy Fathers, we all with one accord teach men to acknowledge one and the same Son, our Lord Jesus Christ, at once complete in Godhead and complete in manhood, truly God and truly man,

consisting also of a reasonable soul and body; of one substance with the Father as regards his Godhead, and at the same time of one substance with us as regards his manhood; like to us in all respects, apart from sin; as regards his Godhead, begotten of the Father before the ages, but yet as regards his manhood begotten, for us men and for our salvation, of Mary the Virgin, the God-bearer; one and the same Christ, Son, Lord, Only-begotten, recognized *in two natures, without confusion, without change, without division, without separation;* the distinction of natures being in no way annulled by the union, but rather the characteristics of each nature being preserved and coming together to form one person and one subsistence, not as parted or separated into two persons, but one and the same Son and Only-begotten God the Word, Lord Jesus Christ . . ."

The Scriptures Proclaim Christ's Deity

1. *The Scriptures Declare that Jesus is God*—Matt. 1:23; John 5:17-18; 20:28; Acts 20:28; Phil. 2:6-7; Col. 2:9; 1 Tim. 3:16; Titus 2:13; 2 Peter 1:1; 1 John 4:3.

2. *The Scriptures Declare that Jesus Fulfills Old Testament Divine Titles:*

Isa. 40:3	with Matt. 3:3 (Jehovah)
Joel 2:32	with Rom. 10:13 (Jehovah)
Isa. 45:23-25	with Rom. 14:10-12 (Jehovah)
Ps. 24:7, 10	with 1 Cor. 2:8; James 2:1 (Jehovah of Glory)
Jer. 23:5-6	with 1 Cor. 1:30 (Jehovah our Righteousness)
Ps. 97:9	with John 3:31 (Jehovah Most High)
Isa. 44:6	with Rev. 1:17 (Jehovah, First and Last)
Isa. 40:10-11	with Heb. 13:20 (Jehovah the Shepherd)
Prov. 16:4	with Col. 1:16 (Jehovah, Creator)
Ps. 102:24-27	with Heb. 1:8, 10-12 (God, Creator)
Hos. 1:7	with Titus 2:13 (God and Saviour)
Ps. 110:1	with Matt. 22:42-45 (Lord)

Ecc. 12:14	with 1 Cor. 4:5; 2 Cor. 5:10 (Judge)
Isa. 7:14	with Matt. 1:23 (Immanuel)
1 Sam. 2:2	with Acts 3:14 (Holy One)
Gen. 2:3	with Matt. 12:8 (Lord of sabbath)

3. *The Scriptures Declare that Jesus is Eternal:*
Old Testament proofs—Isa. 7:14; 9:6; Micah 5:2
New Testament proofs—John 1:1-3, 14; 3:13; 6:38; 7:29; 8:58; 17:5, 24; Col. 1:16-17; Rev. 1:11, 17; 22:12-13, 16.

4. *The Scriptures Declare that Jesus is Omnipresent*—Matt. 18:20; 28:20; John 14:20; 2 Cor. 13:5; Eph. 1:23.

5. *The Scriptures Declare that Jesus is Changeless*—Heb. 1:12; 13:8.

6. *The Scriptures Declare that Jesus is the Creator of the World:* Although the Father (Gen. 1:1; 1 Cor. 8:6) and the Holy Spirit (Gen. 1:2; Job 26:13; 33:4; Ps. 104:30; Isa. 40:12-13) were involved in the act of creation, the Son, too, is attested as having an integral part in this work (John 1:2; Eph. 3:8-9; Col. 1.15-17, Heb. 1:3, 8).

7. *The Scriptures Declare that Jesus is One with the Father:*
To *know* Him was to *know* the Father—John 8:19; 14:7
To *hate* Him was to *hate* the Father—John 15:23
To *believe* Him was to *believe* the Father—Matt. 10:40; John 12:44; 14:1
To *see* Him was to *see* the Father—John 12:45; 14:9
To *honor* Him was to *honor* the Father—John 5:23
To *receive* Him was to *receive* the Father—Mark 9:37

8. *The Scriptures Declare that Jesus is able to Forgive Sins*—Mark 2:5-10.

9. *The Scriptures Declare that Jesus may be Worshiped as God*—Matt. 14:33; 28:9; Luke 24:52; John 5:23; Rom. 10:9-13;

Phil. 2:9-11; Heb. 1:6; Rev. 5:12-14; Note: Men and angels never receive worship—Acts 10:25-26; Heb. 1:6; Rev. 22:8-9.

The Scriptures Proclaim Christ's Humanity: Jesus is not only God; He is *man* as well. He was tempted and limited even as we are. He could feel pain, and He could suffer. Note this listing:

1. Revealed in His Birth, Circumcision, and Growth—Gen. 3:15; Isa. 7:14; 9:6-7; 11:1; Matt. 1:18-25; 2:2; Luke 1:32-35; 2:1-52; Gal. 4:4.

2. Revealed in His being called a babe (Luke 2:16), a child (Isa. 9:6; Acts 4:30), a man (John 8:40; Acts 2:22; 17:31; Rom. 5:12-21), son of Mary (Mark 6:3), and son of Abraham and David (Matt. 1:1).

3. Revealed in His names: Jesus (Matt. 1:21), Son of Man (Matt. 8:20), Master (Matt. 8:19), Rabboni (John 20:16), the last Adam (1 Cor. 15:45), and the second Man (1 Cor. 15:47).

4. Revealed in His body of flesh and bones—Luke 24:39; John 1:14; 19:34; Heb. 2:14-15; 1 John 4:1-6.

5. Revealed in His human limitations. Jesus hungered (Matt. 4:2), slept (Matt. 8:24), thirsted (John 4:7; 19:28), wept (Luke 19:41; John 11:35; Heb. 5:7), grew weary (John 4:6), suffered agony (Luke 22:44), was tempted at all points like all men (Heb. 4:14-16), was scourged (Matt. 27:26), was nailed to a cross (Luke 23:33), died (John 19:30), was pierced in His side (John 19:34), and was buried (Matt. 27:59-60).

6. Revealed in His submission to and reliance upon the Father —John 5:19; 8:26-29; 10:18; 14:28.

7. Revealed in His need to pray—Mark 1:35; 6:46; Luke 22:41-45; Heb. 5:7. Jesus called the Father, "My God" (John 20:17).

8. Revealed in His retaining His manhood after death—1 Tim. 2:5.

Appearances of Christ in the Old Testament

Jesus did not begin to exist as a man at the time of His New Testament birth. He is eternal. He *is* God; He *was* God; He will *forever* be God; but He *became* a man. That is, Jesus consented to divest Himself of His eternal glory with the Father and come to earth in the form of a human (Phil. 2:5-8). But, before Jesus' appearance in the Gospels, He came to earth as God, though in a human form or in manlike appearance. Notice the following teachings of Jesus' prebirth appearances.

Jesus Christ is "The Angel of the Lord"

1. The Angel of the Lord is identified as Jehovah (Gen. 16:7-13; 22:15-18).
2. The Angel of the Lord is identified as a distinct person of the Trinity, apart from Jehovah (Gen. 24:7, 40; Num. 20:16; Zech. 1:12-13).
3. Of the three members of the Godhead, only Jesus Christ serves as the visible expression of God (John 1:18).
4. The Angel of the Lord only appears in the Old Testament. With the advent of Christ, this angel is never mentioned again. (All King James Version designations of *"the* angel of the Lord," should be rendered *"an* angel . . ." when appearing in the New Testament.)

Other Appearances
 1. As the One who walked with Adam—Gen. 3:8
 2. As the Man who met Abraham—Gen 18:1-33
 3. As the face of God before the elders—Ex. 24:9-11
 4. As the cloud—Ex. 33:9-23; 40:38
 5. As the Prince of the host of Jehovah—Josh. 5:13-15

Major Prophecies of Christ in the Old Testament

Direct Prophecy

1. *His Birth*
   a. Bethlehem—Micah 5:2
   b. Approximate date—Dan. 9:24-27
   c. Divine birth—Isa. 7:14; 9:6-7; Micah 5:2
   d. Human birth—Gen. 3:15
   e. He will be Semitic—Gen. 9:26
   f. He will come through Abraham—Gen. 22:18
   g. He will come through the tribe of Judah—Gen. 49:10
   h. He will come through the seed of David—2 Sam. 7:13
   i. He will be taken to Egypt—Hosea 11:1
2. *His Life*
   a. He will be a prophet like Moses—Deut. 18:15
   b. He will trust God from His birth onward—Ps. 22:10
   c. He will bring light to those in Galilee—Isa. 9:1-2
   d. He will be anointed by God's Spirit—Isa. 11:2; 42:1
   e. He will carry our pains and diseases—Isa. 53:4
   f. He will enter Jerusalem on a colt—Zech 9:9
   g. He will perform miracles—Isa. 35:5-6
3. *His Death*
   a. Kings will seek His death—Ps. 2:1-2
   b. He will be forsaken by God—Ps. 22:1
   c. He will be scorned and mocked—Ps. 22:6-8
   d. He will give light to the Gentiles—Isa. 49:6
   e. He will be betrayed for 30 pieces of silver—Zech. 11:12
   f. He will be smitten and pierced—Zech 12:10
   g. He will be cruelly beaten—Isa. 52:14
   h. He will die for world's iniquity—Isa. 53:5, 10
   i. He will have His garments divided—Ps. 22:18
   j. He will be betrayed by a friend—Ps. 41:9
   k. He will not have His bones broken—Ps. 34:20
   l. He will have His beard plucked out—Isa. 50:6
   m. He will be spit upon—Isa. 50:6
4. *His Resurrection*
   a. He will arise after three days—Hosea 6:1-2
   b. He will not see corruption—Ps. 16:10
   c. He will conquer death—Ps. 22:22

5. *His Present Work*
   a. He will function as a priest—Ps. 110:4
   b. He will sit on David's throne—Amos 9:11

Indirect Prophecy: Typology—Christ is Foreshadowed in:
   1. *Persons:* Aaron, Abel, Adam, David, Isaac, Joseph, Joshua, Kinsman-Redeemer, Melchizedek, Moses, etc.
   2. *Things:* sacrifices, feasts, the tabernacle, brazen serpent, smitten rock, cities of refuge, etc.
   3. *Events:* clothing of Adam and Eve, ark in the flood, exodus from Egypt, entrance into Canaan, etc.
   4. *Institutions:* priesthood.

The Childhood of Jesus

He was raised in a godly home—Matt. 2:13-23; Luke 2:39-52
   1. The annual trip to Jerusalem, for a carpenter, would be expensive, but it seems to have been a priority.
   2. Women were not required to go, yet Mary went.
Jesus never attended the schools—Mark 6:2; John 7:15. Jesus must have learned to read (Luke 4:16) and write (John 8:6) largely at home.
Nazareth was a wicked city, being the crossroads of trade routes—John 1:46.
He was obedient to His parents—Luke 2:51.
He grew in stature and wisdom and in favor with both God and men—Luke 2:52.

Why Jesus Came to Earth

To Sit Upon the Earthly Throne of David—His Kingship
   To receive David's throne—Luke 1:33, 67-69
   To be King of the Jews—Matt. 2:2, 6
   To deliver Jerusalem—Luke 2:38
   To preach the kingdom Gospel—Matt. 4:23; Luke 4:18-19
   To destroy Satan's works—1 John 3:8; Heb. 2:14
   To fulfill the Law and the Prophets—Matt. 5:17-18

To Redeem the World—His Priesthood and Prophethood
  To bring salvation—Matt. 1:21; John 3:16-17
  To bring light to the Gentiles—Matt. 12:18-21; Luke 2:32
  To remove sin—John 1:29
  To save the world—John 5:34
  To give His life as a ransom—Matt. 20:28
  To give the abundant life—John 10:10

The Names and Titles of Jesus

Names were very significant in the Semitic world. Names were used to describe the nature or characteristics of someone. Therefore, in the names and titles of Jesus Christ we find a flood of light which brilliantly reflects the many facets of His personality and mission.

Jesus: This word means "Jehovah is salvation" or "Jehovah saves" or "Jehovah will save." See Matt. 1:21

Messiah or Christ: This is the most common designation, besides "Jesus," and preeminently indicates that Jesus is the Davidic King. It means to be God's anointed Servant, and was applied to kings (1 Sam. 9:16; 24:10), priests (Ex. 29:1-9), and prophets (1 Kings 19:16; cf. Isa. 61:1; Zech. 4:1-6). Paul, however, used the word as a proper name.

Son of David: This is a Jewish ascription indicating Jesus' kingly genealogy (Matt. 1:1; 9:27; 12:23; 15:22; 20:30; cf. Jer. 23:5; 33:15).

Son of Man: This was Jesus' favorite way of designating Himself, and excepting Acts 7:56, it only appears in the Gospels. It depicts Jesus in His serving (Luke 19:10), dying (Mark 8:31) and glorified roles (Mark 8:38). Before Caesarea Philippi, the serving aspect is paramount; afterward, His death and eschatological kingdom are dominant.

Son of God: This expression essentially conveys the deity of Christ; God the Son. As the Son, He is God's "firstborn." That is, He occupies the position of absolute sovereignty due to God's choice. See John 5:18.

Lord: This term, the most common Gentile designation, also connotes Jesus' deity; the One possessing all authority in heaven and on earth. As such, it is a reference to His sovereign deity—Mark 12:36-37; Acts 2:36; Phil. 2:11.

The Word or Logos: This rich term refers to the preexistence of Jesus and His role as the divine agent in creation (John 1:1). It also designates Jesus as being the revealer of God (John 1:14).

I Am: The Jews were quick to understand this title as an ascription to being the eternal Yahweh (Jehovah). See John 8:58; Ex. 3:14.

Last Adam or Second Man: These descriptions describe Jesus as the head of the regenerated people of God (1 Cor. 15:45-47).

Other designations include: Almighty, Amen, Alpha and Omega, Advocate, Apostle, the only Potentate, Bread of Life, Captain of salvation, Chief Shepherd, Chief Cornerstone, Deliverer, Door, Immanuel, Faithful Witness, First and Last, God, Good Shepherd, Great High Priest, Head of the Church, Holy One, Just One, King of the Jews, King of kings, Lamb, Lamb of God, Life, Light, Lion of the tribe of Judah, Lord of glory, Lord of all, the Lord our Righteousness, Mediator, Morning Star, Nazarene, Only-begotten, our Passover, Prince of Life, Prince of the kings of the earth, Prophet, Ransom, Redeemer, Resurrection, Rock, Root of David, Saviour, Servant, Shepherd and Bishop of our souls, Sun of Righteousness, True Vine, Truth, Way, and Wonderful Counsellor. See concordance, (chapter 21) for references.

The Character of Jesus

No one has ever been totally like Jesus. His character is impeccable. Jesus is the righteous Pattern whom God has given us to follow. It is because of this that the Father has willed that we be conformed to Christ's image. Observe the likeness into which God is seeking to make you.

Holiness—Mark 1:24; Acts 3:14; 4:27, 30; 1 John 2:20

    He was clean from defilement—2 Cor. 5:21; Heb. 4:15; 7:26; 9:14; 1 Peter 1:19; 1 John 3:3, 5.

        He loved righteousness and hated iniquity—Heb. 1:9

        He was victorious over temptations—Heb. 4:15

        He rebuked sinners—Matt. 23:13-33; John 4:17-18

        He will judge the unbelieving—Matt. 25:31-41; 2 Thes. 1:7-9

Love for the Father—John 14:13
He performed the Father's will—John 4:34; 6:38; 8:55; Phil. 2:8
  He pleased the Father—John 8:29
  He finished the Father's work—John 17:4
  He sought only the Father's glory—John 7:18; 17:1, 4
Love for People
  1. *Who Jesus Loves*
    The Church—Eph. 5:25
    Individuals—Gal. 2:20; Eph. 5:2
    His own—John 13:1; 17:2, 9, 12
    Those who keep His commandments—John 14:21; 15:1-10
    The lost, the ungodly, and the sinners—Luke 19:10; Rom. 5:6, 8
    Children—Mark 10:13-16
    Select people—John 11:5; 19:26
  2. *How Jesus displays His love*
    By becoming poor for our sakes—2 Cor. 8:9
    By giving His life on our behalf—Gal. 2:20; Eph. 5:2; 1 John 3:16
    By forgiving sins—Luke 7:48; Rev. 1:5
    By seeking the lost—Luke 15:4-7
    By healing our sicknesses—Matt. 8:17; 14:14
    By supplying physical needs—Matt. 15:32
    By reproving believers—Rev. 3:19
    By not forsaking us—John 14:18
    By seeking our peace and joy—John 14:1-4, 27; 15:11
    By prayers for people—Luke 22:32; 23:34; John 17:1-26
    By caring for His mother—John 19:26-27
    By calling His own by name—John 10:3
    By keeping His own from becoming lost—John 17:12; 18:8-9
    By feeling what happens to His own—Acts 9:5; Matt. 25:31-45
Compassion
  For the shepherdless sheep—Mark 6:34
  For the hungry who heard Him—Mark 8:2

For the sick—Matt. 14:14; Mark 1:40-41
For the blind—Matt. 20:34
For the demonized—Mark 9:22, 25
For the bereaved—Luke 7:12-13
For the repentant sinner—Luke 15:20
For the neighbor in need—Luke 10:33-36

Prayerfulness
1. *When Christ Prayed*
    At His baptism—Luke 3:21-22
    All night—Luke 6:12
    Early morning—Mark 1:35
    Evening—Matt. 14:23
    Before eating—Matt. 14:19; Luke 24:30
    Before great trials—Luke 22:39-46
    While dying—Luke 23:34, 46
2. *Where Christ Prayed*
    Alone on a mountain—Matt. 14:23; Luke 6:12; John 6:15
    Alone in a solitary place—Mark 1:35
3. *For Whom Christ Prayed*
    God the Father—Matt. 6:9; John 12:28
    Himself—Luke 22:42; John 17:1; Heb. 5:7
    The disciples—John 14:16-17; 17:9, 11
    Those who believe—John 17:20-23; Rom. 8:34; Heb. 7:25
    Peter—Luke 22:31-32
    His enemies—Luke 23:34
4. *How Christ Prayed*
    To the glory of God—Matt. 6:9; John 17:1
    In submission—Matt. 26:42
    On His knees—Luke 22:41
    On His face—Matt. 26:39
    Eyes open toward heaven—Matt. 14:19; John 17:1
    Earnestly—Luke 22:44
    With a strong voice and tears—Heb. 5:7
    With repetition—Matt. 26:44
    With thanksgiving—John 11:41-42

Meekness—Matt. 11:29; 21:5; 2 Cor. 10:1
    Definition: Meekness is that attribute of gentleness in dealing

with the errors of others. (See 1 Cor. 4:21; 2 Cor. 10:1; Gal. 6:1; 2 Tim. 2:24-25; Titus 3:2.)
   Examples—Matt. 12:20; Luke 7:38-50; John 20:29; 21:15-17
Humility—Matt. 11:29
   He did not seek His own glory—John 8:50; Isa. 42:2
   He ate with the sinners—Matt. 9:10; Luke 15:1-2
   He was long-suffering during His cruel trial—Heb. 12:3; 1 Peter 2:23; Isa. 50:5-6; 53:7
   He came to minister, not to be ministered unto—Matt. 20:28
   He washed the disciples' feet—John 13:4-5
   He took on the form of men—Phil. 2:6-7
   He willfully died—Phil. 2:8
Righteousness—Heb. 1:9
Goodness—Matt. 19:16
Faithfulness—Isa. 11:5; 1 Thes. 5:24
Truthfulness—John 1:14; 7:18; 14:6; 1 John 5:20
Just—John 5:30; Acts 22:14
Guileless—Isa. 53:9; 1 Peter 2:22
Spotless—1 Peter 1:19
Harmless—Heb. 7:26
Zealous—Luke 2:49; John 2:17; 8:29
Self-denying—Matt. 8:20; Mark 3:20-21; 2 Cor. 8:9

The Earthly Ministry of Christ

Often we can acquire a good picture of someone by noting what they do and say. Here is a grouping of Jesus' works and words.
Looked at from the Places He Ministered
   The baptism and temptation of Christ—Matt. 3:1—4:11; Mark 1:1-3; Luke 3:1—4:13; John 1:19-34
   Ministry in Judea—John 2:13—4:42
   Ministry in Galilee—Matt. 4:12—18:35; Mark 1:14—9:50; Luke 4:14—9:50; John 4:43—8.59
   Ministry in Perea—Matt. 19:1—20:34; 26:6-13; Mark 10:1-52; 14:3-9; Luke 9:51; 19:28; John 9:1—12:11
   Ministry in Jerusalem—Passion Week—Matt. 21:1—26:5; 26:16—27:66; Mark 11:1—14:2; 14:10—15:47; Luke 19:28—23:56; John 12:12—19:42

Looked at from the Parables He Taught
 The tares—Matt. 13:24-30
 The hidden treasure—Matt. 13:44
 The pearl—Matt. 13:45-46
 The fish net—Matt. 13:47-51
 The unmerciful servant—Matt. 18:23-35
 The laborers in the vineyard—Matt. 20:1-16
 The two sons—Matt. 21:28-32
 The marriage feast—Matt. 22:2-14; cf. Luke 14:16-24
 The ten virgins—Matt. 25:1-13
 The talents—Matt. 25:14-30
 The growing seed—Matt. 4:26-29
 The master takes a far journey—Mark 13:34-37; cf. Luke 19:11-27
 The two debtors—Luke 7:41-43
 The good Samaritan—Luke 10:30-37
 The persistent friend—Luke 11:5-10
 The rich fool—Luke 12:16-21
 The wise stewards—Luke 12:42-48
 The great supper—Luke 14:16-24
 The unfinished tower—Luke 14:28-30
 The king goes to war—Luke 14:31-33
 The prodigal son—Luke 15:11-32
 The unjust steward—Luke 16:1-13
 The persistent woman—Luke 18:2-8
 The Pharisee and the publican—Luke 18:10-14
 The pounds of reward—Luke 19:11-27
 The house on rock and sand—Matt. 7:24-27; Luke 6:47-49
 The leaven—Matt. 13:33; Luke 13:20-21
 The lost sheep—Matt. 18:12-14; Luke 15:3-7
 The candle under a bushel—Matt. 5:15-16; Mark 4:21-22; Luke 8:16-17
 The new cloth and the old garment—Matt. 9:16; Mark 2:21; Luke 5:36
 The new wine and old skins—Matt. 9:17; Mark 2:22; Luke 5:37-38
 The seed sower—Matt. 13:3-9; Mark 4:3-9; Luke 8:5-8

The mustard seed—Matt. 13:31-32; Mark 4:30-32; Luke 13:18-19
　The vineyard—Matt. 21:33-46; Mark 12:1-12; Luke 20:9-19
　The fig tree—Matt. 24:32-35; Mark 13:28-31; Luke 21:29-33
Looked at from the Miracles He Performed
　Two blind men healed—Matt. 9:27-31
　A dumb demoniac healed—Matt. 9:32-35
　Money in the mouth of the fish—Matt. 17:24-27
　A deaf and dumb man healed—Mark 7:32-37
　A blind man healed—Mark 8:22-26
　The large catch of fish—Luke 5:1-11
　Raising the widow's son—Luke 7:11-18
　Healing the crippled woman—Luke 13:11-17
　Healing the man with dropsy—Luke 14:1-6
　Healing the ten lepers—Luke 17:11-19
　Restoring a man's ear—Luke 22:50-51
　Turning water into wine—John 2:1-11
　Healing the nobleman's son—John 4:46-54
　Healing the man at Bethesda—John 5:1-16
　Healing the man born blind—John 9:1-34
　Raising Lazarus from the dead—John 11:1-44
　Large catch of fish—John 21:1-11
　Demoniac in the synagogue cured—Mark 1:21-28; Luke 4:33-37
　Healing a centurion's servant—Matt. 8:5-13; Luke 7:1-10
　Healing the blind and dumb demoniac—Matt. 12:22; Luke 11:14
　Healing the Syrophenician's daughter—Matt. 15:21-28; Mark 7:24-30
　Feeding the four thousand—Matt. 15:32-39; Mark 8:1-9
　Cursing the fig tree—Matt. 21:18-22; Mark 11:12-14
　Healing the leper—Matt. 8:2-4; Mark 1:40-45; Luke 5:12-15
　Healing Peter's mother-in-law—Matt. 8:14-15; Mark 1:30-31; Luke 4:38-39
　Stilling the storm on the Sea of Galilee—Matt. 8:23-27; Mark 4:35-41; Luke 8:22-25
　Healing demoniac(s)—Matt. 8:28-32; Mark 5:1-20; Luke 8:26-35

Healing the man of palsy—Matt. 9:1-8; Mark 2:3-12; Luke 5:18-26

Healing the woman with an issue of blood—Matt. 9:20-22; Mark 5:25-34; Luke 8:43-48

Raising Jairus' daughter—Matt. 9:23-26; Mark 5:38-43; Luke 8:49-56

Healing man with withered hand—Matt. 12:10-13; Mark 3:1-5; Luke 6:6-10

Walking on the water—Matt. 14:22-33; Mark 6:45-52; John 6:15-21

Healing a demoniac child—Matt. 17:14-21; Mark 9:14-29; Luke 9:37-42

Healing a blind man—Matt. 20:30-34; Mark 10:46-52; Luke 18:35-43

Feeding the five thousand—Matt. 14:19-21; Mark 6:32-44; Luke 9:12-17; John 6:1-14

The Trials and Crucifixion of Jesus Christ

The Six Trials of Christ

1. *Before Annas,* immediately after His arrest—John 18:12-24. This trial was illegal, held contrary to Jewish law; no indictment was made; it was conducted at night; no witnesses were presented; and no counsel was provided for the defendant.

2. *Before Caiaphas,* immediately after leaving the high priest, Annas—Matt. 26:57-68; Mark 14:53-65. Two false witnesses were raised, but their testimonies contradicted one another. In answering the question whether He was the Christ, Jesus affirmed it.

3. *Before chief priests and elders,* in the morning—Matt. 27:1-2; Mark 15:1; Luke 22:66-71. Here, Jesus admits to His deity, resulting in His being convicted and referred to Pilate. This session was probably conducted in order to conform to the daylight ruling in Jewish law.

4. *Before Pontius Pilate*—Matt. 27:11-14; Mark 15:1-5; Luke 23:1-7; John 18:28-38. Accusations are made here of Christ's disloyalty to Rome, claiming to be King of the Jews. Pilate refers the case to Herod.

5. *Before Herod*—Luke 23:8-12. Jesus is silent in this trial. Herod had cut off God's voice through beheading John the Baptist; Jesus was to continue this silence. Here, the soldiers mock Christ.

6. *Before Pontius Pilate*—Matt. 27:15-26; Mark 15:6-15; Luke 23:18-25; John 18:29—19:16. Pilate offers to scourge and release Jesus, but the crowd demands His crucifixion, and Pilate succumbs to their cry.

The Fourteen Events on the Cross

1. Christ was offered wine mingled with gall to dull His senses—Matt. 27:33-34; Mark 15:22-23; Luke 23:33; John 19:17.

2. Christ refused this drink and was crucified—Matt. 27:35-38; Mark 15:24-28; Luke 23:33-38; John 19:17-24.

3. The first cry on the cross: "Father, forgive them; for they know not what they do"—Luke 23:34.

4. The soldiers divided the garments, casting lots—Matt. 27:35; Mark 15:24; Luke 23:34; John 19:23-24.

5. The chief priests, scribes, and people mocked Jesus—Matt. 27:39-44; Mark 15:29-32; Luke 23:35-38.

6. One of the thieves believed in Him—Luke 23:39-43.

7. The second cry on the cross: "Today shalt thou be with Me in paradise"—Luke 23:43.

8. The third cry: "Woman, behold thy son," and to John: "Behold, thy mother"—John 19:26-27.

9. Three hours of darkness—Matt. 27:45; Mark 15:33; Luke 23:44.

10. The fourth cry: "My God, my God, why hast Thou forsaken me?"—Matt. 27:46-47; Mark 15:34-36

11. The fifth cry: "I thirst"—John 19:28.

12. The sixth cry: "It is finished"—John 19:30.

13. The seventh cry: "Father, into Thy hands I commend my spirit"—Luke 23:46.

14. Jesus yielded up His spirit—Matt. 27:50; Mark 15:37; Luke 23:46; John 19:30.

The Importance of Christ's Death

1. *The Theme of Scripture*

a. Jesus came that He might die—Matt. 20:28

b. The prophets looked for Christ's death—1 Peter 1:10-11; 1 Cor. 15:1-4

c. The angels took interest in His death—1 Peter 1:12

d. Moses and Elijah took interest in His death—Luke 9:30-31

e. Christ's death is the theme of heaven's song—Rev. 5:8-12

f. In the New Testament alone, there are over 175 references to His death.

2. *The Teaching of Scripture—Why Jesus Died*

a. To take our sins upon Himself—Isa. 53:5, 8, 11-12; Rom. 4:25; 1 Cor. 15:3; 1 Peter 2:24; 3:18.

b. To pay the ransom for our life—Matt. 20:28. The "ransom" is the price paid to deliver all who believe from sin and its penalty.

c. To be the propitiation for our sins—Rom. 3:25; 1 John 4:10. "Propitiation" refers to the turning away of God's wrath toward sinners by means of a sacrifice, resulting in entering into God's favor.

d. To be our Passover—1 Cor. 5:7. The cleansing work that is derived by applying Christ's blood to one's life causes God to pass over him in the time of judgment—cf. Ex. 12:13, 23.

e. To redeem them who were under the judgment of the law—Gal. 4:4-5. "To redeem" means to ransom by means of a payment. That is, to purchase someone in order to deliver him from judgment—cf. Gal. 3:10, 13.

f. To deliver us from this present evil world—Gal 1:4.

g. To bring us to God—1 Peter 3:18.

h. To be Lord over the dead and the living—Rom. 14:9.

3. *The Teaching of Scripture—For Whom Jesus Died*

a. For believers/the Church—Rom. 8:32; 1 Cor. 5:7; 2 Cor. 5:21; Eph. 5:2, 25-27; Titus 2:14.

b. For weak brothers—Rom. 14:15; 1 Cor. 8:11

c. For many—Matt. 20:28

d. For men of every tribe, tongue, and nation—Rev. 5:9

e. For whole world—John 1:29; 1 John 2:2
f. For all—1 Tim. 2:6
g. For every man—Heb. 2:9
h. For the unjust—1 Peter 3:18
i. For sinners—Rom. 5:8
j. For the ungodly—Rom 5:6

The Resurrection and Ascension of Jesus Christ

The Eleven Appearances After The Resurrection
1. To Mary Magdalene—Mark 16:9-11
2. To the other Mary—Matt. 28:1-10
3. To Peter—Luke 24:34; 1 Cor. 15:5
4. To the two disciples on Emmaus road—Mark 16:12-13; Luke 24:13-35
5. To the ten disciples in the upper room—Mark 16:14; Luke 24:36-43; John 20:19-23.
6. To the eleven disciples in the upper room—John 20:26-29.
7. To seven disciples by the Sea of Galilee—John 21:1-23
8. To the five hundred—1 Cor. 15:6
9. To James, the Lord's brother—1 Cor. 15:7
10. To the eleven disciples on a mountain in Galilee—Matt. 28:16-20; Mark 16:15-18
11. To the eleven disciples on the Mount of Olives—Luke 24:44-53; Acts 1:10-11

The Importance of the Resurrection
1. It is the foundation for the Christian faith. If Christ did not rise, our faith is in vain—1 Cor. 15:14, 17.
2. It is foundational to conversion—Rom. 10:9-10.
3. It was central to the preaching of the early church—Acts 1:21-22; 2:24, 29-32; 4:33; 17:18; 23:6; 1 Cor. 15:15.
4. It is mentioned 104 times in the New Testament.
5. It demonstrates God's present power on our behalf—Eph. 1:18-20.
6. Jesus' resurrection guarantees our resurrection—2 Cor. 4:14; 1 Thes. 4:14.

The Six Appearances After the Ascension
1. To Stephen—Acts 7:55-56
2. To Paul—Acts 9:3-6; 22:6-11; 26:13-18
3. To Paul—Gal. 1:12-17
4. To Paul—Acts 9:26-30; 22:17-21
5. To Paul—Acts 23:11
6. To John—Rev. 1:12-20

The Present Work of Christ

Universal Lordship: While God the Father has exercised sovereign rule over all the affairs of creation, this honor is now bestowed upon the Son (Matt. 28:18; Rev. 1:5) who sits at the Father's right hand (Ps. 110:1; Matt. 22:44; Mark 12:36; 16:19; Luke 20:42-43; 22:69; Rom. 8:34; Eph. 1:20-21; Col. 3:1; Heb. 1:3-13; 8:1; 10:12; 12:2; 1 Peter 3:22).

Head of the Church: In this capacity, Jesus provides the life and direction of the Church (John 15:1-8; Acts 1:5; 1 Cor. 12:13; Eph. 1:22-23; 4:11; 5:29; Phil. 4:13; Col. 2:19; Heb. 13:21; 1 John 2:20).

High Priest: As God's Priest, Jesus Christ offered Himself as the perfect and eternal sacrifice in order to atone for the sins of the world (Acts 5:31; Heb. 10:1-18). Also in this regard, Jesus intercedes on the saints' behalf (Rom. 8:34; Heb. 7:25) and defends them as their advocate (1 John 2:1-2) against the accusations of Satan (Rev. 12:10-11). Christ's work as an advocate is based upon His sacrifice and on the saints' continual walking in God's light, thereby continually defeating Satan (1 John 1:7; cf. Heb. 3:1; Rev. 12:11b). Failure to walk in the light deprives one of the privileges of the work of defeating Satan through Jesus' blood.

Forerunner: Jesus has ascended to prepare the way for His own —John 14:2; Heb. 6:20; 9:24.

11 | The Holy Spirit

There are few subjects more important to the Christian than the one concerning the Holy Spirit. For the eternal Spirit of God is the source of the Christian's spiritual life: both its origin and continuation. The Holy Spirit is to our spiritual lives what the Creator is to the world. Without God, the Creator, the world would never have come into existence, and without His continuing, sustaining, preserving work, the world would crash out of existence. Similarly, without the Spirit of God, the Christian would never have been born again, and without the Spirit's ever-present sanctifying influence, the spiritual life of the Christian would drop back into the spiritual deadness from which it came.

From *The Holy Spirit* by Edwin H. Palmer

The Personality of the Holy Spirit

The Holy Spirit is not some impersonal force or influence, or energy that emanates from God's presence. Instead, the Holy Spirit, as the third member of the Godhead, possesses a complete entity and personality of His own. Therefore, the Holy Spirit should never be referred to as "It," but "He" (see John 14:16, 17; 15:26; 16:7-14).

Proofs that the Holy Spirit has personality—the possession of intellect, emotion, and will—are ample. He is said, for instance, to know the deep things of God (1 Cor. 2:10-13; 12:8), to love the saints (Rom. 5:5), and to make decisions (1 Cor. 12:11). Further, He is revealed as One who speaks (Acts 13:2; Rev. 2:7), prays (Rom. 8:26-27), teaches (John 14:26), guides (John 16:13), commands (Acts 16:6-7), and fellowships (2 Cor. 13:14). Finally, He may be grieved (Eph. 4:30), lied to (Acts 5:3), tested (Acts 5:9), vexed (Isa. 63:10), resisted (Acts 7:51), blasphemed (Mark 3:29-30), and quenched (1 Thes. 5:19).

The Deity of the Holy Spirit

There can be no doubt about the deity of the Holy Spirit. This is made plain in His attributes, His titles, and His works.

Attributes of the Holy Spirit
1. Eternal—Heb. 9:14
2. Omniscience—John 14:26; 16:12-13; 1 Cor. 2:10-11
3. Omnipotence—Luke 1:35; Acts 10:38
4. Omnipresence—Ps. 139:7-10
5. Holiness—Rom. 1:4
6. Glory—1 Peter 4:14; 2 Cor. 3:8-18

Titles of the Holy Spirit
1. Titles of Deity
    a. God—Acts 5:3-4; Acts 28:25-27 with Isa. 6:1-3
    b. Lord—2 Cor. 3:18; Heb. 10:15-17 with Jer. 31:31-34
2. Titles Showing Relationship to the Father
    a. Spirit of God—Gen. 1:2; Matt. 3:16
    b. Spirit of the Lord—Luke 4:18
    c. His Spirit—Num. 11:29
    d. Spirit of Yahweh—Jud 3:10
    e. Spirit of the Lord God—Isa. 61:11
    f. Spirit of your Father—Matt. 10:20
    g. Spirit of the living God—2 Cor. 3:3
3. Titles Showing Relationship to Son
    a. Spirit of the Lord—Acts 5:9; 8:39
    b. Spirit of Jesus—Acts 16:7
    c. Spirit of Christ—Rom. 8:9
    d. Spirit of His Son—Gal. 4:6

    e. Spirit of Jesus Christ—Phil. 1:19
    f. The Comforter—John 14:26; 15:26

Works of the Holy Spirit
1. In the Old Testament
   a. Creation—Gen. 1:2; Ps. 104:30; Isa. 40:12-14
   b. Indwelling certain men—Gen. 41:38; Num. 27:18; Dan. 4:8
   c. Convicting men—Gen. 6:3
   d. Enabling men to serve God—Ex. 31:3; Jud. 3:10; 6:34
   e. Writing the Scriptures—1 Peter 1:16; 2 Tim. 3:16
2. In the Life of Christ
   a. His birth—Luke 1:35
   b. His baptism—Luke 3:21-22
   c. His temptation—Matt. 4:1
   d. His anointing—Acts 10:38; see Luke 4:1
   e. His teaching—John 3:34; see Acts 1:1-2
   f. His miracles—Matt. 12:28
   g. His death—Heb. 9:14
   h. His resurrection—Rom. 8:11
3. In the World
   a. Convicts—John 16:8-11
   b. Calls—2 Thes. 2:13-14
   c. Witnesses to Christ—Acts 5:30-32
   d. Regenerates—Titus 3:5; see John 3:3, 5; 2 Cor. 5:17
4. In the Believer
   a. Glorifies Christ—John 16:14; see 1 Cor. 12:3
   b. Indwells—Rom. 8:9; 1 Cor. 6:19
   c. Infills—Eph. 5:18
   d. Imparts fruit of Spirit—Gal. 5:22-23
   e. Imparts gifts of Spirit—Rom. 12:3-7; 1 Cor. 12:1-28
   f. Seals—Eph. 1:13
   g. Communes/Fellowships—2 Cor. 13:14
   h. Teaches—1 John 2:20, 27
   i. Prays—Rom. 8:26-27
   j. Wars with the flesh—Gal. 5:17
   k. Comforts—John 14:16

l. Sanctifies—2 Thes. 2:13
  m. Empowers for service—Acts 1:8
5. In the Church
  a. Forms the body of Christ—1 Cor. 12:12-13; Eph. 2:19-22
  b. Appoints offices—Acts 20:28
  c. Gives guidance—Acts 15:28.

The Symbols of the Holy Spirit

A symbol is a visible object which serves to represent something else. The symbol points beyond itself to the greater reality it seeks to convey. The eight symbols of the Holy Spirit, therefore, are objects of visible reality which in a parallel manner depict some aspect of the Spirit's nature and work. Below is a listing and brief explanation of these symbols.

Dove—depicting gentleness (Matt. 3:16; 10:16).

Clothing—depicting a protective covering, equipment, holiness and power (Jud. 6:34; Luke 24:49; Rom. 13:12; Eph. 4:24; 6:11).

Oil—depicting the Spirit's ministry in producing holiness, sanctification, revelation, illumination, joyfulness, and prayerfulness (Ex. 27:20-21; 40:9-16; Lev. 14:10-29; 21:10; Ps. 45:7; Luke 4:18; Acts 10:38; 2 Cor. 1:21; 1 John 2:27).

Fire—depicting the Lord's presence (Ex. 3:2), the Lord's approval (Lev. 9:24), the Lord's protection (Ex. 13:21), the Lord's disapproval/judgment (Lev. 10:2), the Lord's discipline (Mal. 3:3), and the Word of God (Jer. 5:14; 20:9).

Water—depicting quenching one's thirst for salvation (John 4:14; 7:37-39) and cleansing (Eph. 5:26).

Seal—depicting ownership and safety (2 Cor. 1:22; Eph. 1:13; 4:30).

Earnest—depicting God's down payment and promise for the believer's future inheritance (2 Cor. 1:22; 5:5; Eph. 1:14).

Wind—depicting the sovereign nature of the Spirit (John 3:8) and His ministry of filling believers (Acts 2:4).

The Filling of the Holy Spirit—What It Is
Before discussing *how* to be filled with the Spirit, it will be helpful to first analyze *what* the Spirit's filling is. Below are six foundational truths:

1. Every believer is indwelt by the Holy Spirit from the moment of conversion (Rom. 5:5; 8:9, 11; 1 Cor. 2:12; 3:16; 6:19-20; 2 Cor. 5:5; Gal. 3:2; 4:6; 1 John 3:24; 4:13).

2. There are at least seven synonyms for the "filling" (Acts 2:1-4; 4:31; Eph. 5:18) of the Holy Spirit:
    a. Baptism—Matt. 3:11; Mark 1:4; Luke 3:16; John 1:33; Acts 1:5; 11:16
    b. Comes upon—Acts 1:8; 19:6
    c. Poured out—Acts 2:18; 10:45
    d. Gifts—Acts 2:38
    e. Falls upon—Acts 8:16; 10:44; 11:15
    f. Anoints—Acts 10:38
    g. Receive—Acts 10:47; 19:2.

3. The filling of the Spirit is always a conscious and visible experience, even as salvation is both conscious (Rom. 8:16) and visible (Matt. 3:7-8). If it were not this way, you could have it and never know it, and then lose it and never know that either! One *knows* when he is or is not filled.

4. The filling of the Holy Spirit is always for the purpose(s) of:
    a. Becoming like Christ—Gal. 4:19; Eph. 3:16-19; 4:11-16
    b. Doing God's will—Acts 1:8; Col. 1:9-10
    c. Enduring trials—Matt. 10:16-20.

5. Although every believer receives the Spirit at conversion, and while every believer has the potential for being filled at that time (Acts 2:38), some are not (Acts 8:15-17; 9:17; 19:1-7; see Rom. 12:1-2).

6. There are many fillings of the Spirit (Acts 2:4 with 4:8, 31; Acts 6:5 with 7:55; Acts 9:17 with 11:24; 13:9, 52). Therefore, the real question is not, "Have you been filled with the Spirit?" but *"Are you presently filled with the Spirit?"*
How it comes: God does not function like a machine. We don't push the right buttons and, "presto," receive the Spirit's filling. Nevertheless, some sound principles may be utilized as guidelines. They may be considered in two categories: negative and positive.

Negatively, the Spirit's filling does not come through: (1) church attendance, (2) moral conduct, (3) good works for Christ, (4) witnessing, (5) Bible study, or (6) faithfulness to people.

Positively, the Spirit's filling comes through: (1) a thoroughly repentant attitude, (2) a will which is ready to be broken of all the traits of the self-life, (3) a heart which waits upon God for His daily instructions, and (4) a personality which is ready to accept personal changes and act responsibly.

It is commendable that we pray for the anointing of the Holy Spirit, but too often after such familiar praying, nothing actually happens to our attitudes, our opinions, our actions or our reactions. Honesty demands we confess that in spite of praying, we are frequently never really filled with the Holy Spirit.

Some people teach that we should take the filling of the Spirit by faith alone, but this advice hardly measures up to the multiple proofs which the New Testament offers as evidences of being Spirit-filled.

These basic qualities can always be expected to characterize every Spirit-filled believer: love, joy, peace, long-suffering, gentleness, goodness, faithfulness, meekness, self-control (John 14:26-27; Gal. 5:22-23); faith (Acts 6:5-8; Rom. 12:3); assurance of salvation (Rom. 8:14-16); profound insight into the deep things of God (1 Cor. 2:9-15); spiritual gifts (1 Cor. 12:4-11);

speaking to one another about spiritual things (Eph. 5:18-19); singing in one's heart (Eph. 5:18-19); submission to one another (Eph. 5:18, 21); and a meaningful prayer life (Rom. 8:26-27; Eph. 6:18; Jude 20).

According to the New Testament, these wonderful qualities will distinguish and grace every person who is filled with the Holy Spirit.

The Gifts of the Holy Spirit

Twenty-one gifts are recorded in the New Testament. This listing is probably not intended to be exhaustive, but characteristic of God's workings in believers. Every believer is said to possess at least one gift, so that he may serve Christ's body (1 Cor. 7:7; 12:11). It is entirely possible that someone may have more than a single gift. Below is a listing of the gifts; they are arranged in three natural groupings (see Rom. 12:3-7; 1 Cor. 12:4-11, 28; Eph. 4:11).

OFFICE GIFTS		MINISTRY GIFTS
PROCLAMATION	**PRACTICAL**	**POWER**
1. Apostle	1. Service	A. *Revelation*
2. Prophet	2. Exhortation	1. Wisdom
3. Evangelist	3. Giving	2. Knowledge
4. Pastor-Teacher	4. Leadership	3. Discernment
5. Teacher	5. Mercy	B. *Illumination*
	6. Helps	1. Prophecy
	7. Administration	2. Tongues
		3. Interpretation
		C. *Expectation*
		1. Faith
		2. Healing
		3. Miracles

The Fruit of the Holy Spirit

The fruit or product of the Holy Spirit's reign in a believer's life is: love, joy, peace, patience, kindness, goodness, faithfulness, gentleness, and self-control (Gal. 5:22-23). The first four are qualities of being; they pertain to the inner man. The remaining five are qualities of doing; they pertain to the more visible outer man of actions.

Sinning Against the Holy Spirit

There are two general types of sin which may be committed against the Holy Spirit—forgivable sins and the unforgivable sin. Of the former type, everyone is guilty. These sins include the broad scope of resisting and quenching His will (Eph. 4:30; 1 Thes. 5:19). With one exception, it includes every conceivable sin of omission and commission.

The unforgivable sin differs from forgivable sins on two specific grounds: (1) It can only be committed by a lost person. In the context where this sin is found, it was the unteachable Pharisees who were charged as guilty of this high crime (Matt. 12:22-29). (2) It can only be committed by men so hopelessly depraved that they actually attribute the miracles of the Holy Spirit through Christ to the source of Satan. When Jesus performed miracles, it attested to His deity and the veracity of His message (Mark 2:1-12). Therefore, to reject the Spirit's work in this matter was to reject God's very plan of salvation and thus fall into the unpardonable snare of condemnation.

See Matthew 12:22-23 for the full context of this sin.

12 | Man

Man is the greatest marvel in the universe. Not because his heart beats forty million times a year, driving the bloodstream a distance of over sixty thousand miles in that time; not because of the wonderful mechanism of eye and ear; not because of his conquest over disease and the lengthening of human life; not because of the unique quality of his mind, but because he may walk and talk with God.

The Nazarene Weekly

The Creation of Man

Evolution: There are many *theories* as to where man came from and how he evolved, but the Scriptures alone give us an accurate account of man's origin. It is here that all speculation must give way to facts. Consider for a moment several renowned "discoveries" that were later totally discarded.

1. Java Man. The first major discovery of Java Man came in 1891 at the hands of Eugene Dubois. The findings consisted of parts of a jaw, cranium, and thigh bone. Various attempts were made to prove that this was "the missing link" between ape and men, but authorities now declare that these parts of ancient "man" more closely resemble parts of the ape or chimpanzee.

2. Piltdown Man. In 1911 Charles Dawson discovered por-

tions of a skull that were acclaimed as "the missing link" until 1953. In that year it was discovered that Dawson had taken an ape's skull and scraped it and treated it with chemical to make it look like a primitive form of man!

3. Peking Man. Davidson Black, near Peking, China, in 1927, found a lower molar tooth. From this single tooth he announced the discovery of "the missing link"! Later, other parts were excavated, but the whole findings were ultimately recognized as known animals—not man.

To this list could be added additional named species of ancient man, but the data is no more revealing or conclusive. In fact, the host of divided opinions among these scientists is a jungle in itself.

Countless drawings, many by professionals, have been made showing early mankind as a hunched apelike creature tracing his evolution to modern erect man. Is it possible for an honest artist or scientist to draw such descriptive pictures based on the limited discoverings unearthed so far? The answer is a resounding "No!" To prove this, a man once made a perfect replica of a Saint Bernard dog from a saw horse skeleton. Do not let detailed pictures and long, unpronounceable words or names be a stumbling block to the clear teaching of Scripture. Man did not evolve; he was created (Gen. 1:27; 5:1-2; Deut. 4:32; Ps. 104:30; 1 Cor. 11:9; 1 Tim. 2:13).

Image and Likeness: When God created man, He said, "Let us make man in Our image, after Our likeness" (Gen. 1:26). These two terms, image and likeness, are impossible to dissect into intricate separate meanings. In all probability they are both intended to depict certain moral, emotional, intellectual, volitional, spiritual, and physical aspects of man that correspond to the character and nature of God. It is possible that man's resemblance of God is more specifically his resemblance to the preincarnate body of Jesus. That is, God made Adam with a moral disposition, a mental, emotional, volitional, and spiritual capacity, and a physical shape which corresponded to the features of Jesus' prebirth body (see Rom. 5:14).

What was true of Adam and Eve's creation is also true of our own. Every child, regardless of the time or place of birth, is still made in the image and likeness of God (Gen. 5:1-2; 9:6; James 3:9). While most men do not exemplify the full potential of this creation (often perverting it), it remains God's intention, through salvation, to restore the resemblance of Christ in His own (Gal. 4:19; 2 Cor. 3:18; Phil. 3:21; 1 John 3:2).

Spirit, Soul, and Body. Man is a complex creature. He is more than just matter, such as a plant. He is more than just a soul in the sense that animals are souls (Gen. 1:30). He is spirit, soul, and body (1 Thes. 5:23; Heb. 4:12).

Christian theologians have long been divided on whether man's body is tripartite (spirit, soul, and body) or bipartite (body and soul—with the spirit being but an aspect of the soul). Regardless of how many separate components constitute man's being, most are agreed that man functions on three planes (which we have designated as spirit, soul, and body). Note the diagram below.

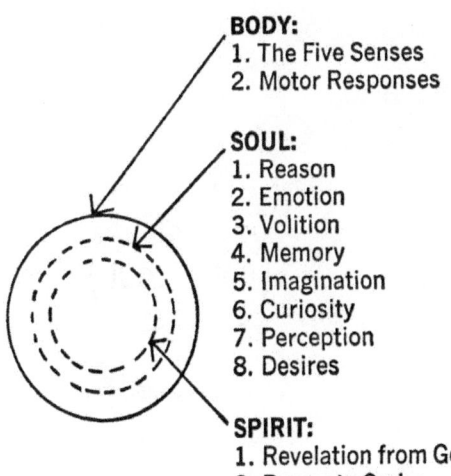

BODY:
1. The Five Senses
2. Motor Responses

SOUL:
1. Reason
2. Emotion
3. Volition
4. Memory
5. Imagination
6. Curiosity
7. Perception
8. Desires

SPIRIT:
1. Revelation from God (or Illumination)
2. Prayer to God
3. Communion with God
4. Fellowship with saints
5. Spiritual inner senses / knowledge / conscience
6. Spiritual fruit
7. Spiritual gifts
8. Spiritual warfare

EMPHASIS

Senses
Lust
Food
Health
Clothes
Comfort
Leisure

EMPHASIS

Reason
Emotion
Self-will
Memory/Knowledge
Curiosity
Imagination
Desire for things

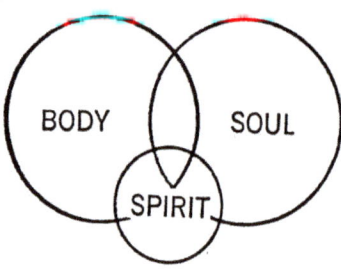

EMPHASIS

Traits of Body &
Traits of Soul

EMPHASIS

Idolatry
Asceticism
Mysticism
Occultism

It is evident that God intended for man to enjoy satisfaction in all three of these levels. In the fall of man, however, the spiritual aspect was shut off from God (though not from Satan or religion). This naturally created an imbalance in man's behavior. The diagrams below demonstrate some of the manners in which this imbalance may manifest itself.

The Fall of Man

After God made man, He placed him in the garden and gave him six tasks—privileges which presupposed responsibilities:

1. Exercise dominion over the fish, fowl, cattle, and creeping things;
2. Be fruitful and multiply;
3. Subdue the natural elements and use them to your advantage;
4. Eat only the herbs which bear seeds;
5. Cultivate the garden;
6. Do not eat of the tree of the knowledge of good and evil (see Gen. 1:26-30; 2:16-17).

These six privileges and responsibilities make it clear that man was designed to live under God's authority. Man was not at liberty to do as he pleased. There were some general and some specific guidelines by which God expected Adam and Eve to operate.

Consequences of the Fall

The "fall of man" occurred when Eve violated God's rules and when Adam followed her in the same rebellion. This transgression brought about 12 staggering consequences:

1. Both Adam and Eve died spiritually the very moment they sinned (Gen. 2:17; see Eph. 2:1-3).
2. They had their eyes of conscience opened (Gen. 3:7-10).
3. Their nakedness became shameful (Gen. 3:7).
4. In recognition of their guilt, they vainly attempted to rectify their sin through covering it with good works (Gen. 3:7).
5. They were alienated from God and made afraid of Him (Gen. 3:8-10).
6. The serpent, as an instrument of Satan, was cursed to crawl on its belly (Gen. 3:14).

7. God made a promise to send a Man, through Eve's seed, who would crush the Serpent—Satan (Gen. 3:15).

8. Satan, nevertheless, would wound the Man's heel; apparently by crucifixion (Gen. 3:15).

9. Between Eve (and all women following her) and serpents in general, God would put enmity (Gen. 3:15).

10. To Eve (and all other women) would come the curse of physical pain in childbearing. Nevertheless, the woman's desire for her husband and the procreation of children would remain. Furthermore, the husband was designated to rule over her (Gen. 3:16).

11. To Adam (and men in general) came the curse of hard labor in thorn-infested territory (Gen. 3:17-19).

12. To Adam and Eve (and to all who follow) physical death would be inevitable (Gen. 3:19). To this end they were sent forth from the garden and from the tree of life (Gen. 3:22-24).

Hope Remains Through Grace: The fall of mankind in Adam is a grim picture; and if the story ended here, how tragic would be our lot! How wonderful it is to know that the story did not stop at this point. Our gracious and merciful Father did not abandon Adam and Eve to a Christless and heavenless eternity. Instead, He did two things to correct their fatal error.

First, He "made coats of skin, and clothed them" (Gen. 3:21). Man-made coverings will never rectify the problems created by sin. Therefore, God graciously taught them that they were unable to earn salvation by their works and that He would provide for their salvation through a work of His own making.

Secondly, God instituted a sacrificial system whereby Adam's family could enjoy the forgiveness of sins and foretaste the work of Jesus Christ on the cross (Gen. 4).

The Miracle of Birth

God's design of procreation has existed since the beginning, but its intense pain is the product of Eve's transgression in the garden (Gen. 3:16; see 35:16). Regarding the birth process, the Scriptures make eight significant statements:

1. *Children come from God*

a. Cain—Gen. 4:1
   b. Seth—Gen. 4:25
   c. Reuben—Gen. 29:32
   d. Simeon—Gen. 29:33
   e. Levi—Gen. 29:34
   f. Judah—Gen. 29:35
   g. Jacob—Gen. 30:17
   h. Zebulun—Gen. 30:20
   i. Joseph—Gen. 30:24
   j. Samson—Jud. 13:1-5, 7, 9-25
   k. Obed—Ruth 4:13, 17
   l. Samuel—1 Sam. 1:27
   m. David—Ps. 139:13-16
   n. General texts—Gen. 33:5; 1 Sam. 2:5, 21; Hosea 9:11, 14.
 2. *God blesses seed for progeneration*
   a. Abraham—Gen. 12:2; 13:16; 15:2-4; 17:2-7, 16-19
   b. Ishmael—Gen. 16:11
   c. Isaac—Gen. 17:19
   d. Jacob—Gen. 28:10-15
   e. David—2 Sam. 7:14-17
 3. *God opens wombs*
   a. Sarai—Gen. 21:1-2
   b. Rebekah—Gen. 25:21
   c. Leah—Gen. 29:31
   d. Rachel—Gen. 30:22
   e. Hannah—1 Sam. 1:19-20
 4. *God closes wombs*
   a. Sarai—Gen. 16:1
   b. Abimelech's household—Gen. 20:17-18
   c. Rachel—Gen. 30:2
   d. Hannah—1 Sam. 1:5-6
 5. *Life begins when God imparts the spirit*—Ps. 139:13-16; Ecc. 12:7; Isa. 57:16; Zech. 12:1.
 6. *Birth is in God's timing*
   a. Isaac—Gen. 17:21; 18:10-14; 21:1-2
   b. Jeremiah—Jer. 1:4-5

c. Jesus Christ—Gal. 4:4
d. All persons—Acts 17:26, 28; Eph. 2:10
7. *God is the Lord of the spirits of all flesh*—Num. 16:22; 27:16; Isa. 57:16; Jer. 38:16; Zech. 12:1; Heb. 12:9.
8. *No one can live unless God ordains it*—Num. 24:33; Deut. 32:39; 1 Sam. 2:6; 2 Kings 5:7; Isa. 42:5; 44:24; Jer. 38:16; Ezek. 18:4.

The Mystery of Sickness and Its Causes

There are four potential causes of illness—*sin* (Lev. 26:14-36; Deut. 28:22-68), *sovereignty* (Job 2:1-7; 38:1—42:17; John 9:1-3), *nature* (Job 5:7; 14:1), and *demons* (Matt. 12:22). In the space below is a thorough listing of the sicknesses that are recorded in the Scriptures along with their causes.

Blindness:
1. Men of Sodom are stricken by angels—Gen. 19:11; Acts 13:11
2. Isaac; due to old age—Gen. 27:1
3. Israel (Jacob); due to old age—Gen. 48:10
4. Men of Israel; cause not stated—Lev. 19:14
5. Eli; due to old age—1 Sam. 3:2; 4:15
6. Ahijah, a prophet, due to old age—1 Kings 14:4
7. Syrian soldiers; due to prophet's curse—2 Kings 6:18
8. Two men; cause unknown—Matt. 9:27
9. One man; cause unknown—Mark 8:22-25
10. One man; cause is sovereignty of God—John 9:1-7
11. In general; cause unknown—Matt. 15:30-31; 21:14; Luke 18:35-43.

Boils:
1. On man and beast in Egypt; cause is sin—Ex. 9:8-11
2. On Job; cause is sovereignty of God—Job 2:7

Crippled:
1. Various persons; cause unknown—Matt. 15:30
2. Woman; cause is spirit of infirmity—Luke 13:11-17

Daniel reacts to visions in illness—Dan. 8:27; 10:16-19
Deadly diseases for Israel; cause is sin—Jer. 16:4
Defects; no son of Aaron with defects (blind, lame, disfigured face,

deformed limbs, broken foot or hand, a hunchback, dwarf, defect in eye, eczema, scabs, or crushed testicles) can enter the holy place—Lev. 21:16-24.
Demoniacs; cause unknown—Matt. 4:23-24; 12:22; 15:22-28; Mark 9:17-29; Luke 4:40-41; 6:17-18; 7:21; 9:1; Acts 8:7; 19:11-12
Discharge; cause is unknown—Lev. 15:1-18
Diseased feet on king Asa; cause is uncertain, though the continuation of the disease is due to his failure to seek God—2 Chron. 16:12
Dislocated thigh of Jacob; cause is wrestling with the angel of the Lord—Gen. 32:24-25, 31-32
Dropsy; cause is unknown—Luke 14:2-4
Dumbness; cause is unknown—Matt. 15:30-32; Mark 7:32-35
Dysentery in Israel; cause is sin—2 Chron. 21:12-19
Epilepsy; cause is unknown—Matt. 4:24; 17:14-18
Exhaustion; cause is overwork—Phil. 2:30
Fever; cause is unknown—Luke 4:38-39; Acts 28:8-9
Hand is dried up; cause is sin—1 Kings 13:4-6
Hemorrhage; cause is unknown—Luke 8:43-48
Irregular menstruation requires a sin offering—Lev. 15:25-31
Lameness; cause is unknown—Matt. 15:30; 21:14; Acts 8:7; 14:8
Leprosy:
  1. On Moses for a sign—Ex. 4:6-9, 30-31
  2. On those in Israel; cause is unknown—Lev. 13:1—14:57
  3. On Miriam; cause is sin—Num. 12:1-12
  4. On Naaman; cause is unkown—2 Kings 5:8-14
  5. On Uzziah; caused by sin—2 Chron. 26:18-22
  6. On one man; cause is unknown—Luke 5:12
  7. On ten men; cause is unknown—Luke 17:11-19
  8. General reference; cause is sin—2 Kings 5:27
Paralysis; cause is unknown—Luke 5:18-25; Acts 8:7-8; 9:33-35
Physical curses for disobedience: Sudden terror, fearful heart, fever that shall cause eyes to waste away, inflammation, boils, hemorrhoids, scab, itch, madness, blindness, bewilderment of heart, hunger, thirst, lack of all things, severe and lasting plagues, miserable and chronic sicknesses—Lev. 26:14-36; Deut. 28:22-68.

Plague; for grumbling—Num. 16:41-50; and harlotry—Num. 25:1-9
Poison; caused by viper bite—Acts 28:3-6
Poor eyes; cause is unknown—Gal. 4:13-15
Sickness:
   1. On Israel (Jacob); cause unknown—Gen. 48:1
   2. On Israel (Nation); cause is impatience and grumbling—Num. 21:4-9
   3. On Ahaziah, a sinful king who fell through a lattice and became ill—2 Kings 1:2-4
   4. On Joram, an evil king; cause is sin—2 Kings 8:16-18, 28-29
   5. On David; cause is sin—Ps. 38:3
   6. General illness; cause is sin—1 Cor. 11:29-30; James 5:14-16
   7. General illness; cause is unknown—2 Kings 13:14; Matt. 9:35; 11:5; 14:35-36; Mark 3:10; 6:5, 13, 56; Luke 7:2-10; 9:1-2, 6, 11; John 4:46-54; 5:1-16; Acts 3:1-11.
Sunstroke; cause is overexposure to the sun—Isa. 49:10
Tumors on Philistines; cause is sin—1 Sam. 5:6, 9, 12
Wasting disease on Israel; cause is sin—Isa. 10:16
Wife suspected of adultery is tested with curse of illness before priest—Num. 5:12-31
Withered hand; cause unknown—Luke 6:6
Wounds on David; cause is iniquity—Ps. 38:3-4

The Message of Man's Certain Death

Mystery has always surrounded the topic of death. Few understand it, and fewer still desire it. But death, for the Christian, is to produce neither fear(Heb. 2:14-15) nor confusion. Notice what the Scriptures teach about this subject.

The Original Source of Death:
   1. Adam's transgression against God in eating from the forbidden tree of knowledge brought *spiritual* death—Gen. 2:17; 3:1-12.
   2. Adam's (and his descendent's) separation from the tree of life brought *physical* death—Gen. 3:22-24.

The Time of Death:
   1. Can be premature:
      a. By murder—Gen. 4:8; 9:5-6; Ex. 21:12

b. By Divine removal without tasting death—Gen. 5:24; 2 Kings 2:11; 1 Cor. 15:51-52; 1 Thes. 4:15, 17
   c. By Divine judgment—Gen. 6:3—7:24; 38:7-10; Ex. 11:4-5
   d. By the pangs of birth—Gen. 35:16-18
   e. By capital punishment—Gen. 9:6; Lev. 20:9
2. Can be prolonged:
   a. By obeying parents—Ex. 20:12; Deut. 5:16
   b. By leaving the mother bird and taking only her young or eggs—Deut. 22:6-7
   c. By honest dealings—Deut. 25:15
   d. By obedience—Deut. 32:47
   e. By prayer—2 Kings 20:1-7; Isa. 38:1-21
3. Is usually unknown:
   a. Isaac—Gen. 27:2
   b. David—Ps. 39:4
4. May be known:
   a. Moses—Num. 20:12; Deut. 31:14, 16
   b. Aaron—Num. 20:23-28
5. Is controlled by God: Ex. 21:13; Deut. 32:39; 1 Sam. 2:6, 27-36; 5:9-12; 6:19; 25:38; 2 Sam. 6:6-7; 12:13-18; 1 Kings 20:35-36, 42; 21:19, 23; 2 Kings 1:4; 2:3, 5, 11; 1 Chron. 10:13-14; 13:10; Pss. 90:3; 135:8, 10; Isa. 25:8; Jer. 28:15-17; Rev. 1:18.

The Description of Death:
1. Breathing last breath (NASB)—Gen. 25:8, 17; 35:29; 49:33; Mark 15:37; Luke 23:46; Acts 5:5, 10.
2. The departure of the soul—Gen. 35:18.
3. The spirit returns to God—Ecc. 12:7.
4. Life is poured out (NASB)—Lam. 2:12; 2 Tim. 4:6.
5. Yielding up one's spirit—Matt. 27:50; John 19:30.
6. The spirit of man ascends upward—Ecc. 3:21.
7. Returning to the dust—Gen. 3:19; Ps. 104:29; Ecc. 3:20; 12:7.
8. Going to thy fathers—Gen. 15:15.
9. Gathered to his people—Gen. 25:8; 49:29.
10. Sleep with thy fathers—Deut. 31:16.

11. Tent cord is plucked up (NASB)—Job 4:21.
12. Like a flower he comes forth and is cut down—Job 14:2.
13. Man goes to his long home—Ecc. 12:5.
14. Sleep—Matt. 9:24; John 11:11; Acts 7:60; 13:36; 1 Cor. 15:18, 51; 1 Thes. 4:14.
15. Swallowed up of life—2 Cor. 5:4.
16. Clothed upon with our house from heaven—2 Cor. 5:2.
17. A departure—Phil. 1:23; 2 Tim. 4:6; 2 Peter 1:15 (NASB).

Death is Desired:
1. By Moses—Num. 11:15
2. By Elijah—1 Kings 19:4
3. By Job—Job 3; 6:8-11; 7:1-3, 15-16; 10:1
4. By Jonah—Jonah 4:8
5. By Simeon—Luke 2:29
6. By Paul—2 Cor. 5:2, 8; Phil. 1:20-23

Death does not end consciousness: Ecc. 12:5, 7; Matt. 17:3; 22:32; Luke 16:19-31; 23:39-43; Acts 7:55-56; 2 Cor. 5:1-8; 2 Tim. 4:6-8; Rev. 6:9-10; 7:9-17; 20:12—22:5.

13 | Sin

> The ultimate proof of the sinner is that he does not recognize his own sin.
>
> Martin Luther

You cannot put your sins behind you until you first face them. Whenever a man is ready to uncover his sins, God is ready to cover them!

The First Two Sins

Originally there was only one will in the universe—God's will. All was bliss. Then certain angels rebelled against this will and a new will emerged—Satan's (Isa. 14:12-17; Ezek. 28:11-19). The bliss vanished and evil entered Creation like a flood. Following this devastating revolt, God created man and gave him dominion over all the earth (Gen. 1:26, 28). In a short time, however, Satan deceived man and usurped his authority over the earth, taking the reins for himself (Gen. 3:1-6; Matt. 4:8-10; John 12:31; 14:30; 2 Cor. 4:3-4). Now the universe is confronted with three wills—

THE THREE WILLS IN THE WORLD		
1. God's	2. Satan's	3. Man's
Matt. 6:10; 7:21	Acts 26:18	Rom. 8:5-8
Heb. 13:21	2 Cor. 4:4; 11:3	1 Cor. 2:14—3:3
1 Peter 4:1-2	Eph. 2:1-3; 6:11-13	Eph. 2:1-3
1 John 2:17		1 Peter 4:2

God's, Satan's, and man's. The last two are the most closely associated, since both of these elected to oppose God's will. See chart below.

The Nature of Sin

There are numerous terms which are used in the Old and New Testaments to convey the concept of disobedience. No single word can capture its fullness. Nevertheless, there are three basic terms which encompass the essential nature of sin. They are:

Sin

The most basic meaning of the word "sin" is "to miss the mark"; that is, to fall short of God's acceptable standard in doing what is good and right (Rom. 3:23). Therefore, it signifies failure, much like a student who hasn't done acceptable work and won't advance to the next grade. Furthermore, it is evident that some of these failures were committed in ignorance (Lev. 4:2; 5:15; Num. 15:28). Such unintentional errors are, nevertheless, sins.

Transgression

The pictorial imagery created in this term is that of going beyond God's boundary of good and crossing over into the territory of evil. Put simply, it means "to revolt against God's right to rule or direct the course of one's life." Such expressions as "a self-made man," "independence," "lawlessness," and "self-will" are apt descriptions of transgression (see 1 Kings 8:50; Ps. 17:3; Isa. 43:27; Rom. 5:14; 1 Tim. 2:14; Heb. 9:15; James 2:9, 11).

Ungodliness

While *sin* designates the failure of man to measure up, and *transgression* depicts willful resistance against God's authority, *ungodliness* describes those wrongs which are directed specifically against mankind (2 Tim. 2:16; Titus 2:12; 2 Peter 2:5; Jude 15, 18). In a nutshell, ungodliness is treating our fellow men in any manner contrary to the way God would treat them.

Analyzed from a slightly different angle, sin may be viewed from three perspectives: (1) Sinning against God (lack of love and reverence toward Him, rebellion, doubt, faithlessness, incomplete obedience, stubbornness, etc.); (2) Sinning against man (lack of love for him, injustice, sexual immorality, arrogance, pride, etc.); and (3) Sinning against self (lack of self-love, sexual immorality, self-will; etc.).

The Scope of Sin

In Heaven: Sin began in the heavenlies with an anointed cherub looking at his own beauty (rather than the Lord's—Ezek. 28:11-19), and boasting his five-fold declaration, all beginning *"I* will . . ." (rather than "Thy will be done"—Isa. 14:12-17). This cherub *became* Satan with these acts. Soon a third of the angelic host followed their leader, sealing their doom for God's eternal fires (Rev. 12:3-4; Matt. 25:41).

On Earth: Nothing was left untouched in the effect of Adam's and Eve's sin. God's curse fell upon nature (Gen. 3:17), serpents (Gen. 3:14), woman (Gen. 3:15-16), and man (Gen. 3:17-19). In brief, the whole Creation suffers from the pains of sin (Rom. 8:18-22).

The Consequences of Sin

It would be impossible to pen all the consequences created by sin. This ten-point list is only suggestive. Sin has caused man's:

1. Alienation from the life of God—Eph. 4:18; Col. 1:20-22
2. Darkened understanding—Eph. 4:17-19
3. Spiritual blindness—2 Cor. 4:3-4
4. Carnal disposition—Rom. 1:18-32; Rom. 8:5-8; Gal. 5:16-21
5. Evil thoughts—Gen. 6:5
6. Corrupt lusts—1 Cor. 6:9-11
7. Subjection to Satan—Eph. 2:1-3; 1 John 3:8-10; John 8:44
8. Physical death—Gen. 2:17; 3:19; Num. 16:29; Rom. 5:12-17
9. Spiritual death—Rom. 5:21; Eph. 2:1-3
10. Eternal death—Matt. 25:41; 2 Thes. 1:9; Rev. 14:11.

14 | Salvation

God is the originating cause of salvation.
Jesus is the meritorious cause.
The Bible is the instrumental cause.
Faith is the conditional cause.
The Spirit is the efficient cause.
In other words:
God thought it.
Jesus brought it.
The Word taught it.
The might caught it.
The soul sought it.
Faith brought it.
The Spirit wrought it.
The devil fought.
But I've got it!

American Holiness Journal

Definition

The term "salvation" is rich in meaning. It means "to deliver, to liberate, to rescue, to help, to give victory, to bring healing and wholeness." The essential ideas of deliverance from danger or demons or disease, and preservation in safety, health, and prosperity are integral to its definition.

In the earlier stages of Scripture the emphasis rested mostly upon the physical elements of salvation, such as deliverance from the hostile hands of an enemy, whereas in the latter stages of Scripture the emphasis settles upon moral, emotional, physical, and spiritual salvation.

The concept of "redemption" is also central to the meaning of salvation. To redeem someone is to recover him from alien hands. Sometimes money was used to purchase back someone (such as a slave) from another party. In the Christian sense, redemption is secured by the price of Christ's precious blood (Matt. 20:28; 1 Peter 1:18-19). It is through this ransom that the Christian experiences deliverance from the world, Satan, sin, self, and death (1 Cor. 15; Eph. 2:1-9; Heb. 2:14).

The Scope of Salvation

From the perspective of *time,* salvation may be said to possess three successive stages:

Justification: This is a legal term and has reference to that past and heavenly activity of God whereby He delivers the believer from all condemnation through the substitutionary death of Jesus Christ (Rom. 3:21—5:21; Gal. 1:4; 1 Peter 3:18).

Sanctification: This is a religious term and refers primarily to God setting us apart for holy purposes, or to make us holy. The believer is further encouraged and strengthened by God to sanctify himself in order to continue the process which began with God. (Eph. 2:1-10; 3:17-19; 1 Thes. 5:23-24; 1 John 2:15; 3:3).

Glorification: This is a term of radiant splendor and has reference to the future and eternal activity of God whereby He delivers the believer (with absolute completeness) from all that is in opposition to His perfect will (Rom. 8:29-30; 1 Cor. 15:51-54; 1 Peter 1:5, 9).

God Calls Men to Salvation

God always takes the first steps in salvation. First, He prepares the plan, and then He invites men to participate in His provisions of grace. There are two types of calls or invitations which God gives:

The External Call: This invitation comes through the instrumentality of men who present the claims and demands of the Gospel of Jesus Christ. It encompasses the basics of a factual presentation (whether formal or informal), an invitation to respond positively to the information, an assurance or promise of the cleansing from sin, and an expectation that the one responding will unashamedly follow in the footsteps of the Saviour. See Matt. 28:19-20; Rom. 10:9-17.

The Internal Call: This invitation comes through the instrumentality of the Holy Spirit who convicts the hearer of the external call. While God speaks indirectly through another human instrument to the outer ear through the external call, He also speaks to the inner ear through the internal call of the Spirit. Hearing both calls is necessary to enter the gates of salvation. See John 1: 13; 6: 63-65; 16:7-11; Acts 2:37-39; 1 Cor. 1:23-24.

Faith Precedes Regeneration

Calvinists teach Monergism, that is, Regeneration precedes Faith. However, there are NO Scriptures that directly say regeneration precedes faith. Calvinist Bruce Demarest even admits that when he says "Faith does not appear to be an effect (result) of regeneration. The Bible teaches FAITH precedes REGENERATION. Ephesians 1:13-14 "In whom ye also trusted, after that ye heard the word of truth, the gospel of your salvation: in whom also after that ye believed, ye were sealed with that holy Spirit of promise, 14 Which is the earnest of our inheritance until the redemption of the purchased possession, unto the praise of his glory."

Conversion and Salvation

Salvation begins with conversion-that turning away from doubt, sin, self, Satan, and the world, and turning toward God, Christ and righteousness•. See Matt. 18:3; Acts 3:19. This turning "from" is called *repentance;* this turning "toward" 'is called *faith.* These two elements-repentance and faith-constitute the negative and positive aspects of conversion.

Repentance involves three areas: (1) *the intellect*—this is an acknowledgement of personal sin or guiltiness before God (Matt. 3:8; Job 42:6); (2) *the emotions*—this is a deep sense of sorrow for the transgressions committed against God (2 Cor. 7:10; James 4:9); and (3) *the will*—this is a positive determination to change—in thoughts, in speech, and in actions (Rom. 12:1-2; 1 Cor. 10:31; Col. 3:17).

Faith involves two qualities: (1) *confidence*—this is a firm persuasion in the Word of God (1 Peter 1:23); and (2) *character*—this is a steadfast adherence to the will of God, as expressed in His Word (2 Tim. 3:16-17; 1 Peter 2:2).

Salvation: Grace and Good Works

It will be helpful to look at salvation in this simple manner—we are saved *by* grace, *through* faith, and *for* good works. Read Ephesians 2:8-10.

Grace declares that God, through Jesus Christ, is for man. God is working to secure for man what He demands, but what man cannot provide for himself. This is grace. It is God's love extended in the form of Jesus Christ's substitutionary death for sinful men (Rom. 5:6-8). Man could never merit, earn or deserve salvation. It is a gift which can only be received.

Good Works are the spontaneous outgrowth of a life which has truly been the recipient of grace. Where good works are absent, there is ample reason to believe that salvation, too, is absent (James 2:14-26; 1 John 3:16-19).

Salvation: Our Standing and Our State

When God looks at a Christian, there are two ways He sees him. First, from the eternal perspective, God sees him in Christ—righteous and holy (1 Cor. 1:30). Second, from the temporal perspective, God sees him either living with unconfessed sins (in which case he would be called "carnal"—1 Cor. 3:1-3) or He sees him living with all sins confessed, washed in Christ's blood (in which case he would be called "spiritual"—1 Cor. 3:1-3; 1 John 1:5-10).

In brief, all believers are saints (from the eternal vantage point), but saints do not always act saintly (from the contemporary vantage point—compare 1 Cor. 1:2 with 3:1-3; note: the italicized words, "to be", are not in the original manuscripts, and therefore, should not be read).

Sixty-Six Things That Happen at Conversion
1. Adoption (new family)—Rom. 8:14-23
2. Redemption (new purchased freedom)—Rom. 3:24-25
3. Propitiation (new covering of sins)—Rom. 3:24-25; 4:7
4. Grace (new favor with God)—Rom. 5:1-2
5. Imputation (new records in heaven)—Rom. 4:1-11
6. Reconciliation (new union)—Rom. 5:10
7. Substitution (new sacrifice; Christ)—Rom 4:3-25
8. Sonship (new birth)—John 1:12
9. Heir (new inheritance)—Rom. 8:17
10. Righteousness (new legal standing)—Rom. 3:21—4:25
11. Retribution (new attitude by God to us)—Heb. 10:30-39
12. Ransom (new deliverance from death)—Matt. 20:28
13. Condemnation Removed (new verdict)—Rom. 8:1
14. Remission (new dismissal)—Matt. 26:28
15. Sanctification (new position/location)—1 Cor. 6:11
16. Justification (new acquittal)—1 Cor. 6:11
17. Washing (new cleansing)—1 Cor. 6:11
18. Preservation (new security)—John 10:27-29
19. Providence (new provision)—John 10; Phil. 4:19
20. Advocate Privileges (new lawyer)—1 John 2:1
21. High Priest's Prayers (new intercessor)—Rom. 8:34
22. Acceptance with God (new relationship)—Eph. 1:6
23. Perfection (new standing)—Heb. 10:14
24. Made Fit (new qualification)—Col. 1:12
25. Translated (new kingdom)—Col. 1:13
26. God's Inheritance (new ownership)—Eph. 1:18
27. God's Beloved—(new lover)—Rom. 1:7
28. Made Rich (new treasure)—Eph. 1:3

SALVATION / 119

29. Predestinated (fulfilling God's outline)—Rom. 8:29-30
30. Foreknown (fulfilling God's love)—Rom. 8:29
31. Foreordained (fulfilling God's work)—1 Peter 1:20
32. Elected (fulfilling God's choice)—Eph. 1:4
33. Called (fulfilling God's invitation)—Acts 2:38-39

Earthly Things:
1. Regeneration (new life)—Titus 3:5
2. Forgiveness (new conscience)—Eph. 1:7
3. Satanic Deliverance (new freedom)—Col. 1:13
4. Deliverance from Self (new freedom)—Rom. 6
5. Deliverance from Law (new freedom)—Rom. 6:14
6. Faith (new hope)—Rom. 12:3
7. Sense of Sonship (new relationship)—Rom. 8:15-16
8. Heir (new wealth)—1 Cor. 3:21-22
9. Access to God (new prayers)—Rom. 5:2
10. Assurance (new confidence)—1 John 5:13
11. Wisdom (new insight)—1 Cor. 1:30
12. Revelation (new knowledge)—Eph. 1:15-18
13. Holy Spirit (new Comforter)—John 14:16-17; Rom. 5:5; 8:9, 11; 1 Cor. 2:12; 6:19-20; 12:13; 2 Cor. 5:5; Gal. 3:2; 4:6; 1 John 3:24; 4:13
14. Fruit of Spirit (new character)—Gal. 5:22-23
15. Gift(s) of Spirit (new equipment)—1 Cor. 7:7; 12:7, 11
16. Eternal Life (new destiny)—1 John 5:11-12
17. Promises (new claims)—2 Cor. 1:20; 2 Peter 1:3-4
18. Made to be Light (new witness)—Eph. 5:8
19. Made Brethren (new family)—1 John 3:14-18
20. Made Child of Abraham (new race)—Gal. 3:7, 29
21. Made Child of Day (new protection)—1 Thes. 5:5
22. Made Child of Resurrection (new eternity)—Luke 20:36
23. Called Christian (new allegiance)—Acts 11:26
24. Made Epistle of Christ (new letter head)—2 Cor. 3:3
25. Member of Holy Nation (new nationality)—1 Peter 2:9
26. Made a Sheep (new Shepherd)—John 10:1-16
27. Made a Living Stone (new function)—1 Peter 2:5
28. Made Salt (new seasoning)—Matt. 5:13

120 / THE VICTOR BIBLE SOURCEBOOK

29. Made Servants (new job)—1 Cor. 7:22
30. Made Vessels unto Honor (new use)—2 Tim. 2:21
31. Made Vessels of Mercy (new favor)—Rom. 9:23
32. Made a Branch (new graft)—John 15:1-8, 16
33. Made an Ambassador (new mission)—2 Cor. 5:20

The Father's, Son's, and the Spirit's Work in Salvation
The relationship of the Father to the Son, and the Son to the Holy Spirit in the plan of salvation is unique. A careful study of the following outline will make this association plain:

The Father's Work: Design the Plan in Eternity
1. Foreknow—Rom. 8:29; 11:2; 1 Peter 1:2, 20.
2. Predestinate—Acts 4:28; Rom. 8:29-30; 1 Cor. 2:7; Eph. 1:5, 11.
3. Choose/Elect—Matt. 20:16; 22:14; 24:22, 24, 31; Mark 13:20, 22, 27; Luke 18:7; Acts 9:15; 22:14; 26:16; Rom. 8:33; 9:11; 11:5, 7, 28; 16:13; Eph. 1:4; Col. 3:12; 1 Thes. 1:4; 2 Thes. 2:13; 2 Tim. 2:10; 1 Peter 1:2; 2:4, 6, 9; 2 Peter 1:10; Rev. 17:14.
4. Call—Matt. 20:16; 22:14; Acts 2:39; Rom. 1:6-7; 8:29-30; 9:7, 11, 24; 11:29; 1 Cor. 1:2, 9, 24, 26; Gal. 1:6, 15; 5:8, 13; Eph. 1:18; 4:1, 4; Phil. 3:14; Col. 3:15; 1 Thes. 2:12; 5:24; 2 Thes. 1:11; 2:14; 1 Tim. 6:12; 2 Tim. 1:9; Heb. 3:1; 9:15; 11:18; 1 Peter 1:15; 2:9, 21; 3:9; 5:10; 2 Peter 1:3, 10; Jude 1; Revelation 17:14.

The Son's Work: Discharge the Plan in Fullness of Time
1. God's eternal covenant with Christ—Real
    a. Matt. 26:54; Mark 14:21; Luke 22:22 with Luke 24:25-27, 46; Acts 2:23; 4:25-28; 13:27-28; 26:22-23; 1 Cor. 15:3-4; 1 Peter 1:11, 20.
    b. Gal. 3:17 with Luke 1:68-79; 2 Cor. 1:20; Heb. 11:13, 17-19, 39-40.
    c. Eph. 3:11 with Eph. 1:3-14; Rom. 8:28-30; 2 Tim. 1:9.
    d. Heb. 10:5-9 with John 4:34; 5:30; 6:38; 17:14; 18:11; Phil. 2:6-8.

e. Isa. 42:6 with Mal. 3:1.
f. Heb. 7:22 with Heb. 9:15-16; 12:24; 13:20.
2. God's eternal covenant with Christ—Revealed
   a. That Christ should be the second federal head of the human race—1 Cor. 15:45, 47.
   b. That Christ would partake of flesh and bones—Heb. 10:5-9.
   c. That Christ would function in a Son and Servant relationship to God—Isa. 43:10; 49:3-6; 52:13; Matt. 12:8-20; John 10:17; 12:49; 14:28, 31; Acts 3:26; Phil. 2:7.
   d. That Christ would die for the sins of the world—Matt. 1:21; 18:11; John 1:29; 12:23, 47; 17:1-5; Acts 3:26; Rom. 5:6; 1 Tim. 1:15; Heb. 2:14-15; 10:5-10; 1 John 3:5, 8; 4:9-10.
   e. That Christ would receive, as His inheritance, the nations, along with all power and authority—Pss. 2:6-8; 8:5-8; 22:27; 110:1-7; Dan. 7:13-14; Matt. 11:27; 28:18; John 3:35; Eph. 1:20-23; Rev. 1:5.

The Spirit's Work: Declare the Plan Daily
1. Propagation—Luke 8:5-15; Rom. 1:16; 10:14-17; 15:18-21; 1 Cor. 1:18-24; Col. 1:4-6; 1 Thes. 1:5-6; 2:13; 2 Thes. 2:13-14; Heb. 4:12; James 1:18, 21; 1 Peter 1:23-25.
2. Conviction—Zech. 12:10; John 16:7-11; 1 Cor. 14:24.
3. Regeneration—John 3:3-7; Titus 3:5.
4. Sanctification—Rom. 15:16; 2 Thes. 2:13; 1 Peter 1:2.

Analyzing Salvation's Eternal Terminology

The Electing Principles
Foreknowledge: This word means "to know beforehand." While the Old Testament sometimes used the term "know" to reveal God's intimate and electing love for His people (Gen. 18:19; Ex. 33:12; Jer. 1:5; Hosea 13:5; Amos 3:2), it was also used merely to indicate God's objective omniscience (Pss. 44:21; 69:5, 19; Amos 5:12). In the New Testament, this former usage of "know" was

still existent, though the expression most frequently carried the weight of "advance knowledge."

1. Election/Chosen: In both the Hebrew and Greek, the terms election and chosen come from the same original word. The term means "to select or pick out." In the Scriptures, Israel, Christ, a lady in a local church, all other saints, and angels are called God's elect (1 Sam. 10:24; 1 Chron. 16:13; 1 Thes. 1:4; 1 Peter 2:6; 2 John 13). In short, any person or body of persons selected by God for any purpose is the chosen of God. It may have reference to choosing for salvation or choosing for certain works (compare Rom. 11:5, 7, 28 and Deut. 21:5).

In the Old Testament, saving election came only through the chosen seed line of corporate Israel. In the New Testament, saving election comes only through the chosen seed of Christ—IN HIS FEDERAL HEADSHIP. In other words, election is never singularly effectual. Rather, election simply designates the *means* through whom (Israel or Christ) salvation is secured. God's electing men to salvation is always corporate (see Rom. 11:7, 14, 17-24, 32). The significant emphasis on election in the New Testament can only be understood in the light of the fact that the corporate election in Israel was being replaced by election in Christ. Compare Romans 11 with Ephesians 1:3-7, 9-10, 12-13.

2. Predestination: This term only occurs in the New Testament and has reference to God's redemptive road map which He designed in eternity. The word is never used for arbitrarily determining an individual's destiny. Instead, the term is only used of God's predetermined *plan* to produce Calvary and of His *goal* that those who believe should become holy and Christ-like (compare Eph. 1:4; Rom. 8:29; Col. 1:21-22 with Col. 1:23).

The Electing Process

1. Calling: The means which God has chosen to use in effecting His eternal plans is a direct invitation or call to become His son/daughter. How does God make this plea? He does it through the call of the Gospel proclamation (2 Thes. 2:13-14) and the convicting, regenerating, and sanctifying work of the Holy Spirit. The whole world is bidden to "come," for God wills the salvation of

every person, everywhere! (Isa. 45:22; 49: 6; 55:1-3; Ezek. 18:23, 32; 33:11; Matt. 28:19; Mark 16:15; John 3:14-17; 6:33, 51; 7:37; 2 Cor. 5:17-19; Eph. 3:6-10; Col. 1:6, 23; 1 Tim. 2:4-6; 4:10; 2 Tim. 4:17; Titus 2:11; 2 Peter 3:9; Rev. 22:17)

2. Faith: Without faith it is impossible to please God and be saved (Heb. 11:6). No man can be regenerated apart from faith, but from where does faith issue? The answer is simple—within every man lies the substance of faith (Ecc. 3:11; Rom. 1:16-21). Certainly the amount of carnality which covers this precious element varies with individuals, but the Scriptures repeatedly imply an inherent faith within all men (Matt. 8:10; John 1:7; 3:14-18; 5:44-47; 7:17; 8:24; 10:37-38; 12:44-48; Rom. 3:21-31; 16:25-26; 1 Thes. 2:13; Heb. 3:1—4:7; 11:1-40; Rev. 22:14-19). Although faith resides in everyone, it is more frequently found to be dormant than active. How does one quicken this suppressed faith? The solution comes to us from Paul: "Faith comes from hearing ... the Word of God" (Rom. 10:17). Faith is brought to life, ignited, or generated at the hearing of God's Word (see Mark 4:26-29; Luke 8:4-15).

15 | Christian Growth and Maturity

An acorn is not an oak tree when it is sprouted. It must go through long summers and fierce winters; it has to endure all that frost and snow and side-striking winds can bring before it is a full grown oak. These are rough teachers; but rugged schoolmasters make rugged pupils. So a man when he is created; he is only begun. His manhood must come with years.

Henry Ward Beecher

Entering the Promised Land

God's immediate desire for newborn believers is that they might zealously pursue both the knowledge of and the practice of His will. It goes without saying that conversion to Christ does not bring about instant perfection. Instead, repentance and faith position us on the threshold of a new way of life. There are stages of development in the Christian life, just as there are in physical life.

A perfect picture of the stages involved in working out God's will in our lives comes to us from the story of Israel's deliverance from Egypt and her ultimate settlement in the Promised Land. There was a goal in Israel's salvation—the Promised Land. It was here that Israel was to receive her inheritance and find her rest (Heb. 3:7—4:11). In like manner, there is a corresponding goal in your salvation—*inheritance rest* (Heb. 3:7—4:11). This is both temporal (Matt. 11:28-30; see 1 Cor. 3:21-23; Eph. 1:13-

14; Heb. 1:14) and eternal (Rom. 8:17, 23-25; Gal. 3:29; Titus 3:7).

Therefore, since the Promised Land represents the objective of our salvation, the stages involved in arriving at the goal are plain:
1. Get out of Egypt;
2. Pass through the wilderness.

| CHARTING THE BELIEVER'S GROWTH PATTERNS |||
I. Out of Egypt	II. Through the Wilderness	III. Into the Land
A. Ruled by Satan B. Interested in self C. Ignorant D. Spiritually dead	A. Ruled by Self B. Trained in godliness C. Becoming informed D. Spiritually alive but carnal	A. Ruled by Christ B. Fulfilling God's will C. Transformed D. Spiritually alive and spiritual

It is one thing to leave Egypt (a picture of salvation). It is another thing to enter the Promised Land (a picture of inheritance rest—both temporally and eternally). A miracle is required to snatch Israel from the heart of Egypt, but no lesser miracle is necessary to snatch Egypt from the heart of Israel, once they have started on their journey to the land of promise.

Separating Egypt and the Promised Land is the wilderness (a picture of testing ground—Ex. 15:22-26; 16:4; Deut. 8:1-2). Here, Israel is to:

1. Bury all self-will and learn obedience—Num. 14:39-45; Deut. 8:1-3.
2. Forsake all human sufficiency and learn Divine might—Ex. 17:8-16.
3. Abandon all her desires for Egypt's pleasures and learn heaven's rewards—Num. 11:4-9; 21:5-9.
4. Resign her possessions and learn spiritual provisions—Lev. 27:30-34.
5. Disregard all human good and learn the necessity of God's righteousness—Ex. 19:9—20:21; Num. 5:1-4; Lev. 10:1-5.
6. Resist insubordination and learn the delegated authority of God's leaders—Num. 12:1-15; 16:1—17:13.

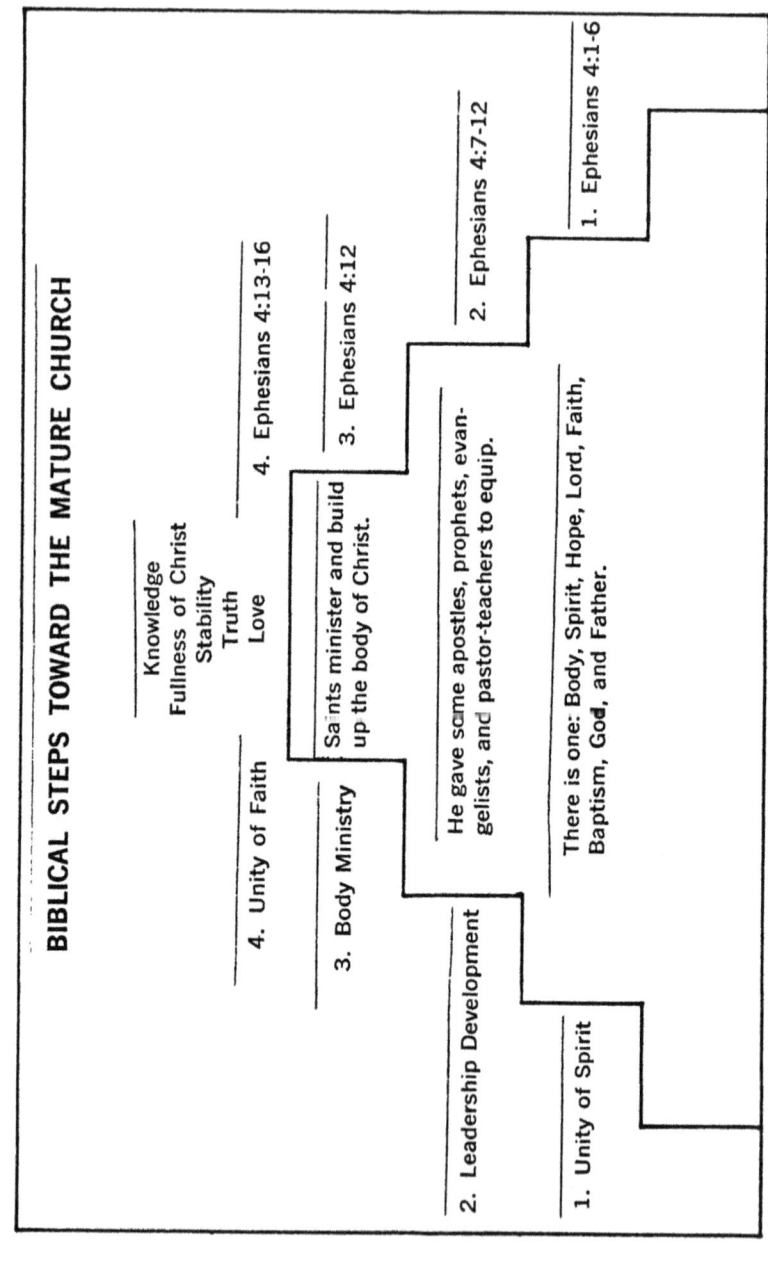

7. Turn from doubt and learn faith in God's Word—Num. 13—14; 20:7-13.

In the wilderness of Sin (Ex. 16:1) God refines disobedience from His people. The wilderness experience is the period of preparation which God's followers must successfully pass through in order to enter the Promised Land of God's complete will (see 1 Peter 4:1-2; Heb. 12:4-11).

The Three Types of People in the World

The whole human race may be divided into various spiritual groupings. There is the obvious redemptive or soteric division (lost and saved), but beyond this broader classification lies the more subtle and refined division of sanctification and maturity (lost—carnal/ordinary or spiritual or mature). Note the following diagram and Scriptures.

THE THREE TYPES OF PEOPLE IN THE WORLD		
LOST	SAVED	
Carnal/Natural Rom.. 8:5-8 1 Cor. 2:14	Carnal/Ordinary 1 Cor. 3:1-3	Spiritual 1 Cor. 3:1-2 Eph. 4:11-16 Col. 1:28 Heb. 5:12—6:2

Lost—Natural: To be lost is to be separated from God's saving grace. Temporally, this means to live in a state of depravity or deviation from the truth. It does not mean that every lost person is as vile as he could possibly be; but it does mean that there is nothing that a lost person can do which will merit or earn acceptance with God. Eternally, this means to live in a state of hell or torment (see Luke 16:19-31; Rev. 14:9-11). The qualitative degree of this unending retribution will be according to the extent of his depravity while on earth (Matt. 23:14; Luke 12:47-48; Rev. 20:10-15).

To be *carnal* is to be sensual or fleshly; that is, to be motivated only by those impulses which arise from a physical source. Such persons are dominated by self-government and are dull to genuinely spiritual matters (see Rom. 6:19; 7:18, 25; Gal. 5:19-21).

To be *natural* (literally, soulical) is to be dominated by mere human knowledge and insight. Such persons have either no perception or only a perverted perception of the *super*natural.

Saved—Carnal: To be *saved* is to be a direct participant in the redemption of God's grace. Temporally, this means to be the recipient of all spiritual blessings in heavenly places (Eph. 1:3); to have all guilt removed (Heb. 9:14); to be given the Holy Spirit for living a holy life (Rom. 8:13), for guidance (Rom. 8:14), for effective prayer (Rom. 8:26-27), for power (Acts 1:8) and for spiritual insight (1 Cor. 2:9-13); to have sound confidence in what the future holds and the One who holds the future (1 Thes. 4:13-18); and much, much more. Eternally, this means to live in the ultimate actualization of all that was begun temporally.

To be *carnal* is to be living in a condition no different (experientially) from a lost person. The dominion of self-government sometimes has its grip on believers too, though this domination is only temporary (1 John 3:9).

Saved—Spiritual: To be spiritual is to be living under the absolute Lordship of Jesus Christ. This implies the absence of all conscious sin (1 John 1:6); the mending, where possible, of relationships Matt. 5:23-26; 18:15-17); the up-to-date filling of the Holy Spirit (Eph. 5:18); a hunger and growth in spiritual things (Phil. 3:12-15); and a vivid display of the Spirit's fruit (Gal. 5:22-23). When a person abides in the spiritual state (making allowances for occasional lapses into carnality), he grows toward maturity. To be *mature* is to be all that is described in the spiritual category, plus the following: he is now stable in character, in knowledge, and in service.

God's Methods for Bringing Us to Maturity

There is no simple, single method that God uses to bring us to the place of Christian maturity. God utilizes many means to nurture us. The following list is suggestive of those ingredients which combine to feed a growing Christian.

Prayer: Acts 3:1; 4:31; 9:40; 12:5, 12; 13:1-4; 1 Thes. 5:17

Bible Study: John 15:7; 17:17; Eph. 5:25-26; 2 Tim. 2:15; 3:16-17
Teachings: Acts 2:42; 18:11, 27-28; 20:27-28; Eph. 4:11-12
Body Ministries: 1 Cor. 14:26; 2 Cor. 1:2-4; Gal. 6:1; Eph. 4:12-16; Col. 3:16; Heb. 3:13; 10:24-25; 12:15
Fellowship: Acts 2:44-46; 1 John 1:1-4
Chastisement: Ps. 119:67, 71; 1 Cor. 11:32; Heb. 12:3-15
Circumstances: John 6:5-6; 2 Cor. 12:1-10; Phil. 4:11-13

This itemization makes it clear that the maturing process entails much more than whipping ourselves into shape in an evening or so. There is the matter of learning how to deal with God through prayer; and there is also the matter of learning how to be dealt with by God through circumstances, chastisement, and Bible study. Additionally, there are fellow brethren who possess that missing ingredient we need in order to make our next step on the upward journey.

God obviously uses many tools to perfect His followers. But the one method which God has designed that carries a higher endorsement than all the rest is the Church, and when the local church is properly surrendered to the Lordship of its Head, Jesus Christ, the plan works. There are four progressive steps in this blueprint for Christian maturity, and they are all explained in the Book of Ephesians.

The Book of Ephesians is a momentous writing on the Christian Faith. In the first three chapters is the *Positional Doctrine* of the believer's *wealth* in Christ. In the remaining three chapters is the *Practical Doctrine* of the believer's *walk* with Christ. This Christian walk is analyzed from five perspectives: (1) the perspective of the corporate Church—4:1-16; (2) the perspective of personal purity —4:17—5:21; (3) the perspective of family relationships—5:22 —6:4; (4) the perspective of employee-employer relationships— 6:5-9; and (5) the perspective of Satanic warfare—6:10-18.

The intent of our investigation is to precisely articulate the practical implications of how the believer is to walk and mature with Christ through his church experience.

The Unity of the Spirit: Ephesians 4:1-6: In the Roman world, religion was both popular and diverse. Peoples' beliefs were constantly being modified and altered. New cults were common, and it wasn't exceptional to see the older views of God, worship and life changed to accomodate these new "insights." Therefore, when the first century Christian movement arose, it doubtlessly gave the impression of being just another cult in the maze of deities already existent.

Into this dark cloud of theologic confusion, Paul presents a forceful teaching that is designed not only to unshackle the Christian from cultic and occultic bondages, but to provide a theological base on which all true believers could and must stand.

Paul identifies this foundation as the *"unity of the Spirit"* (v. 3). There are seven essential ingredients that form this base:

1. "One Body"—the body of Christ, which comprises all genuine believers (see John 3:3, 5; 1 Cor. 12:12, 27).

2. "One Spirit'—the Holy Spirit of God.

3. "One Hope"—the glorious appearing of Christ (Titus 2:13-14).

4. "One Lord"—Jesus Christ, the Lord of lords and King of kings (1 Tim. 6:14-15).

5. "One Faith"—that declaration of truth which is delivered through Christ, His apostles and prophets (John 14:6; Eph. 4:4-5).

6. "One Baptism"—the baptism into the body of Christ (1 Cor. 12:13).

7. "One God and Father"—the only Sovereign in the universe who directs all things after the council of His own will (Eph. 1:1-14).

Therefore, the first step toward Christian maturity is the solid commital of the Church to these seven basic doctrines which constitute the "unity of the Spirit." This is biblical ecumenicity. Without this there can be no real Christian church and no real Christian growth.

Leadership Development: 4:7-12: Following our unity in the Spirit comes the second step on the pilgrimage to Christian maturity—leadership development. Four offices in the church have been set apart to accomplish this task: (1) apostles, (2) prophets, (3) evangelists and (4) pastor-teachers. The main burden of these men is to "equip the saints" (v. 12).

The word "equip" is most significant. In the medical world this word was used to designate the setting of a broken limb or the replacing of a misplaced joint. In the New Testament it was used of mending broken nets (Mark 1:19) and restoring an erring believer (Gal. 6:1). In short, the term means to restore something or someone into its former condition so that it may function as it ought.

It is the duty of these office bearers, therefore, to set, adjust, mend, and restore Christians until they are functioning in the Christian body with full spiritual health. (Their mission is *not* to hold classes on "How to Witness," but to develop believers whose healthy life cannot but automatically witness to the grace of God!)

Thus, biblical leadership development is not so much concerned with spiritual *information* as it is with spiritual *formation*. Its thrust is *sanctification*, not merely *education*. True leadership development is motivated by a key drive—helping believers live the life which reflects the riches they possess in Christ!

Body Ministry: 4:12: In step one we concentrated on the unity of the Spirit (basic doctrines). In step two we focused on the development of leaders (that is, the development of Christians whose lifestyle exhibits the character of Christ). This second step may introduce a different kind of leadership development program than we are accustomed to seeing, because its leaders are not known for their church positions, but for the quality of their stable lives. This single prerequisite enables them to advance to step three in the Christian maturity journey—*body ministry.*

In this level the believer is now ready to lead; or put more specifically, he is now ready to enter "the ministry." The work of "the ministry" is not confined to the few who hold the four offices mentioned earlier. Rather, it is the work of every Christian who has successfully completed steps one and two.

Now, what is this work to which every stable believer has been called? It is simply this—to "edify the body of Christ." But how does this minister "edify" (or spiritually build up) the body? The

BODY MINISTRY—T[

WHO IS CALLED TO BODY MINISTRY	SCRIPTURE
Perfected saints/Every joint (cf. 1 Cor. 12:12-31)	Eph. 4:12-16
Spiritual believers	Gal. 6:1
Brethren not hardened or unbelieving	Heb. 3:12-13
Brethren unwavering in their confession of hope	Heb. 10:23-25
Brethren	1 Thes. 5:14

Into the body of Christ have been placed certain members who are responsible for developing maturity in other members of that body. Once these "trainees" are steadfastly developed into consistent fruit bearing Christians, they are to reproduce this life (of which Christ is the conscious and visible Head) in still other members of the body. We have called this nurturing and reproducing process *body ministry*—the work of believers.

CHRISTIAN GROWTH AND MATURITY / 133

ORK OF BELIEVERS

WHAT IS THE WORK OF BODY MINISTRY
To bring the body to the unity of the faith (a. Full & accurate knowledge of the Son of God; b. Corporate maturity—resemblance of Christ—in character, in service, in stability; c. Grounded in Scripture; d. Caring for one another enough to speak the truth to them in love).
To restore brothers (who have unintentionally and unknowingly slipped—specially from rest into works).
Exhortation (Greek *para* = beside, *kaleo* = to call; to speak to someone intimately and encouragingly about the future. It must deal with unbelief, hardness of heart and steadfastness in our confidence of Christ's work).
Stimulate and exhort one another (to love, to do good works, and to keep coming together for teaching and fellowship).
To admonish (strictly warn) *the unruly* (idle, lazy, undisciplined); *to encourage the fainthearted* (timid); *to support* (hold on to, take an interest in, pay attention to) *the weak* (spiritually weak); *and to be patient toward all men.*

answer is so clear—he does it by helping (the word "minister" means one who serves or helps) his fellow brethren come into the same position of stability and spiritual vitality that he now enjoys. The work of the minister is simply to take immature Christians and reproduce his mature life in them. He says, in essence, "Follow me and I will make you become like Jesus." Read Mark 1:17; 1 Corinthians 4:16; 11:1; Philippians 3:17; 4:9. The only difference between body ministry and leadership development is in the one who does the developing. In one instance it is an office holder; in another it is not.

Unity of the Faith: 4:13-16: What began on a bare foundation ends in a "perfect man" and in "the fullness of Christ" (v. 13). Hallelujah! The climax of the church program is corporate maturity. That is, maturity in knowledge (v. 13), in stature (v. 13), in stability (v. 14), and in service (vv. 15-16).

Let us make two closing observations: (1) Individual Christians can become steadfastly mature, if they submit to authentic leadership development! (2) Every local church can become steadfastly mature, if they will but submit to body ministries!

"I will build my church, and the gates of Hades shall not prevail against it" (Matt. 16:18).

16 | Prayer, Faith, and Fasting

We are constantly on a stretch, if not a strain, to devise new methods, new plans, new organizations to advance the Church. This trend of the day has a tendency to lose sight of the man or sink the man in the plan or organization. God's plan is to make much of the man, far more of him than of anything else. Men are God's method. The Church is looking for better methods; God is looking for better men.

What the Church needs today is not more machinery or better, not new organizations or more and novel methods, but men whom the Holy Ghost can use—men of prayer, men mighty in prayer. The Holy Ghost does not flow through methods, but through men. He does not come upon machinery, but on men. He does not anoint plans, but men—men of prayer.

E. M. Bounds

And without faith it is impossible to please Him, for he who comes to God must believe that He is and that He is a rewarder of those who seek Him.   Hebrews 11:6 (NASB)

One thing is sure, throughout church history the men who laid spiritual foundations that stood the test of time were men who practiced fasting. Martin Luther fasted. John Knox fasted. John Wesley fasted. Charles Finney fasted. Almost every internationally known evangelist of our generation has practiced fasting.   Derek Prince

The Doctrine of Prayer

Original Languages: The most general Old Testament term for prayer is *palal,* and it means "to intercede." Other Old Testament words convey the basic idea of "asking, inquiry and petition." The New Testament terms, and their meanings, are as follows: *proseuchomai,* "to call on God" (it is general and refers to the entirety of prayer—Matt. 6:5); *parakaleo,* "to request, implore" (this is calling on Christ or God to come by one's side for the sake of aid —Matt. 26:53); *erotao* and *aiteo,* "to ask a question or favor" (John 16:26; James 1:5); *deomai,* "to seek, petition, intercession, please" (originally it meant "to lack," but became inverted to convey the idea of "filling all lack by asking"—2 Cor. 1:11); *euchomai,* "to ask and to dedicate/to make a vow" (it is prayer which stems from complete consecration—James 5:16); and *enteuxis,* "to intercede" (1 Tim. 4:5).

Prayer Postures:
Standing—Gen. 24:12-14
Lifting hands—1 Tim. 2:8
Sitting—Jud. 20:26
Kneeling—Mark 1:40
Uplifted eyes—John 17:1
Bowing—Ex. 34:8
On face—Matt. 26:39
Face between knees—1 Kings 18:42
Facing temple—Dan. 6:10
Smiting breast—Luke 18:13

Places of Prayer:
In battle—2 Chron. 13:14-15
In a cave—1 Kings 19:9-10
In a closet—Matt. 6:6
In a garden—Matt. 26:36-44
On a mountain—Luke 6:12
At a riverside—Acts 16:13
At the seashore—Acts 21:5-6
In streets—Matt. 6:5
In God's house—1 Kings 8:27-30
In hades—Luke 16:22-31
Everywhere—1 Tim. 2:8
In bed—Pss. 4:3-4, 8; 63:6
In a home—Acts 9:39-40
In a fish—Jonah 2:1-10
On a housetop—Acts 10:9
In prison—Acts 16:23-26
At the sea—Mark 5:18
In solitude—Mark 1:35
In the wilderness—Luke 5:16
On a cross—Luke 23:33-34, 46
In heaven—Rom 8:34

Times of Prayer:
Early morning—Mark 1:35
Morning—1 Chron. 23:30
Three times a day—Dan. 6:10
Evening—1 Kings 18:36
Before meals—Matt. 14:19
After meals—Deut. 8:10
Ninth hour (3 PM)—Acts 3:1
Bedtime—Ps. 4:4
Midnight—Acts 16:25
Day and night—Luke 2:37; 18:7
Today—Ps. 95:6, 8
Often—Luke 5:33
In youth—Jer. 3:4
In trouble—2 Kings 19:3-14
Daily—Ps. 86:3
Always—Luke 18:1; 1 Thes. 5:17

Fervency of Prayer is Demonstrated By:
Wearing sackcloth—2 Kings 19:1; Neh 9:1; Dan. 9:3; Ps. 35:13
Sitting in ashes/applying ashes to forehead—Job 2:8
Shaving head—Job 1:20-21
Smiting breast—Luke 18:13
Crying—1 Sam. 1:9-10; Jud. 20:26; Ps. 6:6
Applying dust to head—Josh. 7:6; Neh. 9:1
Rending garments—Josh. 7:6; 1 Kings 21:27; 2 Kings 19:1
Fasting—Deut. 9:18; Isa. 58:1-7; Acts 10:30-31; 13:2-3
Sighing—Ex. 2:23; Ps. 12:5; Ezek. 9:4; Mark 7:34
Groaning—Ex. 2:23-24; Ps. 6:4-6; John 11:38-42; Rom. 8:26
Loud crying—Heb. 5:7 (NASB)
Sweating blood—Luke 22:44
Agony—Luke 22:44
Broken heart/spirit—Pss. 34:18; 51:17
Pouring out one's heart—Ps. 62:8; Lam. 2:19
Rending the heart—Joel 2:12-13
Making an oath—2 Chron. 15:12-15; Ps. 132:1-2; Acts 18:18
Making sacrifices—Jud. 20:26; 1 Sam. 7:9-10; Ps. 20:1-3

Hindrances to Answered Prayer:
Failure to heed God's law—Prov. 28:9; Zech. 7:12-13
Lack of humility and turning from sin—2 Chron. 7:14-15
Forsaking God—2 Chron. 15:2
Not helping the poor—Prov. 21:13; Zech. 7:9-13
Any form of sin—Ps. 66:18; Isa. 59:1-2; James 4:8

Selfish desires—James 4:3
Improper respect for wife by husband—1 Peter 3:7
Public display—Matt. 6:5
Meaningless repetitions—Matt. 6:7
Unforgiving spirit—Matt. 6:14-15; Mark 11:25-26
Self-righteousness—Matt. 15:7-9; Luke 18:9-14
Losing heart—Matt. 26:40-44; Luke 18:1-8
Anxiety—Phil. 4:6
Lack of genuine faith—Ps. 37:5; Rom. 14:23; Heb. 11:6
Failure to pray in Jesus' name—John 14:13
Not abiding in Christ—John 15:7
Having idols in heart—Ezek. 14:1-3; 20:31
Requesting contrary to His will—Deut. 3:25-26; 1 John 5:14
Lack of doing good, not faithful and trusting—Ps. 37:3-4
Prayerlessness—1 Sam. 12:23
Wavering—James 1:5-7
Not with the whole heart—Deut. 4:29; 2 Chron. 15:12; 31:21
Without proper fear/awe of God—John 9:31
Not doing His will—John 9:31
Not worshiping God properly—Mal. 1:7-10

Consequences of Prayerlessness:
Wrong decision—Josh. 9:14-16
Judgment—1 Chron. 15:13
Forsaken by God—Ps. 81:11-12
Calamity—Prov. 1:24-28
Lust, murder, war and emptiness—James 4:1-3
Death—1 Chron. 10:13-14
Rejection by God—Jer. 7:13-16
Sickness—2 Chron. 16:12-13
False security—Isa. 30:1-3

Examples of Perseverance in Prayer: See. Gen. 32:24-26; 1 Sam. 7:8; 1 Chron. 16:11; Pss. 27:14; 33:20; 62:1-5; 145:15; Isa. 8:17; 25:9; 30:18-19; 40:31; 62:1, 6-7; Lam. 2:18-19; Hosea 12:6; Micah 7:7; Matt. 26:40-44; Luke 18:1-7; 21:36; Acts 6:4; 12:5; Rom. 1:9; Col. 1:9; 4:12; 2 Thes. 1:3; 2 Tim. 1:3; 1 Thes. 3:10; 5:17.

Examples of Prayers Offered Too Late: See Jud. 10:10-14; 1 Sam.

8:18; 15:24-26; Jer. 11:11, 14; 15:11; Ezek. 8:18; 20:1-3; Hosea 5:6-7; Amos 8:11-12; Micah 3:4-7; Zech. 7:13-14.

Examples of Prayers Forbidden by God: See Jer. 7:16; 11:14; 14:11; 1 John 5:16.

Examples of Unanswered Prayer: See 1 Sam. 28:5-6.

Examples of Prayers Heard But Not Answered: See Ex. 32:30-35; Deut. 3:23-26; Jer. 15:1; 2 Cor. 12:7-9.

Examples of Prayers Not Heard: See Deut. 1:43-45; 1 Sam. 8:18.

Examples of God Giving Petitioner What He Sought When It Was Not God's Will: See Pss. 78:29-31; 106:15.

The Doctrine of Faith

Old Testament: While the word "faith," in the King James Version, occurs only twice (Deut. 32:20; Hab. 2:4), its essence is amply expressed in such other common terms as "believe," "trust," and "hope." Old Testament faith is more frequently exemplified than explained. It is personified by men:
  Who put their confidence in God—Gen. 22:1-14; Prov. 3:26
  Who fear Him—Ex. 18:21; Prov. 1:7
  Who rest in Him—Pss. 16:9; 37:7
  Who wait upon Him—Isa. 40:31; Hosea 12:6
  Who cleave to Him—Deut. 4:4; Josh. 23:8
  Who make Him their Shield—Gen. 15:1; Deut. 33:29
  Who make Him their Rock—Deut. 32:4, 13, 15, 18, 30-31
  Who make Him their Fortress—2 Sam. 22:2; Ps. 18:2
  Who make Him their Refuge—Deut. 33:27; Ps. 46:1

New Testament: The Greek term *pistis* means:
  1. to be firmly persuaded, to have assurance/conviction;
  2. to be faithful, reliable, honest, and promise-keeping.
  Hence, the word for faith embraces both the *confidence* and the

character of the one who possesses it. In the former case, the word is always used of faith in God (Mark 11:22), or Christ (Rom. 3:22) or spiritual things (2 Thes. 2:13). In the latter instance, the term is employed to describe the virtue of those who hold these firm convictions (Matt. 23:23; Rom. 3:3; Gal. 5:22; Titus 2:10; 2 Thes. 1:4).

Therefore, an analysis of the two testaments reveals that the person who orders his life according to the biblical concept of faith will: (a) submit his heart to the way of God, (b) submit his intellect to the Word of God, and (c) submit his volition to the will of God. Genuine faith always affects the whole man—spirit, soul, and body.

The Biblical Definition of Faith—Hebrews 11:1: The writer to the Hebrews defines faith as *"the substance of things hoped for, the evidence of things not seen."* Faith, therefore, embraces two elements: *substance* and *evidence.*

The word *substance* comes from a term which means "that which stands under," like a fountain or a support. In the first century it was used as a legal term. It stood for "the whole body of documents bearing on the ownership of a person's property, deposited in the archives, and forming the evidence of ownership" (James H. Moulton and George Milligan—*Vocabulary of the Greek New Testament,* Eerdmans, 1949). Thus, a suggested translation of *substance* is *title deed.* "Faith is the title deed of things hoped for."

Therefore, from a positive perspective, faith assures or guarantees our inheritance in God's promises. Expressed negatively, without faith we possess no title deed and are without the assurance of ever receiving any inheritance from God.

Looked at from still another angle, faith may be said to stand in the place of that for which we hope (actually expect), even as the title deed only represents what is ours elsewhere. In other words, faith serves as the substance of that which we trust to receive until what we have trusted for is realized or manifested. When you pray, for instance, faith will occupy the substance or the place of that for which you have requested. In God's sight, your faith is regarded as being as good as the real thing, even though it may yet be invisible to you. Your faith takes the shape of your request and it stands as the actual object in God's presence.

Faith is also "the *evidence* of *things* not seen." The word *evidence* means "to have a conviction." The word *things* is a special Greek term, and in this context means "things already done." It is doubtful that these two words should be understood in a manner distinct from substance and hope. Rather, they complement one another. Therefore, an explanatory translation might be rendered as follows: Faith is the title deed which guarantees these things which are hoped and trusted for, and furthermore, faith is firmly convinced that while its expectation is yet unseen by the natural senses, it is a matter already accomplished by God and awaits manifestation in His perfect timing.

"Claiming" God's Promises By Faith: Although the word "claim" does not appear in the Scriptures, its principle is an implicit element of the Word of God. By *claiming* a promise we mean that act of faith whereby we appropriate God's promises as His very will on our behalf. In the words of the Hebrew letter, it is the mixing of faith with the Gospel message that constitutes the claiming of a divine provision (4:2). Put another way, it is believing that God's promises are as much ours today as they were when the Scriptures were first written.

A note of caution must be observed in this regard. There are thousands of promises in God's written Word which cover every conceivable facet of life and death. One is tempted to collect and arrange these promises in such a manner that any adverse circumstance is construed to mean a violation of God's perfect will (as revealed in the promises we've arranged).

Here is the crux of the issue. While God has made promises to meet our needs, we are not always spiritually perceptive enough to assess our actual need. A hungry stomach or a poorly clothed body would naturally give us the impression that our need is food and clothing. Therefore, we might claim God's promises for these essentials. But our Lord, who knows our deeper needs, may have other promises in mind for us to claim—as is demonstrated in the life of Paul.

Listen to Paul's observation in this matter of claiming God's provisions. "I have learned, in whatever state I am, in this to be content. I know both how to be abased, and I know how to abound . . . to be full and to be hungry, both to abound and to suffer need. I can do all things through Christ who strengthens me (Phil. 4:11-13).

Paul, the remarkable miracle man; the man of enormous faith, was occasionally degraded, hungry, and suffering need. How can this be? Didn't Paul know of God's wonderful promises? Certainly he did, but he had yet to learn that we cannot claim God's promises as a child puts a penny in a gum machine to receive his treat. Claiming promises is not a cut-and-dried matter. God's Word and man's life are more complex than this. (Read Hebrews 11:32-40 and especially observe the words "promise" and "faith" in verses 33 and 39).

Return again to the Philippian text, and carefully note the word *learned*. In the Greek, this is a perfect tense verb and could easily be translated by the English phrase, "initiated, little by little." In other words, Paul had to be gradually initiated into the deeper truth that his strength was to be found in Christ, and not in abounding or in being full. Paul was to discover that while *promised blessings* were to be sought, there was still a greater prize in life—*the blessed Promiser*—Christ Himself.

Therefore, before you "claim" just any promise, ask God to direct your heart to the one He has in mind for you to claim. Once you are certain of His specific Word to you, then claim it, confess it as yours, act upon it and do not waver!

The Triangle of Faith: All levels of faith are a gift from God entrusted to man for its cultivation. A measure of faith comes to all men through their creation (Ecc. 3:11; Rom. 1:19-20, 32; 2:14-16), through their association with nature (Pss. 8; 19:1-6; Acts 17:24-29).

In addition to this, another measure of faith comes to certain men through learning the Word of God (Rom. 10:8, 17; see Heb.

4:2; 6:12), through prayer (Luke 17:5; see Jude 20), and through God's sovereign bestowal (1 Cor. 12:9; see Matt. 11:20-27; Rom. 12:3, 6).

These two distinct measures of faith are commonly classified as General Revelation and Special Revelation. The former is given to everyone, while the latter is more narrow in its number of recipients (see Deut. 4:7; 1 Sam. 3:4-10; 1 Chron. 17:10; Ps. 147:9-20; Isa. 29:10; Matt. 11:20-27; Luke 12:47-48; Acts 14:16; 17:30; Rom. 3:1-2; 9:4-5).

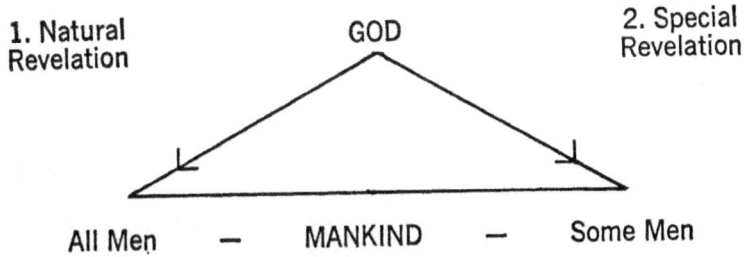

Fifteen Types of Faith:
1. Great faith—Matt. 8:10
2. Mustard seed faith—Matt. 17:20; Luke 17:6
3. Strong faith—Rom. 4:20
4. Weak faith—Rom. 14:1
5. Steadfast faith—Col. 2:5
6. Unfeigned (unhypocritical) faith—1 Tim. 1:5; 2 Tim. 1:5
7. Shipwrecked faith—1 Tim. 1:19-20
8. Bold faith—1 Tim. 3:13
9. First faith—1 Tim. 5:12
10. Overthrown faith—2 Tim. 2:18
11. Common faith—Titus 1:4
12. Sound faith—Titus 1:13
13. Rich faith—James 2:5
14. Precious faith—2 Peter 1:1
15. No faith—Mark 4:40

Ten Nuggets About Faith:
1. It can be seen by our actions—Matt. 9:2; James 2:14-26

2. The just live by means of faith—Gal. 3:11
   3. Faith and law are opposites—Rom. 4:13-15; 10:4-9; Gal. 3:12
   4. The absence of faith is sin—Rom. 14:23; Heb. 11:6
   5. Faith is only useful when exercised in love—1 Cor. 13:2
   6. It may be increased—2 Cor. 10:15; 2 Thes. 1:3
   7. It may be departed from—1 Tim. 4:1; 5:8, 12; 6:10, 21
   8. Faith is a fight—1 Tim. 6:12
   9. It defeats Satan's battle plans—Eph. 6:16
   10. The testing of our faith works to our good—James 1:3; 1 Peter 1:7

What Faith Secures:
   1. Faith obtains:
      Salvation—John 3:16; Rom. 10:9-10, 13; Gal. 3:26; Eph. 2:8
      Propitiation (protection from God's wrath)—Rom. 3:25
      Healing for whole body—Matt. 9:22; Mark 5:34; Luke 7:50; 8:48
      Fullness of the Spirit—Luke 11:13; Gal. 3:2, 5, 14; Eph. 3:14-21.
      Wisdom—James 1:5-7
      Provision for every need—Matt. 21:21-22
   2. By faith we are:
      Justified—Rom. 3:28, 30; 5:1; Gal. 2:16; 3:8, 24
      Made Righteous—Rom. 4:5; 9:30; Gal. 5:5; Heb. 11:7
      Kept—1 Peter 1:5
      Sanctified—Acts 26:18
   3. It is by faith we are to:
      Stand—Rom. 11:20; 1 Cor. 16:13; 2 Cor. 1:24
      Walk—Rom. 4:12; 2 Cor. 5:7
      Live—Rom. 1:17; Gal. 2:20
      Work—1 Thes. 1:3
   4. By faith we can overcome:
      Temptations of the world—1 John 5:4
      Satan's fiery darts—Eph. 6:16
   5. By faith we have·

Access to God—Rom. 5:2
Claim-rights to the promises of God—Heb. 6:12

Fasting

Perception of fasting
1. Old Testament: The Hebrew term for fasting, *tsum*, has the primary meaning of complete abstinence from food. The word comes from an Arabic term which signifies abstinence from food, drink, conversation, and sexual intercourse. A common synonym for fasting is "to afflict one's soul" (Lev. 16:29).
2. New Testament: The Greek word for a fast is *nesteia*. It is a compound of *ne*, a negative prefix, and *esthio*, which means "to eat." Hence, the term literally means "not to eat" and can be used of a voluntary abstinence, in which case fasting is in mind, or it can be used of an involuntary abstinence, in which case "hunger" is in view (2 Cor. 6:5; 11:27).

Put briefly, fasting is the deliberate shunning of food for spiritual purposes.

3. Three Types of Fasts:
   a. The Absolute Fast—This is a fast in which the one fasting abstains from both food and drink. Such fasting is an exceptional form and is used for only critical situations (Deut. 9:9, 18; Ex. 34:28; 1 Kings 19:5-8; Ezra 10:6; Es. 4:16; Acts 9:9).
   b. The Normal Fast—This is the most common type of fast. In this type of fast all foods are avoided, though water is taken.
   c. The Partial Fast—The only illustration of this fast is Daniel. For 21 days he abstained from every "tasty food, nor did meat or wine enter his mouth" (Dan. 10:3). On this type of fast all desirable foods, meats and special drinks are avoided.

Practice of Fasting
In the Great Commission Jesus said, "Go ye therefore and teach all nations . . . teaching them to observe all . . . I have commanded

you" (Matt. 28:19-20). Did Jesus teach on the subject of fasting? Did the early church fast?

1. Jesus' Teaching on Fasting:

In Matthew 6 Jesus taught on three key topics: (a) alms giving, (b) prayer, (c) fasting. Observe how Jesus approached each of these subjects.

    a. "WHEN therefore you give alms . . ." (v. 2).
    b. "WHEN you pray . . ." (v. 5).
    c. "WHENEVER (lit. "when") you fast . . ." (v. 16).

Jesus did not say *"if"* but *"when."* Our Lord took it for granted that a regular part of a saint's piety included fasting. He expected His audience to fast even as He anticipated their praying and giving alms.

Jesus further taught that "when the bridegroom [Jesus] shall be taken from them [His death and resurrection] . . . *then shall they* [His disciples] *fast"* (Matt. 9:15). When Jesus is in the physical presence of His own, it is a time for feasting, not fasting. Hence, Jesus' disciples never fasted when He abode on this earth. Nevertheless, Jesus explicitly taught that once He departed, His disciples would then fast. And fast they did.

2. Complete Biblical Index to Fasting: [1]

Gen. 24:33	Abraham's servant seeking bride for Isaac
Ex. 34:28	Moses' first period of forty days on Sinai
Lev. 16:29, 31	On the day of Atonement
Lev. 23:14	Until sheaf of wave offering was offered
Lev. 23:27, 32	On the day of Atonement
Num. 6:3-4	The law of the Nazarite
Num. 29:7	On the day of Atonement
Deut. 9:9, 18	Moses on Sinai
Jud. 20:26	By Israel after their defeat by Benjamin
1 Sam. 1:7-8	Hannah's prayer for a child

---

1. Arthur Wallis, *God's Chosen Fast* (Fort Washington, Pa.: Christian Literature Crusade, 1968), pp. 117-119.

PRAYER, FAITH, AND FASTING / 147

1 Sam. 7:6	At Mizpah under Samuel
1 Sam. 14:24-30	Saul's curse uttered in battle
1 Sam. 20:34	Jonathan grieved at Saul's hatred of David
1 Sam. 28:20	Saul before his death in battle
1 Sam. 30:11-12	Egyptian servant David found in field
1 Sam. 31:13	By those that buried Saul and his sons
2 Sam. 1:12	By David and his men at news of Saul's death
2 Sam. 3:35	By David at Abner's death
2 Sam. 11:11	Uriah's self-discipline in time of battle
2 Sam. 12:16-23	By David for the child of Bathsheba
1 Kings 13:8-24	By prophet who cried against altar at Bethel
1 Kings 17:6, 14-16	Elijah's restricted diet
1 Kings 19:8	By Elijah on his journey to Horeb
1 Kings 21:4-5	By Ahab after Naboth's refusal
1 Kings 21:9, 12	When Naboth was set on high
1 Kings 21:27	By Ahab in self-humiliation
1 Chron. 10:12	By those who buried Saul and his sons
2 Chron. 20:3	Proclaimed by Jehoshaphat before battle
Ezra 8:21-23	Proclaimed by Ezra
Ezra 10:6	Ezra mourning for faithlessness of exiles
Neh. 1:4	By Nehemiah for the restoration of Jerusalem
Neh. 9:1	By people of Jerusalem, confessing sins
Es. 4:3	By Jews learning of Haman's decree
Es. 4:16	Called by Esther before audience with king
Es. 9:31	In connection with the fast of Purim
Job 33:19-20	As a result of pain or sickness
Ps. 35:13	David on behalf of others who were sick
Ps. 42:3	When the Psalmist's tears became his food

Ps. 69:10	The cause of David being reproached
Ps. 102:4	The Psalmist forgets food in his affliction
Ps. 107:17-18	As a result of sickness
Ps. 109:24	The cause of David's physical sickness
Isa. 58	The kind of fasting which pleases God
Jer. 14:12	That which is unacceptable to God
Jer. 36:6, 9	Baruch reading Jeremiah's scroll on fast day
Dan. 1:12-16	Daniel and companions refuse king's food
Dan. 6:18	Darius when Daniel was in the lions' den
Dan. 9:3	Daniel praying for Jerusalem
Dan. 10:2-3	Daniel's three weeks' partial fast
Joel 1:14	In view of the day of the Lord
Joel 2:12	When returning to God with all the heart
Joel 2:15	Proclaimed by blowing a trumpet
Jonah 3:5-9	Proclaimed by people and king of Nineveh
Zech. 7:3-5	With mourning in the fifth and seventh months
Zech. 8:19	Kept in the fourth, fifth, seventh, and tenth months
Matt. 4:2	By our Lord for forty days
Matt. 6:16-18	Not to be practiced as the hypocrites
Matt. 9:14	By the Pharisees
Matt. 9:15	By the guests when the bridegroom is gone
Matt. 11:18	The abstemious character of John the Baptist
Matt. 15:32	State of the four thousand before our Lord fed them
Mark 2:18	By John's disciples and the Pharisees
Mark 2:19-20	By the guests when the bridegroom is gone

Mark 8:3	State of the four thousand when our Lord fed them
Luke 2:37	By Anna worshiping in the temple
Luke 4:2	By our Lord for forty days
Luke 5:33	By John's disciples and the Pharisees
Luke 5:34-35	By the guests when the bridegroom is gone
Luke 7:33	The abstemious character of John the Baptist
Luke 18:12	By the boastful Pharisee, twice a week
Acts 9:9	Saul of Tarsus after his encounter with Christ
Acts 13:2-3	By prophets and teachers in Antioch
Acts 14:23	At the appointment of elders in the churches
Acts 23:12-21	By Jews under an oath to kill Paul
Acts 27:9	Allusion to the annual day of Atonement
Acts 27:21, 33	By those with Paul before the shipwreck
Rom. 14:21	Abstaining for the sake of a weaker brother
1 Cor. 8:13	Abstaining for the sake of a weaker brother
2 Cor. 6:5	An ingredient of the apostolic ministry
2 Cor. 11:27	In the list of Paul's sufferings
1 Tim. 4:3	False teachers commanding abstinence

Purpose of Fasting

1. To Produce Piety—The Bible places a strong connection between the abundant availability of food and sin (Deut. 8:2-3, 11-14; Ezek. 16:49; Hosea 13:6). Adam and Eve's disobedience to God focused on the appeal of food (Gen. 3:6). In wrath God destroyed all but eight of the earth's inhabitants in part because of their strong desire to only feed their stomachs (Matt. 24:37-38). Esau's uncontrolled appetite led him to sell his valuable birth-

right (Gen. 25:31-33). It is too easy to live to eat, rather than eat to live. If the appetites of the stomach can dominate a man, he is in spiritual peril. Fasting says "NO" to the appeals of the flesh and "YES" to the appeals of the Spirit. It is a means whereby one may humble himself and seek God.

2. To Perfect Prayer—Fasting is always associated with prayer. Fasting demonstrates the earnestness of man. Further it gives to man an opportunity to seek God with his whole and undistracted attention.

3. To Penetrate Problems—There is no better time to fast than in the face of problems. Note what caused various biblical characters to fast.
- a. David fasted during chastisement—2 Sam. 12:16-23;
- b. Ezra fasted for protection on a dangerous journey—Ezra 8:21;
- c. Esther fasted when Israel's destiny was at stake—Esther 4:16;
- d. Paul fasted for safety aboard ship—Acts 27:9, 33;
- e. Jesus fasted when engaged in a spiritual conflict—Matt. 4:1-11;
- f. Various church leaders fasted for guidance—Acts 13:1-4;
- g. Paul and Barnabas fasted before selecting elders to rule a local church—Acts 14:23.

Publicity of Fasting

1. Private: Jesus said, "When ye fast, be not, as the hypocrites, of a sad countenance; for they disfigure their faces, that they may appear unto men to fast. Verily I say unto you, they have their reward. But thou, when thou fastest, anoint thine head, and wash thy face, that thou appear not unto men to fast, but unto thy Father, who is in secret; and thy Father who seeth in secret, shall reward thee openly" (Matt. 6:16-18). Jesus readily denounced fasting for purposes of public display.

2. Public: Joel writes, "Blow the trumpet in Zion, sanctify a

fast, call a solemn assembly. Gather the people, sanctify the congregation, assemble the elders, gather the children, and those that nurse at the breasts; let the bridegroom go forth from his chamber, and the bride out of her room" (Joel 2:15-16).

The Lord's call of a fast through Joel was no private affair. Everyone was informed. We too may tell others that we are on a fast (or of some past fasting experience) if it is in the spirit of humility and edifying to the hearer.

Prolongation of Fasting
The duration of a fast depends on the type of fast undertaken, the need at hand and the one who is fasting. In the Bible we read of one-day fasts, three-day fasts, seven-day fasts, fourteen-day fasts, twenty-one day fasts, and forty-day fasts. The duration was relative to the immediate factors involved in the situation.

God may lead someone on a *one meal fast* and another on a *one week fast*. The point is that the longevity of a fast does not determine its success or spirituality. We must be sensitive to God's leading and act accordingly.

Promises of Fasting
In the fasting chapter of the Bible, Isaiah 58, there is a list of at least nine blessings God desires to award the humble but fervent seeker.
1. New light, insight, illumination—v. 8;
2. Health—v. 8;
3. Increased testimony—vv. 8, 10;
4. Special divine protection—v. 8;
5. Quicker answers to prayer—v. 9;
6. Continual divine guidance—v. 11;
7. Continual satisfaction in drought—v. 11;
8. Our life will bubble up like a spring—v. 11;
9. Our life will be like a watered garden—producing much fruit—v. 11.

17 | The Church

The Church's preoccupation must be Christ. Jesus did not say, "I will build *your* Church; or *you* will build my Church." He said, *"I* will build *My* Church."

Arthur F. Fogartie in *Presbyterian Journal*

The church is not a gallery for the exhibition of eminent Christians, but a school for the education of imperfect ones, a nursery for the care of weak ones, a hospital for the healing of those who need special care.

Henry Ward Beecher

What shall it profit a church if it go round the world to make converts and lose its own sons and daughters?

Definition

Ekklesia: Our English word "church" is the translation of a Greek term, *ekklesia*. It means a body of people who have been assembled together through a call or summons. Therefore, the Christian church is that body of assembled people who have left their homes, at God's calling, to meet together. Furthermore, the idea of gathering is not so much focused on having a meeting as it is focused on meeting the One who called the assembly together—God. The business of the meeting is to hear His voice.

The Universal Church: On several occasions Paul uses the word *ekklesia* to designate the whole body of believers, of all the centuries, the world over (1 Cor. 10:32; 12:28; Phil. 3:6; Heb. 12:23). Below are some other designations for this universal brotherhood of the redeemed.
1. Body of Christ—1 Cor. 12:27; Eph. 1:22-23; 4:12; Col. 1:24
2. Bride of Christ—Rev. 21:9
3. Church of God—Acts 20:28; see 1 Tim. 3:15
4. Family—Eph. 3:15
5. Fold of Christ—John 10:16
6. God's building—1 Cor. 3:9
7. God's field—1 Cor. 3:9
8. Lamb's wife—Eph. 5:22-32; Rev. 19:7-9; 21:9
9. Spiritual house—1 Peter 2:5
10. New Jerusalem—Rev. 21:2

The Local Church: Within the all-embracing universal Church are many local bodies of believers who unite together to fulfill God's will (Rom. 16:1; 1 Cor. 1:2; Gal. 1:2). In the New Testament period these gatherings were usually in homes which had a large enough room to accommodate them (Rom. 16:5; 1 Cor. 16:19; Col. 4:15; Phile. 2).

The Church as an Organism

It is significant to note that the word *ekklesia always* refers to *people* and *never to buildings.* Physical structures are not the Church; they are only the facility into which the Church gathers. *Christians do not attend church; they are the Church!* Technically, therefore, it is improper to use the phrase, "church service" (meaning services in a building called the "church"). Services are actually *to* the church, rather than *in* the church.

There are no *sanctuaries* today. This is an Old Testament term for the holy place in the tabernacle or temple in which God made His permanent dwelling. God no longer inhabits such buildings. Instead, He indwells *people* (1 Cor. 3:16-17; 6:19; 2 Cor. 6:16; Gal. 3:2; 4:6; 1 John 3:24; 4:13).

God's Plan for the Local Church

Offices and Ministries: There are two types of spiritual gifts: (1) those which culminate in *church offices,* and (2) those which end in *personal ministries.* In the former category may be found apostles, prophets, evangelists, pastor-teachers, and teachers (Rom. 12:7; Eph. 4:11). In the latter category may be found service, exhortation, giving, leadership, mercy, helps, administration, word of wisdom, word of knowledge, discerning of spirits, prophecy, kinds of tongues, interpretation of tongues, faith, gifts of healing, and the working of miracles (Rom. 12:3-8; 1 Cor. 12:4-11, 28).

Let me briefly define these five *office gifts.* An *apostle* is someone who is sent forth. This corresponds to our modern day missionary who is specifically engaged in starting new churches. A *prophet* is one who speaks forth a message which is received directly from God. An *evangelist* proclaims the good news to a largely unregenerate audience. And a pastor-teacher or teacher is one who leads local saints through the reproof, correction, and instruction of Scripture.

We may now set before us God's first plan for the local church (as it is revealed in Ephesians 4:11-12): "He (Jesus) gave some . . . apostles . . . prophets . . . evangelists . . . and pastors and teachers for the perfecting of the saints for the work of the ministry, for the edifying of the body of Christ." The preeminent work of the church is decidedly two-fold: (1) The office bearers in the church are to equip the saints, and (2) the equipped saints are to do the work of service, which is the building up of the body of Christ (through ministry gifts). This is God's master design for every local church: equipping and edifying.

Equipping Saints: When Jesus commissioned His intimately trained disciples, He said, "Go make disciples (that is, go reproduce yourselves), *teaching* them." The only authorized prescription for systematic *teaching* of the Word of God. Each of the *office gifts* given by Jesus to the church is a *teaching* gift. Without a comprehensive, in-depth and personally penetrating teaching program serving as the hub of all church activities, there can be no discipleship and no equipping of the saints. It is absolutely impossible.

The word *equipping,* in the Greek, means far more than "preparing" or "training." It is a term which encompasses the idea of mending and repairing. Saints, too, have problems—often serious ones. Numerous Christians suffer from such problems (or sins) as worry, fear, incomplete obedience, anxiety, impatience, anger, doubt, marital difficulties, lusts, a critical and negative attitude, depression, idleness, self-will, and more! Until Christ is wholly enthroned in the Christian, and until the Christian can successfully overcome the obstacles presented by sin, self, Satan, and the world, he is not equipped (Phil. 3:15; 2 Tim. 3:16-17; Heb. 5:11—6:2; James 1:2-8). In short, the mission of the one holding an office-gift is to make saints saintly!

Building up the Body of Christ: Once the saints are equipped, they are to do the work of service or ministry—which is the building up of the body of Christ. (Please carefully observe that a pastor's job is not to soothe a flock's traditional expectations of a do-it-all pastor. The pastor's one job is to perfect imperfect saints through the media of teaching—Acts 6:2-4; 20:28; 2 Tim. 2:2, 15; Titus 1:9; 1 Peter 5:2; Ezek. 34:1-19. He is to be an expert in Bible instruction and solving a disciple's difficulties. Please permit him to do this and see to it that he does nothing else!)

As a saint is equipped, he is to seek out others, according to his *gift(s) of ministry,* and build them up. This saint-to-saint outreach obviously multiplies the effectiveness and growth of any local church. The goal of each saint should be to build up one another "until we all attain to the unity of the faith, and of the knowledge of the Son of God, to a mature man, to the measure of the stature which belongs to the fulness of Christ . . . no longer . . . children, tossed here and there by . . . every wind of doctrine . . . but speaking the truth in love, we are to grow up in all respects into Him, who is the head, even Christ, from whom the whole body, being fitted and held together by that which *every joint supplied* (that is, which saints supply to saints), according to the proper working of each (saint's) individual part, causes the growth of the body for the building up of itself in love" (Eph. 4:13-16, NASB).

Ingredients of the Church Meeting

Teaching and Preaching: Both teaching (that which appeals to the mind) and preaching (that which appeals to the will) are to be common foundational stones of the church meeting (Acts 2:42, 46; 4:2; 5:21, 25, 28, 42; 11:26; 15:35; 18:11, 25; 20:20; 28:31).

Fellowship: In the early church, fellowship was on two levels: public (Acts 2:42—"*the* fellowship") and private (Acts 2:46). The term "fellowship" comes from the Greek word *koinos,* which means "common" or "belonging equally to several." In other words, the goods which were owned by one Christian were equally the property of other believers. Fellowship, therefore, is an intimate relationship with someone of like mind, holding all things as common (Gal. 2:9; 1 John 1:3).

Breaking Bread: At the outset, the Lord's supper and love feast (Communion) were observed daily (Acts 2:42, 46). Later, this practice became a weekly observance (Acts 20:7, 11). (Communion is also mentioned in the *Didache* 4:2; 14:1; 16:2.) The frequency with which this ordinance is to be observed is not stated. Therefore, let every church decide for itself.

Prayer: Paramount was the presence of prayer. The first believers prayed in the upper room (Acts 1:24), in the temple (Acts 3:1), in homes (Acts 9:40; 10:4; 12:5, 12), with church leaders (Acts 13:1-4), at a river side (Acts 16:13, 16) and in prison (Acts 16:25). See also Acts 2:42; 4:23-31; 6:4, 6; 20:36; 28:8.

Mutual Exhortation: The New Testament never envisions the church as being an ordered program with a one-man show! The church is a body and each part, under the Holy Spirit's direction, may contribute to the whole (1 Cor. 12:12-27; 14:1-40; 2 Cor. 1:2-4; Col. 3:16; Heb. 3:13; 10:24-25).

Church Unity

The church began "with one accord" (Acts 2:1, 46; 4:24), "singleness of heart" (Acts 2:46), "one heart and one soul" (Acts 4:32), and "filled with the Holy Spirit" (Acts 2:4; 4:31). Unity was a major key to the success of the early church.

When a church fails to have unity or singleness of heart, the Holy Spirit is grieved and rendered powerless to work effectively in the local church. Notice how the Scriptures plead for unity:

1. Roman 12:16—"Be of the same mind one toward another."
2. 1 Corinthians 1:10—"Now I beseech you . . . that ye all speak the same thing, and that there be no division among you, but that ye be perfectly joined together in the same mind and in the same judgment."
3. 2 Corinthians 13:11—"Be of one mind."
4. Ephesians 4:3—"Endeavoring to keep the unity of the Spirit in the bond of peace."
5. Philippians 1:27—"Stand fast in one spirit, with one mind striving together for the faith of the gospel."
6. Philippians 2:2—"Be like-minded, having the same love, being of one accord, of one mind."

The very instant one sin is intentionally committed, of any size, by any Christian, the church unity suffers. Unity exists when its members are filled with the Holy Spirit (Eph. 5:18). When one member is not under the Spirit's control, the whole church can suffer. The church is a "body" and has many members. Some members are fingers, some are toes, others are elbows or maybe an eye. When one of these ceases to function properly, then the whole body is hindered.

Unity has a price. Negatively, God calls His children to "abhor [utterly detest] that which is evil; cleave to that which is good" (Rom. 12:9); "mortify [kill] the deeds of the body" (Rom. 8:13); "have no fellowship with the unfruitful works of darkness but, rather reprove (rebuke) them" (Eph. 5:11); "warn them that are unruly" (1 Thes. 5:14); "prove all things . . . abstain from all appearances of evil" (1 Thes. 5:21-22); "mark them who cause divisions and offenses contrary to the doctrine which ye have learned and avoid them" (Rom. 16:17); and "a man that is a heretic, after the first and second admonition, reject" (dismiss, drive out).

On the positive side the Lord says: "In lowliness of mind let each esteem others better than themselves, look not every man on his own things, but every man also on the things of others" (Phil. 2:3-4); "Brethren, if a man be overtaken in a fault, ye who are spiritual restore such an one in the spirit of meekness, considering thyself, lest thou also be tempted. Bear ye one another's burdens, and so fulfill the law of Christ" (Gal. 6:1-2); "Comfort yourselves together, and edify one another" (1 Thes. 5:11); "exhort one another daily . . . lest any of you be hardened through the deceitfulness of sin" (Heb. 3:13).

Since the whole effectiveness of the Church lies in its unity to God and to one another, it is mandatory that the weakest links in the chain be strengthened. There are perhaps only a few better questions for the Christian to seriously examine than this: "Do I have 'singleness of heart' with my Lord and my fellow Christians?"

Church Discipline

The Scriptures are by no means silent on how to handle problems that arise between believers. Five disciplining actions are discussed with detail.

Someone Wrongs You: If someone wrongs you, then according to Jesus' words in Matthew 18:15-20, the offended brother is to seek out the offender and attempt reconciliation. If the personal effort fails, the visit is to be made again, this time taking along several others. If the offender still continues in his refusal to listen, then it is to be referred to the whole congregation. If he still refuses to hear, then let him be excommunicated.

You Wrong Someone: Sin is either private or public. If the sin is private, only confession and repentance is necessary for forgiveness (1 John 1:9). If, however, the sin affects another party, the sin must be confessed to the wronged party (Matt. 5:23-24; James 5:16). A failure to attempt reconciliation will result in being out of fellowship with God. God will honor no prayer, worship or offering until restitution has been made.

An Elder's Continual Sin: If an elder is caught by two or three witnesses in the act of a sin which is worthy of excommunication, the elder is to be rebuked openly "before all, that others also may fear" (1 Tim. 5:19-22).

Exhorting, Admonishing and Avoiding: When a fellow Christian begins to walk disorderly, he is to be helped by those who are spiritual (Gal. 6:1-2; Heb. 3:13). If the Christian continues without heeding another's prayerful and scriptural help, then the guilty one is to be avoided. The one who refuses to submit to truth must face the departure of his friends and become "ashamed." Note the following Scriptures:

1. 2 Thessalonians 3:6, 14-15—"Now we command you brethren, in the name of our Lord Jesus Christ, that ye withdraw yourselves from every brother that walks disorderly and not after the tradition which he received of us. And if any man obey not our word by this epistle, note that man, and have no company with him that he may be ashamed. Yet count him not as an enemy, but admonish him as a brother."

2. Romans 16:17—"Now I beseech you, brethren, mark them who cause divisions and offenses contrary to the doctrine which ye have learned, and avoid them."

Excommunication: 1 Cor. 5:1-13; Titus 3:10; Matt. 18:15-20. There are seven specific sins mentioned in the Scriptures for which excommunication is prescribed: (1) immorality [homosexuality, lesbianism, incest]; (2) greed [desire to get gains by base methods]; (3) idolatry [participation in occult practices]; (4) drunkenness; (5) extortion [robbery]; (6) foul tongue [railer, abusing, reviling, slandering, insulting, contentious, speech to injure or damage]; (7) heretic [one who causes divisions by a party spirit, factions, and a self-willed opinion which is substituted for submission to the power of truth and leads to division—W. E. Vine, *An Expository Dictionary of New Testament Words,* Revell].

The procedure of excommunication generally follows the pattern Jesus set forth in Matthew 18:15-20. This is a sad occasion and must be performed out of love and not bitter feelings.

The purpose of excommunication is to "deliver such a one unto Satan for the destruction of the flesh, that the spirit may be saved in the day of the Lord Jesus" (1 Cor. 5:5). The Lord does not want His children to fall away, therefore excommunication is His last corrective measure. The prayer behind excommunication is the repentance and restoring to fellowship of the erring one. Such was the case of the man guilty of fornication in the Corinthian congregation (1 Cor. 5:1-13; 2 Cor. 2:6-11).

18 | Angels

Angels occupy a very prominent place in Scripture. They are spoken of nearly 300 times and under all sorts of circumstances. It would seem that they are a very important part of the great economy of God for His world. I am certain that God wants us to know better these most wonderful creatures, else why would they occupy such a large part of His written Word?

William W. Orr

General Introduction

Definition: The term *angel,* in both the Old Testament Hebrew and the New Testament Greek means "messenger" (Heb. 1:14). Therefore, angels are God's special messengers or agents for delivering and performing His bidding.

Their Creation: The angels were created *by* and *for* Jesus Christ (Col. 1:16). The time of their creation was before the earth (Job 38:4-7). They were all created at the same moment and without number (Dan. 7:10; Heb. 12:22).

Their Nature:
  1. They are greater than man in power—2 Peter 2:11
  2. They do not marry—Matt. 22:30

3. They cannot die—Luke 20:35-36
4. They are increasing in knowledge—1 Cor. 4:9; Eph. 3:10-11; 1 Peter 1:12
5. They eat—Ps. 78:25; Gen. 18:8; 19:3
6. They are meek—2 Peter 2:11; Jude 9
7. They are holy—Mark 8:38
8. They are always referred to in masculine gender—Gen. 18:18
9. They need no rest—Rev. 4:8
10. They travel at speeds comparable to lightning—Ezek. 1:14
11. They possess a language of their own—1 Cor. 13:1
12. They are distinct from man—Heb. 2:6-7; Job 38:7
13. It is doubtful that angels possess wings, since no allusion is ever made to their having any (though the cherubim and seraphim have two sets and three sets of wings respectively).

Two Classifications: There are two classes of angels: God's ("elect") and Satan's ("fallen").
1. Elect Angels: 1 Tim. 5:21. These are those angels who did not follow Satan in the angelic rebellion and as a result have obtained eternal salvation. They are always before God, awaiting His instructions (Matt. 18:10; John 1:51).
2. Fallen Angels: There are four classes in this grouping.
    a. Those bound temporarily in the pit—Rev. 9:1-11
    b. Those bound temporarily in the Euphrates river—Rev. 9:13-21
    c. Those bound until the day of judgment—2 Peter 2:4
    d. Those free to serve Satan—Eph. 6:12.

Organization: The angelic world (both elect and fallen) is highly organized into ranks of power and authority.
1. Angels—occurs 294 times in the Bible
2. Cherubim—Gen. 3:24
3. Seraphim—Isa. 6:1-7
4. Archangels—1 Thes. 4:16; Jude 9
5. Principalities—Rom. 8:38; Eph. 1:21; 3:10; 6:12; Col. 1:16; 2:10

6. Power(s)—Rom. 8:38; 1 Cor. 15:24; Eph. 1:21; 3:10; 6:12; Col. 1:16; 2:10; 1 Peter 3:22
7. Rulers of darkness—Eph. 6:12
8. Spirits of wickedness in high places—Eph. 6:12
9. Power of darkness—Col. 1:13
10. Dominion—Eph. 1:21
11. Thrones—Col. 1:16
12. Rule—1 Cor. 15:24
13. Authority—1 Cor. 15:24; 1 Peter 3:22
14. Princes—Dan. 10:13, 20
15. Chief princes—Dan. 10:13
16. Watchers—Dan. 4:13-23
17. Sons of God—Gen. 6:1-4; Job 1:6; 2:1; 38:7
18. Living creatures—Ezek. 1:5-14; Rev. 4:6-8
19. Assembly—Ps. 89:7
20. Heavenly host—Luke 2:13
21. Kings—Dan. 10:13

Worship: Angels are not to be worshiped—Rev. 22:8-9.

Judgment: The angels are to be judged by believers (1 Cor. 6:3—this may refer to only the fallen angels).

The Elect Angels

Their Ministry: To be before God and worship and serve Him—Pss. 29:1-2; 89:7; 103:20; Matt. 18:10.
1. To rejoice in God's works—Job 38:7; Luke 15:10
2. To serve those who are the heirs of salvation—Heb. 1:14; Gen. 19:11; 1 Kings 19:5-8; 2 Kings 6:15-18; Ps. 91:11-12; Matt. 4:11; 26:53; Luke 22:43; Acts 5:19; 12:8-11; 27:23-24. Without dispute, angels guard believers.
3. To execute God's wrath—Gen. 19:12-13; Matt. 13:24-30, 39-42, 47-50; 25:31-32; Acts 12:21-23; 2 Thes. 1:7-8.
4. To reign in the affairs of the nations—Dan. 10:12-13, 21; 11:1; 12:1. Doubtless, any earthly war is but the manifestation of an angelic conflict. Whoever wins in the heavenlies will likewise

win on earth (see Rev. 16:13-16; Isa. 24:21-23).
   5. To carry believers, at death, into God's presence—Luke 16:22.

Two Names:
   1. Michael. This is one of the "chief princes" and reigns over the nation of Israel—Dan. 10:13, 21; 12:1; Jude 9; Rev. 12:7-12.
   2. Gabriel. He appears four times and always as a messenger or revealer of the Divine purposes—Dan. 8:15-27; 9:20-27; Luke 1:11-20, 26-38.

Satan

Names and Designations:
   1. Satan (adversary, to lie in wait, enemy—used 49 times)—Matt. 4:10
   2. Devil (accuser, slanderer—used 34 times)—1 Peter 5:8
   3. Serpent—Gen. 3:15; Isa. 27:1; Rev. 12:9; 20:2
   4. Oppressor—Isa. 14:4
   5. Leviathan—Isa. 27:1
   6. Anointed cherub—Ezek. 28:14
   7. Tempter—Matt. 4:3; 1 Thes. 3:5
   8. Enemy—Matt. 13:25, 39
   9. Wicked one—Matt. 13:19, 38; 1 John 2:13-14; 3:12; 5:18
   10. Beelzebub (lord of flies [demons]/lord of dung [moral impurity])—Mark 3:22
   11. Prince of demons—Mark 3:22
   12. Strong man—Luke 11:21
   13. Liar—John 8:44; see 1 Kings 22:22
   14. Father of lies—John 8:44
   15. Murderer—John 8:44
   16. Thief—John 10:10
   17. Wolf—John 10:12
   18. Prince of this world—John 12:31; 14:30; 16:11
   19. God of this age—2 Cor. 4:4
   20. Belial (worthlessness)—2 Cor. 6:15
   21. Angel of light—2 Cor. 11:14

22. Prince of the power of the air—Eph. 2:2
23. Adversary—1 Peter 5:8
24. Roaring lion—1 Peter 5:8
25. Wicked one—Matt. 13:19, 38; 1 John 2:13
26. Sinner—1 John 3:8
27. Apollyon (destroyer)—Rev. 9:11
28. Abaddon (destruction)—Rev. 9:11
29. Angel of the abyss—Rev. 9:11
30. Accuser—Rev. 12:10
31. Deceiver—Rev. 12:9
32. Dragon—Rev. 12:3; 20:2
33. Power of darkness—Col. 1:13

The Fall of Satan:
1. Cause. Satan was not always Satan. He, like all the other angelic beings, was created perfect. He *became* Satan by resisting God's will. Some writers think that he began on earth as its prince. Among his duties was the responsibility of bringing earth's worship into the presence of God. Between the greatness of this power and the extreme beauty of his person, he chose to oppose God, resulting in his spiritual fall and the subsequent fall of one-third of the angelic world (see Isa. 14:12-17; Ezek. 28:11-19; Rev. 12:4).
2. Time. Various writers hold that Satan actually fell before Genesis 1:2. This hypothesis declares that a full pre-Adamic world was in existence and judged by the flood waters, chaos and emptiness of Genesis 1:2. Other verses used in support of this theory are Isa. 45:18; Jer. 4:23-26; Job 9:5-7; 38:4-41; 2 Peter 3:5-7. This view conveniently places the age of dinosaurs and "cave men" into this epoch. "Demons" are said, therefore, to be the disembodied spirits of this pre-Adamic race, who wished to follow Satan in his scheme. While the details of this presentation are rejected by certain scholars, all are agreed that Satan had to fall sometime before the events of Genesis chapter three.

The Works of Satan:
1. A careful examination of the "Names and Designations" of Satan will aptly depict this sadistic foe's labors.

2. Additionally, it may be noted that his work includes:
   a. seeking notorious men—John 13:27
   b. leading people to sin—Gen. 3:1-6; Luke 22:31; Acts 5:3
   c. causing sickness—Acts 10:38
   d. setting snares for defeat—1 Tim. 3:7; 2 Tim. 2:26
   e. planting evil thoughts in people's minds—John 13:2; Acts 5:3
   f. blinding the mind of the unbeliever—2 Cor. 4:4
   g. removing God's word from people's hearts—Matt. 13:19
   h. sowing tares amongst the wheat—Matt. 13:39
   i. creating a false salvation—2 Cor. 11:14-15
   j. buffeting God's servants—2 Cor. 12:7
   k. withholding angels with answers to prayer—Dan. 10:13
   l. hindering God's work—1 Thes. 2:18; 2 Cor. 11:3
   m. persecuting the saints—Rev. 2:9-10, 13; 3:9
   n. perverting Scripture—Matt. 4:6
   o. causing apostasy—2 Thes. 2:9; 1 Tim. 4:1
3. Contrasting Jesus' Works and Satan's Works

Jesus' Work	Satan's Work
1. *Reveal Truth*	1. *Conceal Truth*
John 1:17	John 8:44
John 14:6	2 Cor. 4:3-4; 11:3, 14-15
John 18:37-38	Mark 4:1-4, 14-15
	Rev. 12:9
	Acts 5:1-4
	1 Tim. 4:1
2. *Give Life*	2. *Take Life*
John 5:24	John 8:44; 10:10
John 10:10	Rev. 9:11
John 14:6	1 Cor. 10:1-12
	1 Peter 5:8
3. *Produce Spiritual Fruit*	3. *Produce Fleshly Fruit*
John 15:1-8, 16	Eph. 2:1-3; 4:25-27
Gal. 5:22-23	Gal. 5:19-21
	Rom. 1:21-32
	1 Tim. 5:9-15

4. *Test for Maturity*
   John 6:5-6
   James 1:2-4
   Rom. 5:3-5
5. *Set Free*
   Matt. 8:36

6. *Defend Saints*
   1 John 2:1
7. *Destroy Satan's Works*
   Heb. 2:14
   1 John 3:8-10

4. *Tempt for Destruction*
   Matt. 4:3
   1 Thes. 3:5
   1 Cor. 7:3-5
5. *Ensnare*
   1 Tim. 3:6-7
   2 Tim. 2:24-26
   2 Cor. 2:6-11
   1 Thes. 2:18
6. *Accuse/Condemn Saints*
   Rev. 12:10
7. *Destroy Jesus' Works*
   Luke 4:1-13

Limitations on Satan:
1. He cannot inflict diseases without God's permission—Job 1:10, 12.
2. He cannot destroy by death without God's permission—Job 2:6; Heb. 2:14.
3. He cannot touch believers (Job 1:10-12; Luke 22:31-32; 1 John 5:18), unless they open room for his entrance (Eph. 4:27; 1 Peter 5:7-9).
4. He cannot stay when properly resisted—James 4:7.

How You Can Defeat Satan:
1. Recognize that Jesus came into this world for the expressed purpose of defeating Satan (Heb. 2:14; 1 John 3:8-10). Christ is the Victor. You need not worry, for greater is He who is in you than he who is in the world (1 John 4:4).
2. Cast all your cares upon God, become stabilized mentally, and be watchful of your thoughts and speech (1 Peter 5:7-9).
3. Open no room for his entry (Eph. 4:27).
4. Submit to God and resist (stand fast against) the devil by declaring God's Word as your sole source for authority and practice (James 4:7).
5. Do not be ingorant of his devices/strategy (2 Cor. 2:11).

Ask God for insight into demonic activity.

6. Put on the whole armor of God, piece by piece (Eph. 6:12-18).

7. Confess all known sins, having them removed by the blood of Christ (Rev. 12:11; 1 John 1:7, 9).

8. Maintain a strong testimony for Christ in your everyday speech (Rev. 12:11). Because Satan is a liar, continually confess the truth of God's sure Word. Do not accept any mediocre walk with Christ as normal. Usurp Satan of this hold on your power for Christian living.

9. Bring every thought into control so that they all obey Christ (2 Cor. 10:3-5; see Phil. 4:6-9).

10. Flee from temptations (1 Tim. 6:11; 2 Tim. 2:22), and stay in the core of spiritual fellowship (Prov. 19:27; Acts 2:42-47).

Satan's Doom:

1. Ever since Satan's fall, he has been judged; and he will one day be sentenced to the eternal fire, which is presently prepared for him and his angels (Matt. 25:41; John 16:7-11).

2. Jesus Christ came for the expressed purpose of destroying his works (1 John 3:8; Heb. 2:14).

3. On the Cross, Jesus made an open show of triumph over Satan's host (Col. 2:15; John 12:31).

4. Satan's doom is soon to occur—Rom. 16:20.

5. At the second coming of Christ, Satan and his host will be cast into the abyss for 1,000 years. At the end of this period they will be released for one short and final period. After this, he will be cast forever into the lake of fire (Rev. 20:1-3, 7-10).

Demons

Definitions:

1. Demon. This term is derived from a root meaning "to know." Thus, among the pagan Greeks, these spirit beings were considered to be the "intelligent ones" and were viewed as idols or gods. In the New Testament, however, they are equated with "evil spirits,"

"unclean spirit," and "ministers of the devil." (*Note:* The use of the word "devils" in the King James Version is incorrect. There is but one devil, though there are numerous demons.)

2. Demoniac. A demoniac is someone whom the demons can control, usually by entering some portion of a person's mind or body or spirit (Matt. 4:24; 8:16; 9:32).

3. Demonization. Much confusion has been created by the translation of *daimonizomenoi* into the English words "demon possession." This phrase originated with Flavius Josephus, in the first century A.D., but is not in the original biblical text. Instead, this Greek term simply means "to be demonized" or "to be under demonic influence/control." The actual extent of demonic influence has no bearing upon the word. Hence, to make fine distinctions between "possession" (supposedly only internal and of non-Christians) and "oppression" (supposedly only external and of Christians) is nowhere supported by the Scriptures. Many modern writers are wholly convinced of this sobering point.

Only four expressions in the Greek are used to describe demonization:

    a. To *be in* an unclean spirit; that is, to be under the influence of—Mark 1:23; 5:2.

    b. To *have* an unclean spirit—Matt. 11:18; Mark 7:25; 9:17; Luke 4:33; 8:27; 13:11; John 7:20; 8:48-49, 52.

    c. To be *demonized*—Matt. 4:24; 8:16, 28, 33; 9:32; 12:22; 15:22; Mark 1:32; 5:15-16, 18; Luke 8:36.

    d. To be *oppressed*—Acts 10:38.

4. Oppression. This term occurs but once in demonic matters (Acts 10:38) and it is used to describe the whole of Satan's work, over which Jesus was triumphant. The word actually means "to tyrannize, to exercise harsh control over one, to exploit, and to dominate someone." Therefore, it should be viewed as a synonym for "demonization."

5. Exorcism. The act of expelling demons from persons. See chart on the following page for examples.

Description

1. Spirit beings—Luke 24:39. Demons are spirits without mate-

EXORCISM IN THE BIBLE

Scripture	Victim(s)	Key Phrase	Believer or Unbeliever	Symptom(s)
Matt. 4:24	All	Possessed	?	Sickness
Matt. 12:22	Man	Possessed	?	Blind and Dumb
Matt. 15:22-28 Mark 7:25	Daughter	Cruelly Possessed Had	?	Vexation
Mark 1:23-26 Luke 4:33-35	Man	With Had	?	Uncleanness Impurity
Luke 4:40-41 Matt. 8:16	All	Possessed	?	Sickness
Luke 6:17-18	Multitude	With	?	Vexation
Luke 8:26-39 Matt. 8:28-34 Mark 5:2-20	Man	Had Possessed With	?	Extraordinary strength, wild, screaming, self-torture, naked, mental disorder
Luke 9:38-42 Mark 9:14-29 Matt. 17:14-18	Son	Had	?	Fear, screaming pain, foaming at mouth, uncontrolled body movement, dumb, grinding teeth, suicidal
Luke 11:14	Man	?	?	Dumb
Luke 13:10-16	Woman	Had/Bound	?	Crippled body
Acts 5:14-16	All	With	?	Sickness/Vexation
Acts 8:5-7	Many	Had	?	Sickness
Acts 16:16-18	Woman	Had	?	Fortune-teller
Acts 19:11-12	?	?	?	Sickness

rial bodies. This causes some writers to suggest that demons are different from the fallen angels, on four grounds:
- a. Angels fly; demons walk (Matt. 12:43).
- b. Angels inhabit the heavens; demons inhabit the earth (Eph. 6:12; Matt. 12:43).
- c. Angels have bodies; demons desire to enter bodies (Mark 5:12; 1 Cor. 15:39-40; Rev. 16:13-16).
- d. Angels and spirits are discussed separately (Acts 23:8-9).

(*Note:* Frequently, those who distinguish between fallen angels and demons will contend that the latter are disembodied spirits of a pre-Adamic race. Such distinctions, whether legitimate or otherwise, are of little importance to the effects they render today. What matters is to discern how they operate today, not from whence they came.)

2. Personality. Demons are not *things* but *persons*. They can:
   - a. Speak—Mark 1:24, 34.
   - b. Hear—Mark 5:6-10.
   - c. Think/know things—Acts 19:15; 1 Tim. 4:1.
   - d. Feel—Mark 5:7, 12; James 2:19.
   - e. Make decisions—Matt. 12:44; Mark 5:11-13; 2 Peter 2:4; Jude 6.
   - f. Obey Jesus Christ—Mark 1:34; Satan—Mark 3:22; and saints—James 4:7-8.
   - g. Discern between saved and lost—Rev. 9:4.
   - h. Fellowship—1 Cor. 10:20-21.

3. Named. Like their ruler (Satan), all of the demons possess names which identify the nature of their character and work.
   - a. Lilith (Satyr)—Isa. 34:14. This seems to be the name of a female demon who haunted desolate places and kept company with unclean birds, wildcats, and jackals.
   - b. Debher and resheph (pestilence and burning coals)—Hab. 3:5. In Psalm 78:48 the Lord is said to have delivered the livestock of the Egyptians to hail and to "hot thunderbolts" (the reshephs). In Psalm 76:3 God breaks the "arrows" (reshephs) of the bow. And in Job 5:7 the statement appears, "man is born unto trouble, as the sparks (reshephs) fly upward." Thus, the man is beset with

troubles from all quarters—from the natural ground (v. 6) and from the air (v. 7).
  c. Horseleach (or vampire)—Prov. 30:15
  d. Pestilence—Ps. 91:6
  e. Destruction that wastes at noonday—Ps. 91:6
  f. Terror by night—Ps. 91:5; Song 3:8
  g. Arrow that flieth by day—Ps. 91:5; see Job 6:4
  h. Mighty and strong one—Isa. 28:2
  i. King of terrors—Job 18:14
  j. Jealousy—Num. 5:14
  k. Liar—2 Chron. 18:22; see 1 Kings 22:22
  l. Perversion—Isa. 19:14
  m. Deep sleep—Isa. 29:10
  n. Heaviness—Isa. 61:3
  o. Whoredom—Hosea 5:4
  p. Legion—Mark 5:9
  q. Dumbness—Mark 9:17
  r. Divination—Acts 16:16-18
  s. Bondage—Rom. 8:15
  t. Seduction—1 Tim. 4:1
  u. Fear—2 Tim. 1:7
  v. Error—1 John 4:6; see 1 Tim. 4:1
  (*Note:* Universal experience attests to the validity of attaching names to demons. With amazing unity these names reoccur throughout the world. It appears that for every potential manifestation of the flesh, there is a corresponding demon (see Rom. 1:24-32; Gal. 5:19-21; Col. 3:5-9).

4. Nature. Demons vary in their wickedness (Matt. 12:43-45; 2 Cor. 11:13-15). Some are extremely base in their nature, while others appear almost righteous. Nevertheless, all demons are:
  a. wicked—Matt. 12:45; Eph. 6:16; 2 Thes. 2:8
  b. unclean—Zech. 13:2; Matt. 10:1; 12:43; Acts 5:16
  c. foul—Mark 9:25; Rev. 18:2
  d. deceitful—1 Tim. 4:1
  e. evil—Luke 7:21
5. Appearance. Although demons are normally invisible, one's

ANGELS / 173

eyes may be opened to see them. John gives two descriptions in his demonic visions:
   a. locustlike—Rev. 9:1-12
   b. froglike—Rev. 16:13-14
6. Powerful
   a. Manifested in the natural realm—wind (Job 1:19; Mark 4:35-41), human strength (Mark 5:4), thoughts (1 Chron. 21:1; Acts 5:1-11; 2 Cor. 11:3; 2 Cor. 4:3-4), and death (Heb. 2:14).
   b. Manifested in the magical realm—rods turned to serpents (Ex. 7:11-12), water turned to blood (Ex. 7:20-22), creation of frogs (Ex. 8:6-7), fire falling from heaven (Job 1:16), and great wonders (Rev. 13:13; see 2 Thes. 2:10-13).
7. Organized into Ranks.
   a. principalities—Rom. 8:38; Eph. 6:12; Col. 2:15
   b. powers—Rom. 8:38; 1 Cor. 15:24; Eph. 6:12; Col. 2:15
   c. power of darkness—Col. 1:13
   d. spirits of wickedness in high places—Eph. 6:12
   e. rule—1 Cor. 15:24
   f. authority—1 Cor. 15:24; 1 Peter 3:22
   g. ruler of darkness—Eph. 6:12
   h. princes—Dan. 10:13, 20
   i. kings—Dan. 10:13

Spiritism/Occult—Deut. 18:9-14
1. All such practices are strictly forbidden:
   a. passing through the fire—child sacrifices; worship of Molech—the sun god (Lev. 18:21).
   b. divination—acquiring information from spirits. This encompasses all forms of fortune-telling: reading tea leaves, palm or card reading, handwriting analysis, crystal balls, Ouija boards, astrology, etc.
   c. sorcery—occult power, practices, and spells. This includes anyone who deals with evil spirits, potions, drugs, spells, or anyone given to the psychic, telepathy, ESP, etc.
   d. necromancy—contact with the dead, a séance.

2. Other Scriptures demonstrate the seriousness of the occult:
   a. Ex. 22:18—kill witches
   b. Lev. 20:6, 27—kill mediums and wizards
   c. 1 Chron. 10:13—Saul dies for seeking a medium
   d. Isa. 47:13-14—astrologers shall burn
   e. 1 Cor. 5:11—excommunication for idolatry

Can a Believer Be Demonized?
1. A woman, whom Jesus called a "daughter of Abraham," had a demon (Luke 13:10-16). This designation seems to mean that she was a believer (see Rom. 4:9-11; Gal. 3:7).
2. Peter, a saved man (John 13:10-11; 17:2-8), was capable of speaking both the Father's words (Matt. 16:13-17) and Satan's words (Matt. 16:21-23).
3. Ananias and Sapphira were Spirit-filled Christians—at least a few days before Satan filled their heart—Acts 4:31—5:6. Proof that they were Christians is plain—they lied to the indwelling Holy Spirit.
4. The gifts of the Holy Spirit are for the profit of believers (1 Cor. 12:7; 14:3). Why then is the gift of discerning of spirits (demonic spirits) among this list unless it too profits the believer? (1 Cor. 12:10)
5. Paul wrote of his concern that the Corinthian congregation might "receive another spirit," other than the Holy Spirit (2 Cor. 11:3-4).
6. The Galatians were said to have been "bewitched" (led astray by some spell or witchcraft) and guilty of returning to the "beggarly elemental spirits" who once enslaved them—3:1-2; 4:3, 8-9. The word "spirits" here is not the normal word for demons. It is difficult to discern fully whether the elementary teaching of the world or actual demonic spirits are in view; both are highly possible (see Eph. 2:1-3).
7. Believers can be seduced by demons, and thereby depart from the faith (1 Tim. 4:1-3).
8. Also see Acts 8:5-8; 16:16-18; 1 Cor. 7:3-5; 10:1-12, 16-22; 2 Cor. 2:6-11; 10:3-5; Eph. 4:25-27; 6:11-18; 1 Tim. 3:6-7; 5:9-15; 2 Tim. 2:24-26; James 3:5-17.

(*Note:* While all believers are prospects for demonic vexation, none need to be dominated by evil spirits. If: (1) God is loved preeminently, (2) all sins are confessed, (3) all personal relationships are pure, and (4) Satan is resisted at the point of temptation, then the believer is shielded from the enemy. However, if the believer fails in these four areas, then he is a candidate for demonic problems (Matt. 12:43-45).

How to Detect Demonic Activity
1. The most certain method is to consult with someone who has the gift of "discerning of spirits" (1 Cor. 12:10).
2. If a believer's problem is nondemonic (fleshly), then it will yield to prayer and submission to God. For example, fear will disappear when filled with the Holy Spirit (2 Tim. 1:7; 1 John 4:18). However, if a believer's problem, such as fear, does not depart with prayer and submission to God, then the problem may very well be demonic.
3. When a believer is habitually plagued with uncontrollable thoughts or speech, worry, resentment, hatred, doubt, indecision, lust, lying, addictions, or any other sinful inclination, then the source of such forceful compulsions may be demonic.
4. Perhaps the chief characteristic is the projection of a new personality in the victim.

Extent of Demonization: It is evident that not all demonic victims manifest the same symptoms. Some appear perfectly normal and others appear as madmen. The reason for such a variance is easily explained. Demons vary in wickedness; plus, the number which inhabit a body can vary from one to thousands (see Mark 5). Obviously the type and number of demons harrassing an individual will dictate the corresponding manifestation.

How You Can Overcome Demonic Assault: Follow the points in this chapter on *How You Can Defeat Satan.*

19 | Prophecy

When God gives a prophecy, faith believes it, hope anticipates it, love shares it and patience awaits it. The children of God have been granted the "sure word of prophecy . . . that shines in a dark place, until the day dawns" (2 Peter 1:19). On this we stand, by this we live and for this we die!

Prophecy is one of the most fascinating subjects found in the Scriptures. It is also possibly the most intricate and difficult to interpret. No person can carefully examine the complexities of biblical predictions and fail to be humbled. The multiple usages of symbols, the incomparable obstacles of chronology, the telescoping of events, the intentional ambiguity of prophetic language and the host of divided scholarship makes dogmatism an attitude for only the novice and the proud. Let us advance into a study of specific data.

The Bible is a Prophetic Book: Over one-fourth of the Scriptures were speaking of future events at the time they were written—over 8,000 verses! J. Barton Payne notes that 1,817 predictions are made on 737 separate topics and occupy 28½% of the Old Testament and 21½% of the New Testament (J. Barton Payne, *Encyclopedia of Biblical Prophecy,* Harper and Row, 1973).

Jesus Christ is the Cornerstone of all Prophecy: The Bible is preeminently a book about God, and particularly His Son, Jesus Christ (see Gen. 1:1; Matt. 5:17; 26:24, 54; Luke 18:31; 24:44; John 5:39; 1 Peter 1:10-12). Man is a secondary theme, and considered only as he relates to the triune Godhead.

The pivotal thrust of the prophetic oracles, therefore, must *not* centralize on the Antichrist, or the great tribulation, or the rapture, or any other man-centered event. The impetus behind predictions is not *what* is going to happen, or *when* it will occur, or *how* it will transpire. Rather, the momentum of prophecy is the Lord Jesus Christ Himself—*"the testimony of Jesus is the spirit of prophecy"* (Rev. 19:10). If He is not the foundation upon which all is built, and the capstone under which all has been mounting and directed, then the intended impact of the message has been eluded and is yet to be perceived.

The Two Basic Themes of Prophecy: The two most basic themes of prophecy are the first and second comings of Jesus Christ. Numerous writers have noted that the Old Testament predicts the first coming of Christ some 333 times. The mathematical possibility of all 333 prophecies actually coming to pass is 1 in 1 with 110 zeros added! How marvelous is our God in keeping His Word. Regarding the second coming of Christ, René Pache declares that this event is mentioned 1,527 times in the Old Testament and that 1 out of 25 verses in the New Testament speak of this blessed event—319 verses (René Pache, *The Return of Jesus Christ,* Moody Press, 1955).

Personal Value of Knowing Prophecy: Life is, at best, only an existence of deceptive pleasures if one does not know what the future holds and the One who holds the future (Luke 12:16-20). When the eye cannot see beyond the temporal world of momentary fancies, how futile everything can become. Knowledge of the prophetic calendar, however, can provide the following benefits:

1. Comfort for the mourning—1 Thes. 4:18; 5:1-11; John 14:1-4.

2. Hope for the afflicted—1 Peter 1:5-11; 4:13; 2 Peter 3:1-14; 1:3, 9.

3. Holiness for the backsliding—Rom. 13:12; 1 Cor. 4:5; 1 Thes. 5:1-11; 1 Peter 1:13; 4:7; 2 Peter 3:10-14; 1 John 3:2-3.
4. Answers for the confused—Matt. 24:3—25:46; 2 Thes. 2:1-17.
5. Stimulus for service—Matt. 25:14-30; Luke 12:42-48; 1 Cor. 3:11-15; 2 Cor. 5:10; 2 Tim. 4:8; 1 Peter 5:2-4.
6. Endurance for the weak—Heb. 10:36-37; James 5:7-8.

Digest of Prophetic Topics

Prophet: Although there were prophets and prophecy long before the time of Moses (Enoch—Jude 14-15; Noah—Gen. 9:25-27; Abraham—Gen. 20:7; Jacob—Gen. 49:1-33), he, nevertheless, serves as the pattern for all future prophets (Deut. 18:15-19). In a real sense, the official origin of the prophetic *institution* may be said to begin here.

It is through Moses that God sets forth the function of the prophet—"I will put My words in his mouth, and he shall speak to them all that I command him" (Deut. 18:18). The function is clear; the prophet serves as God's spokesman (see Ex. 4:14-16; 7:1; 1 Kings 8:15; Isa. 32:2; Jer. 1:17).

The message of the prophet may be divided into two general categories: *foretelling,* the predicting of certain future events, and *forthtelling,* the edification, exhortation, and consolation for certain contemporary events.

Two final points need attention. One, when the prophet prophesies, he is delivering words which have their immediate and direct source from God. The prophet, therefore, is not the true speaker, but God. The prophet is merely God's instrument. This, obviously, is not to be confused with popular preaching or teaching, since these latter gifts anticipate preparation and the secondary or indirect usage of God's written word. Two, the only ultimate proof that a prophet has indeed spoken God's words is to be found in the fulfillment of the prophecy itself. Genuine prophecies always come to pass (Deut. 18:1-5).

Time, Ages and Eternity: Defining the distinguishing between time and eternity is no simple matter. Nevertheless, several basic observations will greatly benefit one's grasp of prophetic matters.

1. Time: Time is that period of events which occupies the space between "the beginning" of Genesis 1:1 and "the end" of 1 Corinthians 15:24. As such it includes every occurrence from the creation to the consummation. It began with God making the heavens and the earth, and it will end with Christ returning the kingdom of heaven and earth to the Father.

2. Ages: The Scriptures divide time into three periods—*past* (Amos 9:11; Jer. 18:15; Luke 1:70; John 9:32; Acts 3:21; Col. 1:26), *present* (Matt 12:32; Mark 10:29-30; Rom. 3:26) and *future* (Matt. 12:32; Mark 10:29-30; Eph. 1:21; 2:7; 3:21).

Past time has reference to that period between the creation and the first advent of Jesus Christ. *Present time* refers to the dispensation between the first and second advents of Christ. *Future* time, as odd as it may seem, began where "present time" got its start—the first coming of Christ; and it will have no experiential end or climax (though it may be said to have an official or theological end —see Time above).

Jesus' first coming marked the end of time (Gal. 4:4; Heb. 1:1-2; 9:26). This is why faith in Him brings eternal life, *immediately* (John 5:24; 1 John 3:14). Put another way, the powers of the age to come have invaded the present age. There is an overlap between these periods. Note the chart below.

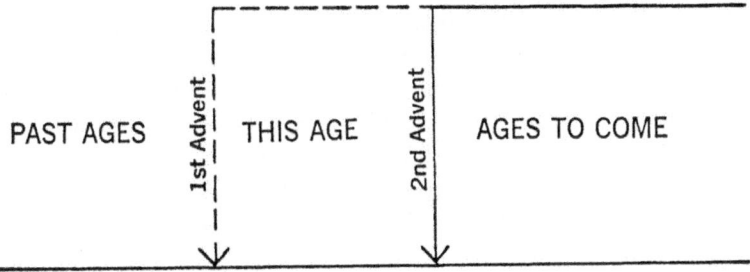

3. Eternity: The Bible presents time from two perspectives: God's and man's. From the human point of view, time is temporal and may be measured by the duration of one's own life or the

longevity of the present earth. From the divine perspective, however, eternity is an endless time-line (without beginning or end), to which temporal time is both attached and detached. This paradoxical union might be drawn in the following manner.

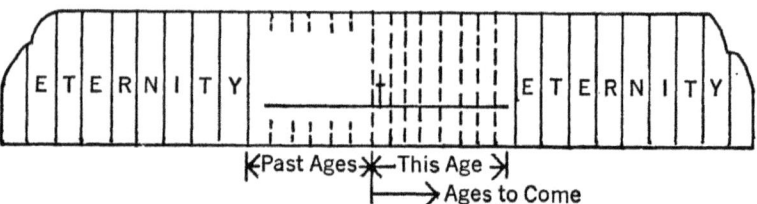

Time is detached from eternity by nature of its temporal qualities. On the other hand, it is attached to eternity by the fact that God, who inhabits eternity, also dwells within time. Furthermore, the presence of the age to come has invaded and overlapped the present age.

Sovereignty of God: Christians view God in many ways, but there is one foundational attribute of God that is too often ignored—*sovereignty*. This unfortunate oversight has produced a conception of God which is by far too human, too fleshly, too man-made. The modern picture of God is to see Him in heaven as reigning supreme in every event, and to see Him in earth as doing the very best He can under the turbulent circumstances! In other words, most people (saved or lost) find it easy to believe in a benevolent God who seeks all men's highest good and who would never directly interfere in the immediate affairs of men to effect His own plans. This so-called "god" is not the God presented in the Scriptures.

Sovereignty affirms God's absolute authority to govern the course of men and nations, and to execute His will in any manner which best fits His eternal, wise, holy and loving counsels. This is the God of the Bible—autonomous, self-sufficient, independent and at liberty to exercise all His decrees with no one to stay His activities.

God controls the world of nature, animals, angels, and men. The Scriptures are bold and plain in their declaration that God regulates all events (Pss. 115:3; 119:89-91; 135:6; Isa. 14:24-27; 45:21-23; 46:10-11; Jer. 27:5-7), and that no one or nothing hinders His hand (Ex. 9:29; Num. 23:19; Ecc. 3:14; Dan. 4:35; Eph. 4:6; Rev. 1:5). See chapter 9 for further Scriptures.

Due to their misunderstanding many saints cringe, and even detest the idea of sovereignty. Indeed, into whose hands would one prefer to place this most excellent attribute? Surely if man or Satan were granted sovereignty, the world would encounter indescribable horror, not to mention the fact that God would thereby be made nothing more than a mere creator, rather than the awesome Creator. Of a certainty, the reins of the universe have been placed into the hands of Him who created it, sustains it, directs it, and most of all, loves it.

Let us rejoice in knowing this grand feature of God's impeccable character. Rains cannot fall, winds cannot blow, lightning cannot flash, floods cannot rise—the whole of creation cannot move without God's permission! There is no bitter test in one's path, no antagonistic person in one's way, but what God is in full control. There are no accidents in the universe. *None.* They simply cannot exist in the always present, all-powerful, sovereign God.

Therefore, when we look at future events, such as the reign of the cruel Antichrist, the persecution of the saints, and the devastation which will come upon the earth, remember, they cannot transpire without divine recognition and control (Dan. 7:25; 8:12; 2 Thes. 2:7-12; Rev. 12:13-16; 13:5, 7; 17:17)! It is not a period to fear (see 2 Tim. 1:7; 1 John 4:18), but one in which to rejoice, for it marks the fleeting seconds before Christ's wonderful return in triumph!

Eschatology: Eschatology is a specialized study of the events which are to transpire in the last time. There are over seventy eschatological expressions used throughout the Scriptures to identify, either in part or in whole, the last day time zone. Certain terms are very localized and specific, while others cover a vast sweep of time. There are, to total, some twelve distinct periods or phases within the breadth of the last days. Below is this chronological listing with some leading references.

1. The future of Israel—Gen. 49:1; Num. 24:14; Deut. 4:30; 31:29. An examination of these prophecies reveals that much of this is now history. It is difficult, however, to determine accurately the precise extent of time these predictions were intended to cover.

2. The reign of Antiochus Epiphanes IV-(175-164 B.C.)—Dan. 8:17, 19, 23; 11:27, 35.

3. The times of the Gentiles (which spans a period from at least 605 B.C. to the second coming of Christ)—Luke 21:24; see Dan. 2; 7.

4. The first advent of Christ—Gal. 4:4; Heb. 1:2; 9:26.

5. The Church age—Acts 2:17; 1 Cor. 10:11; James 5:3; 1 Peter 1:5, 20; 4:7; 1 John 2:18.

6. The fulness of the Gentiles (a period beginning at Pentecost and extending to the second advent)—Rom. 11:25.

7. The last days of the Church age—1 Tim. 4:1; 2 Tim. 3:1; 2 Peter 3:3; Jude 18.

8. The great tribulation (this may correspond to the point above)—Rev. 7:14.

9. The second advent of Christ—Jer. 23:20; 30:24; 48:47; 1 Cor. 1:8.

10. The day of resurrection—John 6:39-40, 44, 54; 11:24.

11. The earthly phase of the kingdom—Isa. 2:2; Ezek. 38:8, 16; Hosea 3:5.

12. The day of judgment—John 12:48.

One final eschatological item remains for our unveiling: What do the Old and New Testament present as the eschatological hope? On what events did these saints fix their gaze? In the following two concise paragraphs are brief descriptions of the major prophetic views held within the two testaments.

Old Testament Prophecy: The Old Testament hope of the end is never presented climactically, in the sense of an absolute cessation of one order and the initiation of some new existence. To the contrary, the end is always pictured as transpiring in phases, with each phase bringing one closer to a new, though not detailed, culmination. For Israel, the end would begin with the great resurrection, which was preceded by an awesome time of tribulation and followed by the judgment of the righteous and the wicked (Dan. 12:1-3). At this same juncture a Davidic Messiah would sit on the throne, inaugurating a new and unending age, with Satan and his angelic host being bound (Isa. 24:21-22). This King would vindicate Yahweh and His people, judging (or ruling) the world with righteousness from Jerusalem (Pss. 9:8; 96:13; 98:9; Isa. 2:2). The earth would then be filled with the knowledge of the Lord (Isa. 11:9; Hab. 2:14), and complete dominion would be given to the saints (Dan. 7:27). This is also the time when the new heaven and earth seem to appear (Isa. 65:17; 66:22), but apparently births, deaths and rebellion to God are anticipated for a portion of this final state (Isa. 65:20; 66:19-24; Zech. 14:16-21). It is further discernible that this earthly reign would be marked with a distinct terminal point (Dan. 7:12; Isa. 24:21-22), after which God would swallow up death for all time (Isa. 25:8).

New Testament Prophecy: Like the Old Testament, the New Testament perspective of the end is to come in stages and be in-

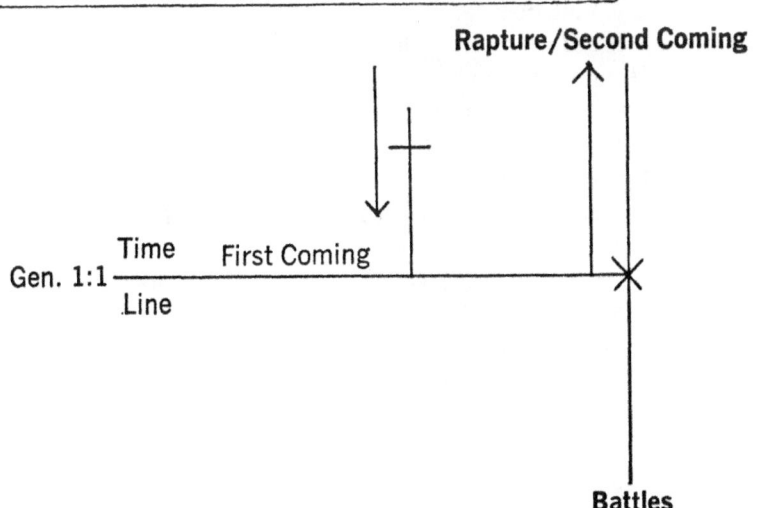

**Chart Number One:
Events of the Second Coming**

augurated by a messianic kingdom. The new Testament, however, envisions this kingdom as coming in two overlapping phases. With the first advent of Christ came phase one—"the time is fulfilled, and the kingdom of God is at hand" (Mark 1:15). The kingdom came with the King (Matt. 12:28; Luke 17:20; Acts 15:14-19; Col. 1:13), yet the kingdom is still to come; this is phase two and occurs at Christ's second advent (Matt. 25:31-46; 1 Cor. 15:50). What happens at the Second Coming basically compares with the Old Testament hope, excluding the resurrection of the unjust, which will transpire after the 1,000-year earthly reign of the Davidic Messiah. Near the close of this millennial era, Satan will be released to test the nations; a host will follow him in earth's final war (Rev. 20:7-10). Immediately after this brief episode all the dead will be raised and judged (Rev. 20:11-15). The Christ will then return the kingdom to God, having subjected all things under His feet, including death (1 Cor. 15:24-28).

Chronology of Events with Scriptures

Rapture: This is the snatching away of all true Christians from the earth, whether dead or alive (1 Thes. 4:13-17). The actual sequence is noted below.

1. The Lord descends with a shout, the voice of the archangel, and the trumpet of God.
2. God will bring with Him (Jesus Christ) those (disembodied, but conscious, spirits—2 Cor. 5:1-8; Phil. 1:21-23) who have died in Christ.
3. The dead (i.e. the physical bodies of the dead) in Christ will rise first.
4. Then we who are alive in Christ will be snatched up together with them.
5. We shall meet the Lord in the air.
6. The marriage of the Lamb—Rev. 19:7-8; see 2 Cor. 11:2; Eph. 5:25-27.

Battles: There will be three major campaigns at the time of the second coming of Christ.

1. Battle of Edom—Isa. 34:8-15; 63:1-6.
2. Battle in the valley of Jehoshaphat—Joel 3; Zech. 8; 12:9.
3. Battle at Armageddon—Rev. 16:16-21; 19:11-21.

Chart Number Two:
Events Following the Second Coming

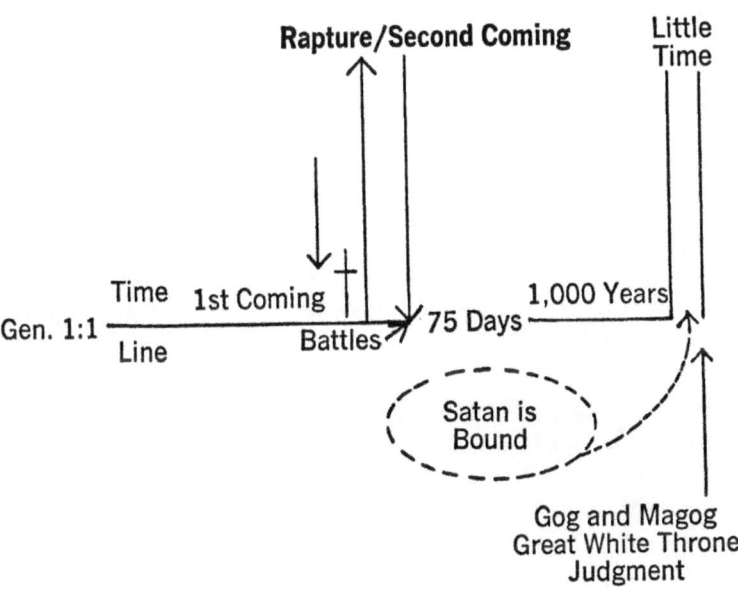

Seventy-Five Days: This complex period is divided into two sections—a 30-day section (Dan. 12:11) and a 45-day section (Dan. 12:12). The following events seem to occur during this brief period.

1. The temporary judgment of Satan and his host—Isa. 24:21-23; Rev. 20:1-3.
2. The judgment of unbelieving Jews—Ezek. 20:33-38; Zeph. 3:11; Matt. 25:1-30.
3. The salvation of true Israel—Zech. 12:10—13:1; Rom. 11:25-29.

4. The witnessing of the converted Jews to Gentiles who have not heard of Christ—Isa. 2:2-4; 66:18-21; Zech. 2:11; 3:8-10; see Rom. 11:11-12.
  5. The judgment of unbelieving Gentiles—Matt. 25:31-40.
  6. The rewarding of all resurrected believers—Luke 14:14; 2 Cor. 5:10.
  7. The marriage supper—Rev. 19:9; see Matt. 22:1-14; Luke 14:15-24.
  8. The new heavens and earth—2 Peter 3:10-14; Rev. 21—22.

1,000 Years: This refers to that period in which Christ will rule the whole earth, allowing for no resistance to His will (Pss. 2; 110:1-2; Dan. 2:44-45; Rev. 19:6-16).

Little Time: At the close of the 1,000 years, the abyss will be opened, releasing Satan and his host. He will go forth to deceive various nations and together they will march to Jerusalem for war with God (Rev. 20:7-10).

Gog and Magog: These words designate the great, but very brief, battle of Satan's host against God (Rev. 20:8-9).

Great White Throne Judgment: At this judgment, all those who have died without salvation will be resurrected, sentenced to their appropriate level of punishment and cast into the lake of fire (Rev. 20:11-15).

The Tribulation Period: The English term "tribulation" is derived from the Latin *tribulum,* which was an agricultural tool used for separating the husks from the corn by a rigorous process. The imagery of roughness and intensity is paramount.
  In the New Testament the word translated "tribulation" is *thlipsis,* and it means "to press, squash, rub, afflict, oppress, and harass." It is used both of distress that is brought about by outward circumstances (Acts 11:19; Rom. 5:3; 12:12; 2 Cor. 1:8; 6:4) and of distress that is mental and spiritual in nature (2 Cor. 2:4; Phil. 1:16-17).

Of the 54 occurrences of the word tribulation (including both verbal and noun forms) its usage is quite uniform. They inevitably describe a period of pain, pressure, or persecution. In the general sense, therefore, tribulation depicts the distresses and trials of all Christians in every period of history (Matt. 7:14; John 16:33).

More specifically, however, it is clear that the word tribulation possesses a distinctly prophetic aspect too. In the Book of Revelation, John records seeing a great multitude from every nation who were standing before the throne of God and before the Lamb (7:9-17). Next, John is given the identity of this heavenly host—"These are they who came out of the great tribulation" (7:14). The context makes it plain that these saints are the martyrs of a three-and-a-half-year span which immediately precedes the Second Coming (see Rev. 6:9; 13:1-7; 20:4).

The chronology is very plain: (1) general tribulation—for all saints in all periods of history; (2) specific tribulation—immediately before the second coming of Christ; and (3) the Lord's return to earth.

The Antichrist: The "great tribulation" which precedes Christ's return, will be marred by many ills (wars, famines, earthquakes, false prophets, deception, persecution, and so forth), but the greatest cancer will reside in its key personage—the Antichrist. Like spokes on a wheel, every event within this cataclysmic epoch will attach itself to this single figure.

Interestingly, almost every generation since Christ has "located" and pronounced the identity of the Antichrist. Before the New Testament canon was completed, two Roman emperors had already been selected as the Antichrist: Caligula (who reigned from A.D. 37-41) and Nero (who ruled from A.D. 54-68). The former attempted to place his image in the Jerusalem temple; the latter cruelly persecuted the Christians in Rome.

In the second and third centuries, the Church Fathers commonly held that when the Roman empire fell, it would be instantly followed by the ten-toed kingdom of Daniel's prophecies (chapter 2 and 7). Over this ten-body empire would rule the Antichrist. Irenaeus (c A.D. 200) thought he would be a Jew from the idolatrous tribe of Dan and that his appearance would be three-and-a-half years before the Second Coming. Tertullian (c. A.D. 190) held to the view of a personal Antichrist, though he need not be a Jew. Cyprian (c. A.D. 235) concluded that the end was very near and that the reign of the Antichrist was upon them.

This attitude was common during the early years of the church, but when Constantine legalized the Christian movement, people's prophetic views shifted. While certain emperors (those who persecuted the church after Constantine's time) were regarded as the Antichrist, a great variety of other views emerged. By the time of the Reformation, however, almost everyone was agreed (excluding the Roman heirarchy) that the papal system and/or the pope himself was the Antichrist. To date, this view has not been largely altered (though such men as Nietzsche, Hitler, and Mussolini have been candidates).

From a scriptural perspective, the word "Antichrist" is used five times, and only by John in his first and second letters (1 John 2:18, 22; 4:3; 2 John 7). Six general conclusions may be drawn from these five appearances:

1. The Christians of John's day anticipated the appearance of one particular antichrist, who apparently had not yet arrived.

2. There are many antichrists (those within whom abides the spirit of antichrist).

3. The "last hour" (probably a designation for the whole church age) is at hand when antichrists are present.

4. A denial of the Father or the Son or the messiahship of Jesus constitutes one as an antichrist.

5. Everyone not acknowledging the full deity and humanity of Jesus Christ is an antichrist.

6. The Antichrist is a deceiver.

Therefore, according to John, the coming Antichrist of antichrists will be a man of deception and denial, repudiating and disowning the person and work of Jesus Christ.

Other scriptural designations for this personage include: little horn (Dan. 7), man of sin (2 Thes. 2), son of perdition (2 Thes. 2), beast (Rev. 11:7, 13, 17), The Assyrian (Isa. 10:5-12; see 31:4—32:20) and the king of Babylon (Isa. 14:1-5).

Contrasts Between Antichrist and Christ

Antichrist	Christ
1. Has 10 horns Rev. 13.1	1. Has 7 horns Rev. 5:6
2. A king of earth Dan. 7:8, 24	2. Ruler of earth's kings Rev. 1:5
3. Claims deity Dan. 11:36	3. Is deity John 20:28
4. Proud Dan. 7:25	4. Meek Matt. 11:29
5. Blasphemous speech Rev. 13:5	5. Speech controlled by Father—John 14:10
6. Deceiver Dan. 8:23	6. Guileless 1 Peter 2:22
7. Fights saints Dan. 7:21	7. Comforts saints Rev. 7:7-17
8. Sheds blood Rev. 6:2-10	8. Gave His blood Rev. 5:9
9. Devours earth Dan. 7:23	9. Smites nations Rev. 19:15
10. Speaks great words Dan. 7:25	10. Speaks words of life John 6:63
11. Reign is limited Dan. 7:25	11. Reign is limited 1 Cor. 15:24-28; Rev. 20:4-6
12. Rules from Jerusalem 2 Thes. 2:4	12. Rules from Jerusalem Isa. 2:2-4
13. His power is not his own Dan. 8:24	13. His power is not His own Matt. 28:18
14. Called a prince Dan. 9:26	14. Called the Prince of princes—Dan. 8:25
15. Breaks covenant with Israel—Dan. 9:26-27	15. Fulfills covenant with Israel—Zech. 12:10—13:1; Rom. 11:25-27
16. Acts according to his will Dan. 11:36	16. Acts according to Father's will—Mark 14:36

17. Is worshiped Rev. 13:4	17. Is worshiped Rev. 5:8-14
18. Son of perdition 2 Thes. 2:3	18. Son of God John 1:14
19. Man of sin 2 Thes. 2:3	19. Sun of righteousness Mal. 4:2
20. Called wicked one 2 Thes. 2:8	20. Called Lord of glory James 2:1
21. Wears a crown *(stephanos)* Rev. 6:2	21. Wears crowns *(diadems)* Rev. 19:12
22. Rides white horse Rev. 6:2	22. Rides white horse Rev. 19:11
23. Has bow in his hand Rev. 6:2	23. Has sword Rev. 19:15
24. Gathers armies for Armageddon—Rev. 16:13-16	24. Brings armies to Armageddon—Rev. 19:14
25. Ascends from the pit Rev. 11:7	25. Descends from heaven Rev. 19:11
26. Symbolized as a leopard, bear, lion, and beast—Rev. 13:1-2	26. Symbolized as a lion and lamb—Rev. 5:5-6
27. Wounded to death Rev. 13:3, 12, 14	27. Wounded to death Rev. 5:6
28. Death wound healed Rev. 13:3, 12, 14	28. Death wound healed Col. 2:12
29. Hailed as a king Rev. 13:4	29. Hailed as a king Luke 19:38
30. Demon-possessed Rev. 16:13-14	30. Spirit-controlled Luke 4:1
31. Mark of Antichrist Rev. 13:15-18	31. Mark of Christ Rev. 3:12
32. Comes in his own name John 5:43	32. Came in His Father's name—John 5:43
33. Comes to destroy Rev. 13:1-10	33. Came to save Luke 19:10

The Rapture: Central to the joy of every Christian's heart is *hope*—

that confident expectation with regard to the unseen and the future (Rom. 8:24-25; 15:13; Heb. 6:11). The saint possesses hope in the resurrection from the dead (Acts 23:6), in the promises of God (Acts 26:6), in divine providence (Rom. 5:4-5), in a future experiential righteousness (Gal. 5:5), in salvation (Eph. 4:4), in eternal life (Titus 1:2; 3:7), and in a yet to be bestowed glorified body which will be fashioned after Christ's very own glorious body (1 John 3:2). There is still another hope—one which outshines all these optimistic anticipations. The hope is Jesus Christ Himself (1 Thes. 1:3; 1 Tim. 1:1) and specifically His blessed return (Titus 2:13). The pinnacle expectation of every true child of God is to see Jesus—face to face (1 John 3:3-4; Rev. 22:4). The theological title for this event is "the rapture."

The term "rapture" is derived from the Latin *rapio,* and means "to seize," "to transport," and "to snatch" so as to remove something or someone from one place to another. Although the exact word "rapture" does not appear in the Scriptures, its Greek equivalent is found in 1 Thessalonians 4:17. Here the word *harpagesometha* (from *harpazo*) is used and is appropriately translated "caught up."

The verb *harpazo* appears thirteen times in the New Testament, of which four particular occurrences merit attention. In Acts, "the Spirit of the Lord caught *away* Philip" (8:39); in 2 Corinthians, Paul was said to be *"caught up* to the third heaven . . . *caught up* to paradise" (12:2, 4); and in Revelation, the Male Child (Jesus Christ) was *"caught up* to God and to His throne" (12:5). These references make it clear that the rapture is a physical removal of the saints from the earth (also see 1 Cor. 15:51-53; Rev. 20:4-6).

The subject of Christ's return and appearing is a most magnificent one, but regrettably marred with confusion as to the time of His manifestation. Essentially the debate centers around the relationship of the rapture to the tribulation period. There are no less than five positions on this critical issue.

1. Pretribulationalism: The pretribulationalists view the second coming of Christ as a two-fold event. The first aspect of His return is secret, and it focuses only upon the rapturing of the Church

FIGURE XXI.

THE RAPTURE VISUALIZED

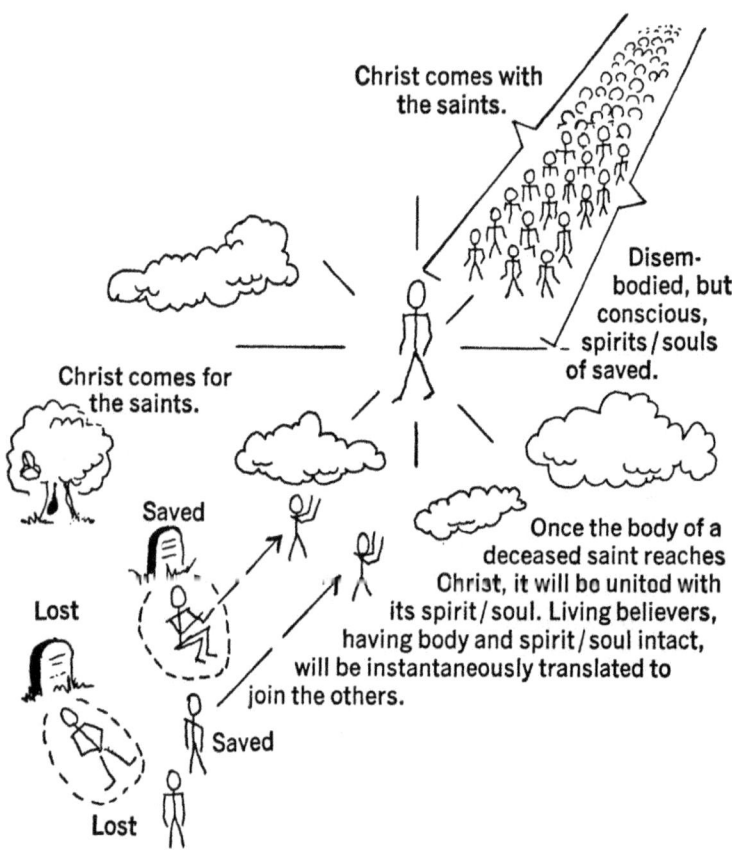

ORDER OF EVENTS:
1. Resurrection of deceased saint's body to unite with his spirit/soul, which God brings with Christ at His coming in the air.
2. Translation of living saints.
3. Marriage of the Lamb.
4. Descent to earth; the second coming.

FIGURE XXII.

DIAGRAMS OF THE FIVE RAPTURE POSITIONS

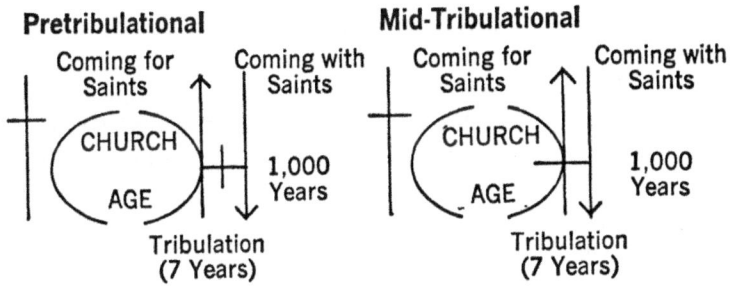

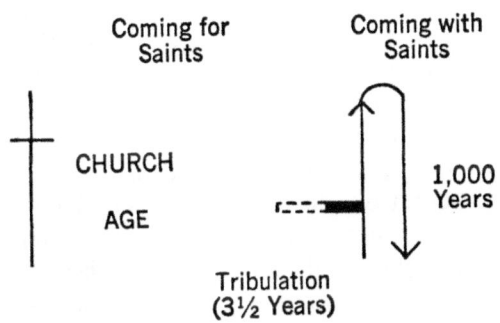

before the period of the tribulation. This coming is only in the air. The second phase of His coming, this time to the earth, occurs seven years later (after Israel's 70th week) and focuses upon Armageddon, multiple judgments and setting up the millennial kingdom.

2. Midtribulationalism: The proponents of this position hold that Christ will not return for His Church until *midway* through Israel's 70th week, between the second and the third woes of John's Apocalypse (11:3-14). Like pretribulationalists, they too, hold that the Second Coming has two distinct phases.

3. Posttribulationalism: This body of interpreters believes that the Second Coming and the Rapture constitute a single event—*after* the tribulation period.

4. Partial Rapture: The followers of this particular view hold that only a prepared and expectant section of believers will be raptured before the tribulation period, with the remainder being caught up at the end of Israel's 70th week.

5. Potential Past-Tribulation: This position asserts the possibility that the tribulation (a period of trial immediately before the Lord's second advent but distinct from Israel's 70th week, which is held to be already past) is potentially already completed.

A study of the following diagrams illustrate these five positions.

Each of the above positions is held by biblical scholars who love the Lord Jesus Christ and who seek only to properly interpret the Scriptures. Doubtless, the intent of each proponent is to inform, comfort, and edify the body of Christ. Therefore, regardless of the personal appeal of any one specific interpretation, let each child of God hold his own convictions firmly, but also with humility. Christian unity does not depend upon our unanimity to the "proper" succession of prophetic events. In the final analysis only time will prove the accuracy and inaccuracies of these varied positions.

At the time of the Rapture the saints are given their new bodies. Eleven traits are discussed in the Scriptures regarding these new abodes. (This assumes that the resurrected body of Jesus will be analogous to the believer's new body—1 John 3:2 with Rom. 8:29; 2 Peter 1:4).

1. They will be able to pass through solid objects—John 20:19-20.
2. They will retain a semblance of the earthly body—John 20:26-28.
3. They will be capable of eating food—John 21:12-14; Rev. 19:9.
4. They will have flesh and bones (obviously different from our present flesh and bones)—Luke 24:39.
5. They will vary in their glory; that is, to the extent that they will shine—Dan. 12:2-3; 1 Cor. 15:40-42.
6. They will be incorruptible; hence, they cannot sin or be affected by disease—1 Cor. 15:42, 53-54.
7. They will possess power; therefore, they will never tire or need rest—1 Cor. 15:43; see Rev. 22:5.
8. They will be spiritual bodies—1 Cor. 15:44-49.
9. They will be immortal; they will never die—1 Cor. 15:51-57.
10. They will not be given in marriage—Matt. 22:30.
11. They will be given a mind that has no remembrance of earth, but instead, this mind will think God's very thoughts after Him—Isa. 65:17; Rev. 3:12. Paul states it in this fashion: "Then I shall know fully, just as I also have been fully known"—1 Cor. 13:12 (NASB).

Hell: There are seven key words on the topic of hell which require individual attention.
1. Sheol: This Hebrew word occurs 65 times and is translated "grave," "hell," and "pit." The best rendering of this term is *the place of the dead.* It has reference to both the righteous dead (Ps. 16:10) and the unrighteous dead (Num. 16:33). It is a place of conscious existence and is regarded as a temporary abode, with the righteous ones eventually being resurrected out of it (Pss. 16:9-11; 17:15).
2. Hades: The Greek term "hades" refers to the temporary or intermediate abode of only the unrighteous dead and is translated "hell" (Matt. 11:23). The actual location of the unrighteous dead (of sheol and hades) is "beneath the oceans" (Job 26:5) and in the "heart of the earth" (Matt. 12:40; see Ps. 63:9).

3. Pit: This unique word has reference to the dwelling place of imprisoned fallen angels (Rev. 11:7; 17:8; 20:1, 3).

4. Tartarus: This word only occurs once and is translated "hell" (2 Peter 2:4). It seems to be another word for "pit" (1 Peter 3:19; Jude 6-7).

5. Gehenna: Twelve times this word occurs and it always appears as "hell" (Matt. 5:22, 29-30). While *hades* is the intermediate state of the unrighteous dead, *gehenna* is the eternal state. All those in *hades* will be resurrected at the close of the millennium, judged, and cast into their everlasting dwelling—hell or the lake of fire (Rev. 20:11-15).

6. Abraham's Bosom: This occurs but twice and speaks of the separate abode for the righteous dead in *sheol* (Luke 16:22-23).

7. Paradise: There are only three references to this term (Luke 23:43; 2 Cor. 12:4; Rev. 2:7). Paradise is doubtless in the immediate presence of God. Some theologians are persuaded that the inhabitants of Abraham's bosom were transported into paradise at the resurrection of Christ (see Eph. 4:8-10).

One final aspect needs consideration—"What is hell like?" Below are six basic characteristics of the horrors of hell.

1. Vision—people can see in hell (Luke 16:19-23).
2. Torments—
   a. levels of punishment (Matt. 23:14; Luke 12:47-48; Rev. 20:11-15)
   b. darkness (Matt. 8:12)
   c. prison (Job 17:16; Isa. 38:10; Jude 6)
   d. smoke (Rev. 14:9-11)
   e. fire (Isa. 33:14; 66:24)
   f. no rest (Rev. 14:9-11)
   g. weeping and wailing (Matt. 13:42; Matt. 22:13)
   h. gnashing of teeth (Matt. 22:13)
   i. worms die not (Isa. 66:24)
   j. eternal (Mark 9:45-48; Rev. 20:10)
3. Speech—Luke 16:19-31
4. Remembrance—Luke 16:19-31
5. No escape—Luke 16:19-31
6. Burden for lost souls—Luke 16:28

Heaven: The Hebrew (*shamayim*) and the Greek (*ouranos*) words for heaven have closely related meanings. The former means "the heights" while the latter means "that which is raised up." Both convey the central concept of that which is lofty and above men or the earth.

Although the term "heaven" or "heavens" appears over 700 times in the Scriptures, very little is really known about the eternal home of the righteous. This is due largely to the fact that the word "heaven" is used to express three distinct entities.

1. The First Heaven—Atmosphere. Frequently the Scriptures speak of heaven as the place where the rains fall (Deut. 11:11), frost is sent (Job 38:29), dew comes (Deut. 33:13), clouds dwell (Ps. 147:8), winds blow (Zech. 2:6) and birds fly (Prov 23:5).

2. The Second Heaven—Planetary. Naturally, this heaven includes the sun, the moon, and the stars (Gen. 1:14; 15:5; Heb. 1:10). Among the planets, Venus and Saturn are expressly identified (Isa. 14:12; Amos 5:26). Two constellations are even named —Pleiades and Orion (Job 9:9; 38:31; Amos 5:8).

3. The Third Heaven—God's Abode. The occupants of this heaven include: God (Deut. 26:15), Jesus Christ (John 14:2-3), the Holy Spirit (Rev. 4:5), angels (Matt. 18:10), cherubim (Gen. 3:24; Ex. 25:18-22), seraphim (Isa. 6:2-7), the archangel (1 Thes. 4:16; see Dan. 10:13-14, 20-21), the host of Yahweh (1 Sam. 4:4), living creatures (Rev. 4:6-11), Satan (Rev. 12:10; see Job 1:6; 2:1) and the spirits of the departed saints (Luke 16:19-31; 23:43; Acts 7:55; 2 Cor. 5:6-8; Phil. 1:21; Rev. 6:11).

What are the saints doing in heaven? We would all enjoy an answer to this question, but the Scriptures are silent as to the immediate activities of these saints. We may rest confident, however, that they enjoy perfect bliss. Regarding future activities of the saints in heaven (which must partially cover the present activities of the saints), the record states that the saints will: look upon His face (Rev. 22:4), worship God (Rev. 19:1-8), sing (Rev. 5:9; 14:3; 15:2-4), serve God (Rev. 22:3), reign over the nations (Luke 19:17-19; Matt. 25:21-23; 1 Cor. 6:2; Rev. 2:26-27; 20:4, 6), judge angels (1 Cor. 6:3), fellowship (Rev. 19:9; 21:3-4), and rest from earth's labors (Rev. 14:13).

Part 3

Glossary and Concordance

20 | Concise Bible Dictionary

A

Abba. The Aramaic term for "father," recorded in Mark 14:36; Rom. 8:15; and Gal. 4:6. It is always used in conjunction with the normal Greek word for "father," and therefore suggests either an added intimacy in its usage or a translation added for the non-Aramaic reader. Jewish law forbade slaves to use this word in addressing the head of a family. Its use was especially reserved for those of a most personal bond.

abide. With reference to place, it means to tarry as a guest or to maintain an unbroken fellowship (Matt. 10:11; John 15:4, 6-7, 10). With reference to quality, it means to remain as one is (1 Cor. 13:13). With reference to time, it means to continue or endure (2 Tim. 2:13).

abomination. Something to be abhorred and considered evil or wicked, such as idolatry (Matt. 24:15; Mark 13:14), or unlawful practices (Acts 10:28; 1 Peter 4:3), or deception (Titus 1:16).

abstain. Refers to the act of refraining or the keeping of oneself from evil practices (Acts 15:20, 29; 1 Thes. 4:3; 5:22; 1 Tim. 4:3; 1 Peter 2:11).

abyss. Appears in the *New International Version,* replacing the *Authorized Version's* phrase of "bottomless pit" (Rev. 9:1-2, 11; 11:7; 17:8; 20:1, 3) and "deep" (Luke 8:31; Rom. 10:7). It designates the underworld, the regions of Sheol, and it is occupied with demons or fallen angels.

access. A leading or a bringing into the presence of another. It denotes the freedom to enter due to the assistance or favor of another (Rom. 5:2; Eph. 2:18).

accountability. The quality or state of holding each person responsible for his or her own actions (Rom. 1:20; 14:12; Heb. 4:13; 13:17).

admonition. Means literally, "to put into the mind." What is put into the mind is a verbal warning to someone needing correction (Rom. 15:14; 1 Cor. 4:14; Col. 1:28; 3:16; 1 Thes. 5:12, 14; 2 Thes. 3:15).

adoption. Occurs five times in the New Testament and denotes God's act of grace whereby He accepts believers into His family (Rom. 8:15, 23; 9:4; Gal. 4:5; Eph. 1:5).

adultery. The act of sexual intercourse by a married person with any person other than the lawful spouse (Luke 18:11; 1 Cor. 6:9-10; Heb. 13:4).

advocate. Appears only once in the Authorized Version (1 John 2:1) and means "one who is called to the side of another," especially in a court situation. Therefore, it might be rightly rendered "lawyer" or "defense attorney." Elsewhere, the word is translated "comforter" (John 14:16, 26; 15:26; 16:7). This translation comes from the Latin, meaning "Strengthener." The best idea seems to be that of a Counsellor, One who gives advice and encouragement.

affliction. Suffering resulting from the pressures of circumstances or from antagonistic people (1 Thes. 3:4; 2 Thes. 1:6-7; 1 Tim. 5:9-10). The idea of sickness is not within the scope of the term.

age. "Era" is an appropriate synonym. It may refer to the past (Luke 1:70; Acts 3:2; 15:18), the future (Matt. 21:19; John 6:51, 58; Heb. 5:6; 6:20), and the present (Matt. 12:32; Eph. 1:21).

allegory. A literary term that is used to classify statements which go beyond the literal meaning of the narrative. Paul used this word to convey a spiritual principle that resided deeper than the literal story (Gal. 4:24). While this is occasionally a valid method of interpretation, it must always be carefully balanced with the broader explicit witness of Scripture.

alms. Any act of benevolence, such as giving to the poor (Deut. 15:7; 24:13), constitutes "almsgiving" (Matt. 6:1-4; Acts 10:2; 24:17).

alpha and omega. The first and last letters of the Greek alphabet. Its usage indicates the totality of a thing (Rev. 1:8; 21:6; 22:13).

ambassador. The Roman Emperor's official emissary was given this title. Christians, in like manner, are sent forth as representatives of the King of kings, to deliver His message (2 Cor. 5:20; Eph. 6:20).

amen. This Hebrew word means "to be reliable, sure, and true." When used at the end of a doxology, it signifies, "yes, indeed!" (See Pss. 41:13; 72:19.) When the listener uses the term, he indicates his hearty assent (1 Kings 1:36; Jer. 11:5). And when it is applied to Christ, as a proper name, it depicts His faithfulness in carrying out His works (Rev. 3:14).

anathema. A strong word which implies moral worthlessness and accursedness, or that which brings disfavor before God (1 Cor. 16:22; "accursed" is this word—Rom. 9:3; 1 Cor. 12:3).

anoint. This is a general term for applying either an ointment or a perfumed oil upon persons or things (Ruth 3:3; John 11:2; James 5:14). When the anointing comes from the Holy Spirit, it indicates that the one being anointed is rendered holy or separated unto God (Acts 10:38; 1 John 2:20, 27).

Antichrist. Opposition to Christ is the obvious meaning of this compound. It is used of people who are antagonistic to the truth of Christ (1 John 2:18, 22; 2 John 7), of the spirit of this age (1 John 4:3), and of one final figure who will openly oppose Christ (1 John 2:18).

apostle. One who is sent forth, like Christ from heaven (Heb. 3:1), or the twelve from Jesus (Luke 6:13), or the missionaries from the early church (Acts 14:4, 14; 2 Cor. 8:23), is an "apostle."

Armageddon. The place of the awesome and decisive battle between certain armies of the earth and Jesus Christ at His second coming (Rev. 16:16).

atonement. Best described by the term "reconciliation." It is the divine process of bringing those who are enemies of God into unity (at-one-ment) with Himself. Christ died, taking our sins unto His own body and bearing man's punishment, that we might, by personally appropriating this finished work, stand accepted before God (Mark 10:45; Rom. 5:11; 2 Cor. 5:14, 18-19).

B

backbiter. To speak down or against someone is to backbite (Rom. 1:30; James 4:11; 1 Peter 2:12).
baptism. The process or the act of immersing or submerging something into water though other symbolic forms such as sprinkling or pouring are also called baptism. As a Christian ceremony, it symbolizes the convert's death, burial, and resurrection with Christ (Rom. 6:3-4; 1 Cor. 1:13-17; Gal. 3:27; Col. 2:12).
barbarian. This designation was used of those persons who spoke a language other than the common Greek. It is applied in both a derogatory and a nonderogatory fashion (Acts 28:2, 4; Rom. 1:14; 1 Cor. 14:11; Col. 3:11).
base. This denotes someone of low birth and who is of no account (1 Cor. 1:28).
Beelzebub. In the Old Testament this term refers to the god of the Philistines and meant, "lord of the flies" (2 Kings 1:2ff.). The scribes used the term to designate the ruler of the demons (Mark 3:22).
beget. To beget someone does not always imply immediate parentage; sometimes only direct descent is meant. "Begotten" conveys a similar idea—"to be born of" (Matt. 1:1-16).
beguile. To practice deception (2 Cor. 11:3; 1 Tim. 2:14).
behooved. "To owe." The term indicates an obligation (Luke 24:46; Heb. 2:17).
Belial. Originally this word meant "extreme wickedness." Later, it came to be used as a name of Satan (Deut. 13:13; 2 Cor. 6:15).
believe. To be persuaded to accept a statement about something or someone as true. It denotes confidence, trust, and personal reliance (Luke 8:50; John 14:1; John 16:30).

benediction. A blessing or the act or pronouncement of a blessing (Num. 6:22-27; 2 Cor. 13:14; Eph. 3:20-21; Heb. 13:20-21; Jude 24-25).

binding and loosing. The authority of the church to include or exclude certain ones from its membership is expressed in these terms (Matt. 16:19; Matt. 18:18).

birthright. The firstborn child was to receive special blessing and authority which constituted his birthright (Gen. 27:29; 49:3; Deut. 21:17; 1 Chron. 5:1-2).

bishop. An "overseer" or shepherd (Acts 20:28; Phil. 1:1; 1 Tim. 3:2; Titus 1:7). It is another designation for "elder."

blasphemy. The act of speaking evil of someone. It is generally used as defamatory speech directed against God. Sometimes it is translated "railing." (See. Matt. 15:19; Mark 3:28; Rom. 2:24; Eph. 4:31; Jude 9.)

bless. To speak well of. With regard to God, it means to thank or praise Him (Pss. 16:7; 103:1; Rom. 12:14).

bosom. The chest of one's body (John 13:23) and is figuratively used of the place of blessedness and honor (Luke 16:22-23; John 1:18).

bowels. The intestines are here designated as the seat of affection and compassion (Phil. 1:8; 2:1; 1 John 3:17).

busybody. Someone who meddles in another's business (2 Thes. 3:11). Someone who is engaged with the trifles of life (1 Tim. 5:13).

C

carnal. The description of a person who is controlled by his natural or human nature, instead of by the Holy Spirit. It is used of both the unbeliever (Rom. 8:5-8) and the believer (1 Cor. 3:1-3). The term literally means "fleshly."

censer. A vessel for carrying or dispensing burning incense (2 Chron. 26:19; Heb. 9:4).

centurion. A military officer who commanded from 50 to 100 men (Matt. 8:5, 8).

chaff. The outer husk of the grain, from which the grain has been removed (Matt. 3:12).

charity. See **love**.

chaste. Pure or free from fault or defilement (2 Cor. 7:11; Phil. 4:8; 1 Tim. 5:22; 1 Peter 3:2; 1 John 3:3).

chastisement. Punishment or child training and education. The learning may come through corrective speech (1 Tim. 1:20; 2 Tim. 2:25) and/or through adverse circumstances (1 Cor. 11:32; 2 Cor. 6:9; Heb. 12:6-10).

cherubim. See "Angels" in the Doctrinal section of this book.

circumcision. The Jewish rite of cutting off the foreskin of the male sex organ (Gen. 17:11).

comely. Beautiful, graceful, or fitting. Comeliness refers to one's elegance of figure (Pss. 33:1; 147:1; 1 Cor. 11:13; 12:24).

communion. A partnership; having things in common. It may be used of common experiences (Gal. 2:9), common knowledge (1 Cor. 1:9), sharing in Christ's sufferings (Phil. 3:10) or of the intimate discourse that is derived from the indwelling Holy Spirit (2 Cor. 13:14).

concision. A cutting down, a mutilation, or a hacking; it is used of that Jewish party which insisted upon circumcision for Christians (Phil. 3:2).

confession. An agreement or assent to one's guilt. Literally, "to say the same thing" God says of our sin (John 1:20; Heb. 11:13; 1 John 1:9).

contrition. Deep sorrow for sin (2 Cor. 7:9-10).

conversation. In the King James Version it means "behavior" or "manner of life" (Acts 23:1; Phil. 1:27; Heb. 13:5).

conversion. A turning—turning around, or returning (either physically or spiritually). It encompasses turning from evil (Jer. 18:8) and turning unto the Lord (Mal. 3:7; Matt. 18:3; Acts 3:19; 28:27).

conviction. More than the discovery of personal faults; it also includes a shame for their practice (John 8:46; 16:8).

corban. Appears only in Mark 7:11. It means "offering" or "sacrifice."

countenance. Personal appearance, usually facial (Prov. 15:13; Matt. 6:16; Luke 9:29; Rev. 1:16).

covenant. An agreement between two parties which mutually binds them. It may be looked upon as a solemn promise. Covenants were made between men and between God and men (Gen. 12:1-3; Jer. 11:4; Luke 1:72; Heb. 7:22; 8:6, 8, 10; 9:4; 10:16).

covet. To fix one's eyes of desire on something, to long for, or lust after something. It is usually used of inordinate or improper desires (Luke 12:15; Rom. 7:7; 13:9), but see 1 Cor. 14:1.

cruse. A vessel used for holding liquids (1 Kings 17:12). The alabaster box, so called because of the alabaster stone from which the vessel was made, was one kind of cruse (Matt. 26:7).

cubit. The distance between the elbow joint to the tip of the middle finger—about eighteen inches (Matt. 6:27; Luke 12:25). There is some evidence that such a measure was arbitrarily set by measuring the king's or other ruler's arm length.

D

dayspring. The rising of the sun (Luke 1:78).

deacon. The official order of servants who aid in the work of the church (Phil. 1:1; 1 Tim. 3:8-13). The term actually means "servant" and should not be confused with the church leadership, which is the responsibility of the elders.

demon. Originally, among the Greeks, demons were regarded as gods. The New Testament uses this term for evil spirits who serve as Satan's agents. See "Angels" in the Doctrinal section.

desolation. Something that is laid waste, brought to nought, or made useless (Matt. 12:25; 24:15).

despite. Insulting or injurious treatment (Rom. 1:30; 1 Tim. 1:13).

destitute. The state of lacking something needed or desirable (Heb. 11:37; James 2:15).

devils. See demon.

diadem. A kingly ornament worn on the head. Hence, a symbol of authority (Rev. 12:3; 13:1; 19:12).

discreet. Sober-minded, self-controlled, and temperate (Titus 1:8; 2:2, 5).

dispensation. In Greek a compound of the words "house" and "law." Hence, the meaning is the administration or management of a household. It also includes the concept of stewardship (Luke 16:2-4). Its broader usages include one's entrustment with spiritual things (1 Cor. 9:17). Also the period of time in which God manages His affairs here on earth (Eph. 1:10; 3:2, 9).

dispersion. Scatter abroad. It is used most often of the Jews who lived outside the border of Israel (see Diaspora—James 1:1).

dissimulation. This term comes from the Greek stage where an actor would play several roles and wear masks to depict the various roles. He was called a hypocrite (Rom. 12:9; Gal. 2:13; 2 Cor. 6:6; 1 Tim. 1:5).

divers. Diversities or manifold (James 1:2).

divination. The pagan skill of obtaining information from demons (Deut. 18:10-14; Ezek. 21:21; 1 Sam. 28; Acts 16:16).

doctrine. The teaching or the content of what is taught (1 Tim. 1:10; Titus 2:1). It usually relates to truths about God and His relationship to man and the world.

dull. Slow or sluggish (Heb. 5:11).

dung. Either human excrement or discarded food, garbage (Phil. 3:8).

E

edification. A term to describe construction of a house. Hence, when a believer is edified, he is being built up or developed more completely in the Christian way (Rom. 15:2; 1 Cor. 14:3; 2 Cor. 10:8; 13:10).

effectual. Powerful in force or effective in results (1 Cor. 16:9; Heb. 4:12).

effulgence. Brightness or radiance (Heb. 1:3).

elder. The elders of Israel were often regarded as the local administrators of the law (Ex. 3:16; Jud. 8:14; 1 Sam. 4:3). In the New Testament they are regarded as the leaders of the church, upon whom rested the responsibility of pastoral oversight (Acts 15:2, 6, 23; 20:17, 28; 1 Tim. 3:1-7; Titus 1:5-9). This same word is also translated "presbyter."

ensample. The word "type" is a more common designation for this term. It means to strike something so that an impression is left (John 20:25). It is also used in the sense of a mold or pattern (1 Cor. 10:6, 11; 1 Peter 5:3).

entreat. Request or ask (Phil. 4:3).

envy. Suggests either a desire for the possessions of another, or the grudge one feels when someone else receives something he does not himself possess (Gal. 5:21; Phil. 1:15; 1 Tim. 6:4-5).

err. To lead astray or deceive (Heb. 3:10).

eunuch. An emasculated man (Matt. 19:12).

eventide. Evening (Acts 4:3).

exhortation. The admonishment, comfort, or strengthening of someone in the course he should follow (Phil. 4:2; 1 Thes. 4:10; Heb. 13:19, 22).

exorcist. Someone who practices the casting out of demons (Acts 19:13).

expedient. Profitable or advantageous (John 11:50; 2 Cor. 8:10).

extort. To rob, seize, or plunder (Matt. 23:25).

F

faith. The firm persuasion and conviction about the trustworthiness of the object in which the faith is placed. In the New Testament it is only used of faith in God, Christ, and spiritual things. Additionally, the term may be translated "faithfulness." This note strongly suggests that anyone who exercises genuine faith in divine matters will invariably personify these convictions with steadfast loyalty (Gal. 5:22; Titus 2:10).

fasting. The practice of abstaining from food for spiritual purposes. In some cases even water was abstained from (Es. 4:16-17), while in others, only certain kinds of foods were avoided (Dan. 10:2-3). Normally, all foods are not eaten during the fasting period, which may be of any duration (Matt. 4:2; 6:16; Acts 12:2-3; 27:33; Isa. 58).

feign. To act as a hypocrite or play actor (Luke 20:20).

fellowship. See **communion**.

fidelity. Faithfulness or dependability (Titus 2:10).

firkin. A liquid measure of about nine gallons (John 2:6).
firstborn. See **begotten**.
flesh. See **carnal**.
forbear. To endure (Eph. 4:2) or to withhold (Rom. 2:4; 3:25).
foreknowledge. God's foresight, which involves the whole course of earthly events (Acts 2:23; 15:18; Gal. 1:15-16; Eph. 1:5, 11; 1 Peter 1:2).
fornication. Illicit sexual intercourse, which may include the sexual union between married or unmarried persons (1 Cor. 5:1; 6:13, 18).
furlong. A distance of 220 yards (Luke 24:13).

G

gainsay. To oppose, contradict, and question (Rom. 10:21; Titus 2:9; Heb. 12:3).
gentiles. Non-Jewish people (Matt. 4:15; Rom. 3:29).
glorify. To extol, magnify, and praise (Matt. 5:16; Rom. 11:13; 1 Cor. 6:20).
glutton. One who overeats or is given to food (Matt. 11:19; Titus 1:12).
gnash. To grind with the teeth (Matt. 8:12; Acts 7:54).
goad. A sting: a pointed stick for prodding animals (Acts 9:5; 26:14).
godliness. Acting as God would act. Holy righteous behavior (1 Tim. 2:2; 3:16; 2 Tim. 3:5).
Gospel. The good news regarding the kingdom of God (Mark 1:14-15). It includes the good news of salvation (Eph. 1:13), peace (Eph. 6:15), and eternal life (Col. 1:23) through Jesus Christ's death, burial, and resurrection (Acts 15:7; 20:24; 1 Cor. 15).
grace. The divine act whereby God shows undeserved favor, mercy, kindness, benefit, or salvation to man (Ex. 33:13; Rom. 11:6; Eph. 2:7).
guile. Deceit, bait, or a snare (2 Cor. 12:16; 1 Peter 2:1). Someone who is guileless, therefore, is someone without deceptive, crafty, and subtle speech or actions (John 1:47).

H

Hades. The present or temporary abode of the wicked dead (Matt. 11:23; 16:18; Rev. 6:8). The eternal dwelling place of these occupants is "hell" (literally Gehenna) or the "lake of fire" (Rev. 20:10-15).

hallowed. Made holy or set apart for God's glory (Matt. 6:9).

harlot. A prostitute or one who sells her body for sexual purposes (Matt. 21:31-32; James 2:25).

haughty. The act of placing oneself above others in an arrogant manner (Rom. 1:30; 2 Tim. 3:2).

havoc. (n) Wide or general destruction; (v) to lay waste (Acts 8:3; 9:21).

hearken. Hear, listen (Mark 4:3; Acts 4:19).

heaven. Three heavens are referred to in Scripture (2 Cor. 12:2): 1. The sky—Matt. 6:26 (translated "air"); 2. The solar system—Matt. 24:29, 35; and 3. The abode of God—Matt. 5:16.

heir. The recipient of an inheritance (Matt. 21:38; Rom. 4:13-14; 8:17; Gal. 3:29).

heresies. Destructive opinions or false teachings which persons (heretics) spread as truth. This is more than a mistaken interpretation of some single passage; it embraces the notion of a deliberate denial of the revealed truth, resulting in a sect or schism (Acts 5:17; 15:5; 24:14; 28:22; 1 Cor. 11:19).

hireling. A hired servant (John 10:12-13).

holy. A two-fold concept which includes: 1. separation from all that is evil, and 2. consecration to all that is of God (Ps. 1; 2 Cor. 7:1; 1 Thes. 3:13; 1 Peter 1:16). In the original languages this same root is used to form the words "saint" and "sanctification." The meaning of these latter terms is the same as "holy."

hope. A confident expectation, not mere wishing. It pertains to the future and the unseen (Rom. 8:24-25; Col. 1:23).

hosanna. Is taken from Psalm 118:26 and means, "Save, now, we pray" (Matt. 21:9, 15).

host: A large crowd, as an army of angels (Luke 2:13; Acts 7:42).

humility. The absence of self-consciousness. The act of rendering selfless service for others (Acts 20:19; Phil. 2:3).

husbandman. One who cultivates the ground (John 15:1; 1 Cor. 3:9; Heb. 6:7).
hypocrisy. See dissimulation.

I

idle. Inactive or unfruitful (1 Tim. 5:13; Titus 1:12).
idol. An image or representation of a false god (Acts 7:41; 1 Cor. 12:2). Paul calls these so-called gods "demons" (1 Cor. 10:19). Idolatry is the worship of, or devotion to, these gods. Greed and idolatry are considered to be identical (Eph. 5:5).
immortality. Deathlessness (1 Cor. 15:53-54).
immutability. Changeless (Heb. 6:18).
impediment. A speech difficulty (Mark 7:32).
implacable. Incapable of being appeased or pacified (2 Tim. 3:3).
importunity. Shameless persistence (Luke 11:8).
impotent. Without strength (Acts 4:9).
impute. The doctrine of imputation is important in the understanding of Christ's sacrifice. Essentially, the term means to reckon to another's account. As such, it refers to: 1. Adam's sin being placed on all persons (Rom. 5:12-21); 2. Man's sin being placed on Christ (Isa. 53:4-6; 2 Cor. 5:21); and 3. God's righteousness being placed on the believer (Rom. 3:21—5:21).
incontinent. Lacking self-control; one who dwells in excesses, (Matt. 23:25; 1 Cor. 7:5; 2 Tim. 3:3).
indignation. To be moved with anger (2 Cor. 7:11).
infirmity. Any weakness or disability (excluding a sickness caused by disease—Rom. 8:26; 2 Cor. 12:5, 9-10).
inheritance. See heir.
inn. A house for the reception of strangers. It may even include a sheltered area for their animals (Luke 10:34).
insolent. To be verbally injurious (Rom. 1:30).
inspiration. God-breathed; it is used of the writing of the Scriptures (2 Tim. 3:16).
intercession. The act of seeking God in prayer in behalf of others (Rom. 8:27; Heb. 7:25).
intreaty. To ask or beseech (Phil. 4:3).

J

jealousy. The emotion which will not tolerate rivalry or unfaithfulness. It is used of God toward His people (Ex. 20:5; 34:14). The expression may also be used of God's people who serve Him with faithfulness and godly jealousy (2 Cor. 11:2).

jesting. Originally this word described the versatility one possessed in social dialogue. In New Testament translations, however, it is used to denote coarse, foolish, or unserious speech (Eph. 5:4).

jot. The smallest Hebrew letter (Matt. 5:18).

just. To conduct oneself in a proper manner (same word in the original—Rom. 1:17; 2:13; 5:7). Since no one can conduct himself wholly in a just manner, a divine remedy was necessary. Through the death of Christ, upon whom was rested all of man's unrighteousness, God could justify sinners (Rom. 3:23—5:21). Therefore, a person who is justified is one who has been judicially released from the sentence which once loomed before him. He is made guiltless in God's sight. See **impute.**

K

kingdom of God. essentially denotes the sphere of God's sovereign rule in the affairs of earth. As such, it extends throughout all of time. Presently, the realm of the kingdom's authority includes all those who are in Jesus Christ (Matt. 28:18; Luke 17:21). At this moment He rules as King of kings and Lord of lords (1 Tim. 6:14-15; Rev. 1:5). At His return, Jesus will manifest this authority before all men and demand allegiance (Rev. 19—20). After an earthly reign of a thousand years, Jesus will then return the rule back to God the Father (1 Cor. 15:24-28).

L

lasciviousness. Licentious, lewd, wanton, or indecent conduct (Gal. 5:19).

law. The Scriptures use this term to identify authoritative instruction (Prov. 1:8). In some cases the word refers only to the writings of Moses (Matt. 5:17); more frequently, however, the whole counsel and will of God is in view.

leaven. Leaven, a form of yeast, was used to produce fermentation in dough. All sacrifices were void of yeast (Lev. 2:11), since it symbolized a mixture of purity with evil (Matt. 13:33; Mark 8:15; 1 Cor. 5:7-8).

leprosy. A chronic disease (Lev. 13).

Levites. The descendents of Levi who served Israel in the functions of the tabernacle and temple. They served in a lesser role than the priests (who descended from Aaron). One of their tasks was teaching the law (Deut. 33:10; Neh. 8:7).

lord. Used in a variety of ways. With reference to man, it refers to his headship, either as the leader of the family or the owner and master of servants (2 Kings 5:1-3). With reference to God, it denotes superiority and authority (Rom. 14:19).

lot casting. Small pieces of wood or stone (sometimes with names affixed) were placed in a large and loose pocket of someone's garment, out of which they were cast, after being shaken. The first lot landing outside the garment was chosen (see Lev. 16:8; Josh. 18:5-10; Jonah 1:7; 1 Sam. 10:19-21; Matt. 27:35; Acts 1:24-26).

love. The sacrificing of self for others is love. It is best defined by the way it acts—see 1 Corinthians 13.

lucre. Material wealth (Titus 1:11).

lust. A strong desire, usually fleshly (good—Luke 22:15; Phil. 1:23; bad—Rom. 6:12; 13:14; Eph. 2:3; 2 Peter 2:18).

M

malefactor. One who practices evil (Luke 23:32-33).

malice. A trait of moral deficiency which results in wickedness and ill will. See 1 Cor. 5:8; 14:20; Eph. 4:31.

malignity. An evil disposition or corrupt character (Rom. 1:29).

mammon. An Aramaic word for riches (Matt. 6:24).

manna. The food with which God fed Israel in their wilderness wanderings (Ex. 16:15). It is called the corn of heaven or angels' food (Ps. 78:24-25).

mansions. Literally, dwelling places (John 14:2).
Maranatha. Only used once in the Bible (1 Cor. 16:22); it is a petition meaning, "Our Lord, come!"
meek. A humility describing one's contrition of spirit before God and man (Ps. 147:6; Isa. 61:1; 1 Cor. 4:21).
memorial. That which keeps alive the memory of someone or something is a memorial (Matt. 26:13).
mercy. The outward display of pity (Matt. 18:23-35; Eph. 2:4).
Messiah. Although rare in its appearance in Scripture (Dan. 9:25; John 1:41; 4:25), its equivalent translations are "Anointed One" or "Christ."
minister. One who serves (Mark 10:43; Rom. 13:4; 15:8; see deacon). In the New Testament the work of the ministry is the responsibility of each believer (Eph. 4:11-16).
mite. A small copper coin of minimal value (Mark 12:42).
mock. To ridicule or insult (Luke 22:63).
moderation. Gentleness or considerateness (Phil. 4:5).
mortal. That which is subject to death (Rom. 6:12).
mortify. To put to death (Rom. 8:13; Col. 3:5).
mote. A small piece of wood or straw used by birds to build their nests. A speck, usually of dust. It is contrasted with a beam, which was used in supporting the roof of a building (Matt. 7:3-5).
murmur. To grumble or complain (Luke 5:30; 1 Cor. 10:10).
mystery. Something secret or hidden, requiring divine revelation to unlock its appearance. In the New Testament it occurs twenty-seven times, and it usually pertains to God's plan of salvation (Matt. 13:11; Rom. 11:25; Eph. 3:3-4).

N

novice. Literally means, newly planted. It depicts a new convert (1 Tim. 3:6).

O

offense. A snare or stumblingblock set in path of another (Matt. 11:6; Rom. 16:17; Gal. 5:11).

offscouring. That which is wiped or washed off. It denotes rubbish and refuse (1 Cor. 4:13).
oracle. A word or divine utterance (Acts 7:38; Heb. 5:12).
ordain. To appoint (Acts 10:42; 16:4; 1 Cor. 7:17; Titus 1:5; Heb. 5:1; 8:3).
ordinance. An action prescribed by God for our obedience (Rom. 13:2; Eph. 2:15).

P

paradise. Heaven, on one occasion called Abraham's bosom (Luke 23:43; 2 Cor. 12:4).
Passover. A feast celebrated by the Jews commemorating their deliverance from Egypt (Ex. 23:14-17; Deut. 16:1).
pastor. Pastor and shepherd are from the same Greek word. Therefore, a pastor is one who tends, cares for, protects and feeds his flock (Eph. 4:11).
patriarch. From the word for father, this term designates the family heads of the Jewish race before Moses (Gen. 12—50; 7:8-9; Heb. 7:4).
penny. A Roman coin, *denarius*, of small value (Matt. 20:2).
peradventure. Lest or perhaps (Gen. 18:32; Rom. 5:7).
perdition. Destruction (Phil. 1:28).
perfection. Ethical and spiritual maturity or wholeness (Deut. 25:15; 27·6; 2 Cor. 13:9; Eph. 4:12; Phil. 3:15).
pervert. To distort or twist (Acts 13:10; Phil. 2:15).
pestilence. Any deadly, infectious disease (Lev. 26:25; Acts 24:5).
Pharisees. An Aramaic word meaning separated ones, set apart from the general public. It came to designate a religious body in Israel which was more conservative than the Sadducees, accepting the doctrine of the resurrection from the dead, belief in angels, and in future rewards and punishments (Acts 23:8). The Pharisees ran the synagogues and taught school.
phylactery. Also called a "frontlet." A small piece of parchment with portions of the Law written on it. It was fastened by a leather strap to either the left arm, next to the heart, or around the forehead (Ex. 13:16; Deut. 6:18; Matt. 23:5).

piety. Reverence or godly actions (Acts 17:23; 1 Tim. 5:4).

pinnacle. The highest ledge of a building as in the temple structure (Matt. 4:5).

pit. See **abyss.**

pity. Compassion or tenderheartedness (1 Peter 3:8).

pomp. A show of bragging display (Acts 25:23).

praise. The act of ascribing to God His unspeakable worth in some medium of worship. It is the action of glorifying God (Ps. 50:23).

prate. To raise false accusations or to talk nonsense (3 John 10).

prayer. The act of calling on God is prayer. It encompasses petition, adoration, thanksgiving, and intercession (Matt. 21:22; Acts 6:4; Phil. 4:6).

preach. To preach is to declare God's good news (Isaiah 61:1; Mark 1:15; Luke 1:19; 2 Tim. 4:2). It should not be sharply distinguished from teaching, since the two are inseparably mixed together (preaching, appealing to the will; and teaching, appealing to the mind).

predestinate. To set a definite boundary beforehand (Acts 2:23; 4:27-28; Rom. 8:29-30; 9:11-12, 23; Eph. 1:5, 11).

preeminence. To have first place (Col. 1:18).

presbytery. See **elder.**

priest. One who is in charge of spiritual things and offers up sacrifices is a priest. In Old Testament times the priests were only of the lineage of Aaron. In the New Testament period all believers are priests (1 Peter 2:5, 9; Rev. 1:6; 5:10; 20:6).

principality. Government or rule (Eph. 3:10).

privily. Secretly (Matt. 1:19; 2:7).

profane/profanity. The opposite of holiness. It means to take something out of the sacred realm and use it in everyday life. Profanity, therefore, is the nonspiritual use of God's name (Lev. 18:21; 20:3).

prophecy/prophesy. Literally, "speaking forth," the divine will as He gives the utterance (Jer. 1:9). This is to be distinguished from preaching, which anticipates preparation (see 1 Cor. 12:28; Eph. 2:20; 4:11).

propitiation. The turning away of God's wrath by the offering of a sacrifice (Luke 18:13; Heb. 2:17).

proselyte. A Gentile convert to Judaism (Matt. 23:15; Acts 2:10). It may also speak of an alien living within the borders of Israel (Ex. 12:49; Deut. 5:14).

providence. Although this exact word does not appear in the Scriptures except in its cognates—provide and provision. The term describes God's foresight of man's needs and His willful supply of those lacks (Ps. 136:25; Matt. 6:25-34).

province. An administrative division of the Roman Empire over which a magistrate exercised authority (Acts 23:34; 25:1).

provocation. An act which provokes or arouses anger (Acts 17:16; 1 Cor. 13:5).

prudence. Intelligence or practical wisdom (Prov. 8:12; 19:25; 1 Cor. 1:19).

purge. To cleanse (John 15:2; 1 Cor. 5:7).

purification. The act of making something clean or pure; that is, to make it free from sin (Lev. 15:12; Heb. 9:13-23).

Q

quaternion. This is a group of four men posted as a guard, two being chained to the prisoner and two keeping watch (Acts 12:4).

quench. To quench something is to put it out, as placing water on a flame (Eph. 6:16; 1 Thes. 5:19).

quicken. To make alive or to give life (Eph. 2:5).

R

rabbi. A title of respect that was used to address teachers (Matt. 26:25, 49; Mark 9:5; John 1:38).

rabboni. An intensification of the address of Rabbi. It means, "My great Master/Teacher," and was applied only to the president of the Sanhedrin (John 20:16).

raca. Empty-headed or intellectually void (Matt. 5:22)

rail. To speak in an evil manner (1 Cor. 5:11; Eph. 4:31; Col. 3:8; 1 Tim. 6:4; 2 Peter 2:10).

Rapture. See concordance section of this book along with the doctrinal section, under Prophecy.

ransom. To loose a life from slavery with a price is to ransom someone (or to redeem someone—Ex. 21:30; Jer. 31:11; Matt. 20:28; Mark 10:45).

ravening. Devouring (Matt. 7:15).

rebuke. The act of reprimanding someone for their improper attitudes, speech or actions (Lev. 19:17; Luke 17:3; 1 Tim. 5:20). Failure to reprove a sinning brother or sister is equivalent to partaking of the sin itself.

reckon. To calculate or count or consider (Luke 22:37; Rom. 2:26; 4:3-24).

recompense. A giving back in return; this term designates a payment—either in a good sense, as in a reward (Luke 14:12; Heb. 11:26), or in a bad sense, as in punishment (Rom. 11:9; Heb. 2:2).

reconciliation. The changing of a relationship from a state of enmity to a state of harmony and friendship. It may occur between men (1 Sam. 29:4; Matt. 5:24; 1 Cor. 7:11) or between God and men (Rom. 5:1-11; 2 Cor. 5:18-21; Eph. 2:16).

redeem. See **ransom.**

regeneration. The new birth of man which restores his relationship with God through Jesus Christ (John 3:3-5; Titus 3:5). While the stress is upon the inception of a new life, the transformation of the whole life in godliness is strongly present (Rom. 12:1-2; Eph. 4:17-24).

reins. Literally, the kidneys, denoting the will and affections (Ps. 7:9; Jer. 11:20; Rev. 2:23).

remission. To remit a sin or a debt is to forgive it or to pass over it (Matt. 26:28; Acts 2:38; 5:31; Rom. 3:25).

remnant. Literally means, that which is left, or the rest. It is used in the Scriptures to designate those who were left after a famine or a conquest. It is also used to contrast the vast numbers of people in Israel, out of which only a small number, a remnant, was actually accepted by God (Rom. 9:27; 11:5).

rend. To tear (Matt. 26:65).

repent. To repent means to change one's mind about something or someone. It is a sober afterthought which culminates in a decisive change of opinion and action (Matt. 3:8; Acts 20:21; Rom. 2:4; 2 Tim. 2:25).

reproach. The act of bringing reproach upon someone; to bring shame and disgrace upon them (Matt. 11:20; Heb. 11:26).

reprobate. When someone does not stand the test and is rejected, he is said to be reprobate (Rom. 1:28; 2 Cor. 13:5-7).

reproof. See **rebuke.**

restitution. Restoration or giving back to someone what was taken from them, and usually with high interest (Ex. 22:4, 7; 2 Sam. 12:6; Prov. 6:31; Luke 19:8).

revelation. The act of uncovering or revealing (1 Cor. 1:7; Eph. 1:17; 1 Peter 1:7; Rev. 1:1).

revel. To riot or carouse (Rom. 13:13).

reverence. Worshipful fear or awe (Mark 12:6).

revile. To use abusive speech (John 9:28; Acts 23:4; 1 Cor. 4:12).

righteousness. To act righteously is to act rightly. It is that quality of character that corresponds to God's likeness (Matt. 6:33). See **just.**

S

sabaoth. Host or armies (Rom. 9:29; James 5:4).

Sabbath. This term means to cease from labor, referring to the Jewish day of rest and worship. It began at sunset Friday night and ran for twenty-four hours (Gen. 2:2-3; Ex. 16:23-30; 20:8-11).

sackcloth. A material made from either goat's or camel's hair (Matt. 11:21; Rev. 6:12).

sacred. Devoted solely to God (2 Tim. 2:21).

Sadducees. A small religious group of wealthy, aristocratic families who controlled the temple (Acts 4:1-2). They only accepted Moses' writings as authoritative; disclaiming the doctrines of angels, the resurrection, rewards, and punishments. See **Pharisee.**

salvation. Deliverance, liberation, victory, wholeness, and preservation. See the Doctrinal section for a complete discussion.

sanctify. To sanctify something or someone is to set it or them apart for God's use (1 Cor. 1:30; 2 Thes. 2:13; 1 Peter 1:2). See **holy.**

sanctuary. A dwelling place. When God indwelt the holy of holies in the Old Testament tabernacle and temple, that structure was said to be holy or a sanctuary, because of His presence (Ex. 25:8). Obviously, no man-made structure today can qualify to be called a sanctuary since God no longer indwells buildings, but instead inhabits people (1 Cor. 6:19-20).
Sanhedrin. The ruling body of religious affairs in Israel (Matt. 26:59; Acts 4:15).
Satan. See "Angels" in the Doctrinal section of this volume.
Saviour. Deliverer and Preserver—see "Salvation" in the Doctrinal unit of this book.
savor. Fragrance or taste (2 Cor. 2:14; Eph. 5:2).
schism. Division (1 Cor. 12:24-25).
scourge. A whip made of leather thongs and imbedded with sharp pieces of either bone or lead. When someone was scourged, he would be stripped of his clothing and tied to a pillar in a bending position or stretched on a frame. The lashing would naturally tear the flesh from the back. It was so severe that the victim might readily die from its cruel pain (John 19:1; Acts 22:25).
scribes. The teachers of the Law in the synagogues (Mark 1:22).
sedition. A dissension or insurrection (Acts 24:5; Gal. 5:20).
seduce. To cause to wander astray (1 John 2:26).
sepulchre. A burial place or tomb (Matt. 27:61).
sergeant. An officer who both accompanied and executed the magistrate's orders. They would carry a bundle of rods, in which rested an axe for beheading offenders (Acts 16:35, 38).
similitude. Likeness (Rom. 5:14; James 3:9).
sin. Many different words in the Hebrew and Greek languages describe sin. Essentially, however, they convey a missing of the mark or a falling short of God's moral requirements. See "Sin" in the Doctrinal section of this book.
sincere. Pure or genuine (2 Cor. 8:8; Phil. 1:16).
slanderer. One who accuses falsely (1 Tim. 3:11; 2 Tim. 3:3).
slothful. Sluggish, dull and lazy (Heb. 6:12).
sober. Self-controlled and mentally alert (1 Peter 1:13; 5:8).
sobriety. Mental alertness (1 Tim. 2:9, 15).
sojourn. To dwell in a place as a stranger (Luke 24:18; Heb. 11:9).

soothsaying. To practice divination or to call upon evil spirits (Acts 16:16).
sop. A piece of food dipped in a liquid (John 13:26).
sorcerer. A magician or wizard who practices special powers through the arts of witchcraft (Acts 13:6, 8), especially through the use of drugs, potions, and spells. It is from this word that we derive our English term, pharmacy (Gal. 5:20; Rev. 9:21; 18:23).
soul. A designation of either the total essence of man (Ex. 1:5) or his intellectual, volitional, and emotional personality (Matt. 11:29; Heb. 6:19). See "Man" in the Doctrinal unit of this book.
spirit. Used in both Hebrew and Greek for wind, breath, and that part of man which gives him God-awareness (John 3:8; 2 Thes. 2:8; James 2:26). See "Man" in the Doctrinal unit of this book.
spiritual. In harmony (intellectually, volitionally, and emotionally) with the will and character of God. It is the natural state of all genuine believers (1 Cor. 3:1-3; Gal. 6:1).
stanch. To cause to stand (Luke 8:44).
steward. One who manages or administers (Luke 12:42; 1 Cor. 4:2).
stubble. A corn stalk (1 Cor. 3:12).
suborn. To procure (Acts 6:11).
subvert. To plunder or overthrow (Acts 15:24).
sumptuously. Lavishly or with great expense (Luke 16:19).
sup. When used literally, this refers to the primary meal of the day (Luke 17:8). When used figuratively, it designates intimate spiritual communion between Christ and the obedient believer (Rev. 3:20).
superfluous. Abundant or more than sufficient (2 Cor. 9:1).
supplication. To petition or to ask (1 Tim. 2:1).
surety. A person who takes the responsibility for a debt or the engagement of another party. It also signifies the bail that is paid as a security against any loss or damage (Acts 12:11; Heb. 7:22).
surfeiting. Overindulgence in food or wine (Luke 21:34).
synagogue. The assembly or meeting place for Jewish religious services was the synagogue (Matt. 6:2; James 2:2; Rev. 2:9).

T

tabernacle. The religious structure God commanded to be built during Israel's period in the wilderness (Ex. 25—27; 30—31; 35—40). It served to demonstrate God's presence in the midst of Israel, and to provide a means whereby sinful men could approach the thrice-holy God (Heb. 9). Later, this tent structure was superceded with the temple, during the reign of Solomon (1 Kings 8).

tares. A plant greatly resembling the wheat stalk, but produces instead only a seed that is poisonous to man. See Matt. 13:25-30.

temperance. Self-control (Gal. 5:23; 2 Peter 1:6).

tempest. Storm or whirlwind (Acts 27:20).

temple. See **tabernacle.**

temptation. A divinely permitted or sent trial with the ultimate intent of improving the character of the one tested (Luke 22:28; James 1:2, 1 Peter 1:6). Occasionally, however, temptations (from Satan) are solely designed to lead one into sin (Luke 4:13; 8:13; 1 Tim. 6:9).

tetrarch. A governor of a fourth part of a region (Matt. 14:1).

thorn in the flesh. Possibly a figure of speech describing antagonistic people or a physical ailment of the body (Num. 33:55; Ezek. 28:24; Hosea 2:6; 2 Cor. 12:7).

tidings. A message (Luke 1:19; 2:10; 3:18).

tithe. From a word meaning tenth, it designates an offering God required of the Jews. There were, in all, three tithes—two were annual (Num. 18:21-24; Deut. 14:22-26) and one came every three years (Deut. 14:28-29). Therefore, each year the Jews were expected to give 23 1/3% of their goods to God as a minimal requirement. This amount, however, is not to be compared with the requirement of the New Testament, which comes to 100% (Luke 14:33).

tittle. The small strokes that were made on Hebrew consonants so as to distinguish certain letters (Matt. 5:18).

transgression. To go beyond the allotted boundary. (See "Sin" in the Doctrinal unit.)

travail. Labor (such as childbirth) involving painful effort (Isa. 53:11; 2 Cor. 11:27).

tribulation. Pressure generated by antagonistic people and/or besetting circumstances (Acts 14:22; Rom. 8:35; 12:12).

tumult. A noise or uproar (Matt. 27:24).

CONCISE BIBLE DICTIONARY / 223

U

uncomely. Shapeless (1 Cor. 12:23). See **comely.**
unction. See **anoint.**
unfeigned. See **dissimulation.**

V

vanity. Empty results (Eph. 4:17; 2 Peter 2:18).
vaunt. To boast (1 Cor. 13:4).
verily. Truly or indeed (1 John 2:5).
vesture. An outer garment (Matt. 27:35).
vexed. To be tormented or troubled, especially by evil spirits (Matt. 17:15; Acts 5:16).
vile. Filthy or dirty (James 2:2; Rev. 22:11).
virgin. A person who has not engaged in any sexual activity (Matt. 1:23; see Acts 21:9; 1 Cor. 7:25, 28, 34; 2 Cor. 11:2; Rev. 14:4).

W

wantonness. Unruly or rude (2 Peter 2:18; see **laciviousness**).
wiles. Craft and deceit (Eph. 6:11).
worship. While this word, in both testaments, means to manifest reverential fear and adoring awe, it more essentially means to render service (Acts 7:42; 24:14; Phil. 3:3).
wranglings. Disrupting or irritations (1 Tim. 6:5).
wroth. Very angry (Matt. 2:16).

Y

yokefellow. Fellow laborer (Phil. 4:3).

Z

zealous. To be full of uncompromising fervency (Acts 21:20; 22:3; 1 Cor. 14:12; Gal. 1:14; Titus 2:14).

21 | An Abbreviated Topical Concordance

A

abomination of desolation. Dan. 9:27; 11:31; 12:11; Matt. 24:15
Abraham's bosom. Luke 16:22-23
acceptance with God. Acts 10:35; 2 Cor. 5:9; Eph. 1:6
access to God. Rom. 5:2; Eph. 2:13; 3:12; Heb. 7:19, 25; 10:19
adoption by God. Deut. 14:1; Rom. 9:4, 8, 26
adultery. Ex. 20:14; Acts 15:20, 29; 1 Cor. 5:9-11; 6:13-18
advocate. John 14:16, 26; 15:26; 1 John 2:1
alms. Matt. 5:42; 19:21; 1 Tim. 6:18
ambassadors. 2 Cor. 5:20; Eph. 6:20
anointing for healing. Mark 6:13; James 5:14; Rev. 3:18
anointing for learning. 1 John 2:20, 27
Antichrist. 1 John 2:18, 22; 4:3; 2 John 7
anxiety. Matt. 6:25-34; 1 Cor. 7:32; Phil. 4:6; 1 Peter 5:7
apostasy of last days. Matt. 24:12; 2 Thes. 2:3; 1 Tim. 4:1-3; 2 Tim. 3:1-9; 4:3-4
apostles (other than twelve). Acts 14:4, 14; Rom. 16:7; 1 Cor. 4:6-9; Gal. 1:19
Armageddon. Rev. 16:16; see Jud. 5:19-20; 2 Kings 23:29-30; Zech. 12:11

armor of God. Rom. 13:12; 2 Cor. 6:7; Eph. 6:12-17
assurance of salvation. 2 Tim. 1:12; Heb. 10:22; 1 John 5:13
astrology. Isa. 47:13-14; Jer. 10:1-2; Dan. 1:20; 2:27
atonement. Ex. 30:10; Romans 3:24; Eph. 2:13-15, Heb. 9:12-15, 25-26

B

Babel. Gen. 11:1-9
Babylon. Gen. 10:8, 10; Dan. 1:1; Zech. 5:11; 1 Peter 5:13; Rev. 17—18
backsliding. 1 Sam. 15:11; Kings 11:9; Jer. 8:5; Gal. 3:1-3
Balaam. Num. 24:1-25; 2 Peter 2:15-16; Jude 11; Rev. 2:14-15
baptism in Spirit. Matt. 3:11; Luke 3:16; John 1:33; Acts 1:5; 11:16
baptism in water. Matt. 28:19; Mark 16:15-16; Acts 2:38; 8:37-38; 16:15
binding and loosing. Matt. 16:19; 18:18
bishop. Phil 1:1; 1 Tim. 3:1-7; Titus 1:5, 7; 1 Peter 2:25
blasphemy. Lev. 24:16; Matt. 12:31; 1 Tim. 1:13, 20; Heb. 10:29; Rev. 2:9
blood of Christ. Matt. 26:28; Rom. 3:24-25; 5:9; Eph. 2:13, 16; Heb. 10:19
boldness. Prov. 28:1; Acts 4:31; 18:26; 19:8; Eph. 6:20 Heb. 13:6

C

carnality. Rom. 8:6-8, 13; 1 Cor. 3:1-3
character of saints. Gal. 5:22-23; Col. 3:1-17; 2 Peter 1:3-9
chastisement. Heb. 12:5-10; Rev. 3:19
citizens of heaven. Phil. 3:20; Col. 1:13
Commandments (the Ten). Ex. 20:3-17; Deut. 5:6-21

communion. 1 Cor. 10:16; Matt. 26:26-28; 2 Cor. 6:14; 13:14
communion of the saints. Acts 2:42; 2 Cor. 8:4; Phil. 1:5; 1 John 1:3
confession of Christ. Matt. 10:32; Rom. 10:9-11; 1 Cor. 12:1-3
confession of sin. Numbers 21:7; James 5:16; 1 John 1:8-10
conscience. Acts 24:16; Rom. 2:14-15; 9:1; 1 Tim. 1:5, 19; Heb. 10:22
consecration. Rom. 6:11-19; 12:1-2; 1 Cor. 10:31
conversion. Acts 3:19, 26; 11:21; 2 Cor. 5:17; 1 Thes. 1:9
conviction. John 8:9; 16:6-11; Acts 2:37
courage. Deut. 31:6; Joshua 1:6-7; Ps. 27:14; 1 Cor. 16:13; Eph. 6:10; 2 Tim. 1:7
covetousness. Ex. 20:17; Ps. 10:3; Matt. 6:19-21; Col. 3:5; 1 Tim. 6:9-11; Titus 1:7
crowns of reward. 1 Cor. 9:25; 2 Tim. 4:8; James 1:12; 1 Peter 5:4; Rev. 2:10; 3:11
curse. Gen. 8:21; Ex. 22:28; Num. 22:12; Matt. 5:44; Rom. 12:14

D

damnation. Matt. 5:29; 10:28; 23:14, 33; 2 Thes. 1:9; Jude 6-7
deacon. 1 Tim. 3:8-13; see Acts 6:1-6
deaconess. Rom.16:1
diligence. Rom. 12:10-12; 2 Cor. 8:7; Heb. 6:11; 11:6
discipleship. Matt. 10:32-39; Luke 9:23-26, 57-62; 14:25-35
discipline of self. 1 Cor. 9:24-27; 1 Tim. 4:7 (NASB)
divorce. Ex. 21:7-11; Deut. 21:10-14; 24:1-4; Matt. 5:31-32; 19:3-11; 1 Cor. 7:10-16
doubt. Matt. 14:31; 21:21; Luke 12:29
drunkard. Deut. 21:20-21; 1 Cor. 5:11; 6:9-10; Gal. 5:19-21

E

elders. Acts 14:23; 1 Tim. 3:1-7; Titus 1:5-9
election. John 15:16; 17:6; Rom. 9:11; Eph. 1:4; 1 Thes. 1:4; 1 Peter 2:9
envy. Rom. 13:13; 1 Cor. 3:3; 13:4; Gal. 5:19-21
Eucharist. Matt. 26:17-29; Acts 2:42; 20:7; 1 Cor. 11:23-34
evangelist. Acts 21:8; Eph. 4:11-12; 2 Tim. 4:5
excommunication. Matt. 18:15-17; 1 Cor. 5:1-13; 1 Tim. 1:20

F

faith. Mark 11:22-24; Rom. 12:3; 14:22-23; Heb. 11; James 1:4-8
falsehood. Ex. 20:16; Eph. 4:25, 29; Col. 3:9; 1 Tim. 1:9-10
family unity. Eph. 5:22—6:9
fasting. Isa. 58; Matt. 6:16-18; 17:21; Acts 13:3; 14:23; 27:9, 33-34
fear of God. Job 28:28; Ps. 19:9; Prov. 1:7; 8:13; 9:10; 14:27; Acts 10:34-35
fellowship with God. Ex. 33:11-17; John 17:20-23; 2 Cor. 13:11; 1 John 1:3-7
fellowship with Christ. 1 Cor. 1:9; 10:16; 1 John 1:3-7; Rev. 3:20
fellowship with Spirit. John 14:16-17; Rom. 8:9; 1 Cor. 3:16; 2 Cor. 13:14
fellowship with believers. Acts 2:42-47; Rom. 15:6-7; Col. 2:2; 1 Peter 3:8-9
fellowship with wicked. Ex. 34:12-16; Rom. 16:17; 1 Cor. 5:1-11; 1 Tim. 6:3-5
firstborn. Ex. 4:22; Deut. 21:15-17; Col. 1:15; Heb. 1:6
fool. Prov. 1:17; 10:8, 10; 18:6-7; 20:3; 29:9, 11; Matt. 25:1-13; Titus 3:3
forgiveness by believers. Matt. 6:12-15; 18:21-35; Mark 11:25

forgiveness by God. 1 John 1:7, 9

G

gifts of Spirit. Rom. 12:3-8; 1 Cor. 12—14; Eph. 4:11; 1 Peter 4:10
giving. Matt. 6:1-4; 1 Cor. 16:2; 2 Cor. 8:7-15; 9:6-15
glorification. Rom. 8:18-25; 1 Cor. 15:35-57; 1 John 3:2
gluttony. Deut. 21:20-21; 1 Cor. 9:25-27; 10:31; Phil. 3:17-19
gnashing of teeth. Matt. 8:12; 13:42; 22:13; 24:51; 25:30
gossip. Ps. 50:20; Prov. 10:18; 20:19; Eph. 4:31
grace of God. Eph. 1:6; 2:8-9; Titus 2:11; Heb. 4:16; 1 Peter 1:10

H

healing promised. Ex. 15:26; Ps. 103:3; Prov. 3:7-8; James 5:14-16
heart for God. Deut. 6:5-6; Ps. 101:2; Matt. 22:37; Col. 3:22; James 4:8
heaven. Matt. 5:12; Phil. 3:20; 1 Thes. 4:13-18; Rev. 2:7; 3:21; 4—5; 21—22
hell. Matt. 5:22, 29-30; 10:28; 18:9; 23:15, 33; Rev. 20:11-15
heresy. 2 Cor. 11:4; Gal. 1:7; 2:4; 2 Peter 2; Jude 3-16; Rev. 2:2
holiness of saints. 2 Cor. 6:17—7:1; Col. 3:5-14; 1 Thes. 3:13; Heb. 12:14
honesty. Rom. 12:17; 13:13; Phil. 4:8; 1 Thes. 4:11-12; 1 Peter 2:11-12
hope in God. Ps. 31:24; Rom. 15:13; Heb. 6:18-19; 1 Peter 1:21
hospitality. Rom. 12:13; 1 Tim. 3:2; 5:9-10; Heb. 13:2; 1 Peter 4:9-10
humility. Prov. 15:33; Luke 14:11; Eph. 4:2; Phil. 2:3; James 4:6
hypocrisy. Is. 32:6; 21:27; Mal. 1:6-14; Matt. 6:2; 23:28; James 3:17

I

idleness. Prov. 6:6-11; 21:25-26; Luke 19:20-24; 2 Thes. 3:10-11; 1 Tim. 5:13
idolatry. 1 Cor. 6:9-10; 10:14, 20-22; 1 John 5:21; Rev. 21:8
immortality. Matt. 25:46; Luke 10:25-28; 1 Cor. 15:12-54; 2 Cor. 5:1
inheritance of saints. Matt. 25:34; Acts 20:32; Rom. 8:16-17; Eph. 1:14
inspiration of Scripture. 2 Tim. 3:16; 2 Peter 1:21; Rev. 22: 6-7
intercession. Jer. 27:18; Rom. 8:34; Eph. 6:18; 1 Thes. 5:25; 1 Tim. 2:1-4; James 5:16

J

jealousy of man. Gen. 4:5-6; Luke 15:25-32; Rom. 13:13
judgment. Ecc. 12:14; Matt. 25; Heb. 6:2; 2 Peter 2:4; Rev. 20:11-15
justification. Rom. 1:16-17; 3:20-25; 4:6; 5:1; 8:30; Gal. 2:14-21

K

kindness. 1 Cor. 13:4-7; Col. 3:12; 1 Peter 3:8-9; 1 John 3:17-18
kiss, holy. Rom. 16:16; 2 Cor. 13:12; 1 Thes. 5:26; 1 Peter 5:14

L

Lamb of God. John 1:29, 36; Rev. 5:6, 8, 12-13; 6:1, 16; 7:9-10, 14; 22:1, 3
lasciviousness. Mark 7:21; 1 Cor. 6:13-18; Gal. 5:19-21; Col. 3:5; 1 Thes. 4:3-6; Jude 4, 7
Law (Ten Commandments). Ex. 20:3-17; Deut. 5:6-21; Matt. 5:17-48

laying on of hands. Matt. 19:13-15; Mark 16:18; Acts 6:1-6; 8:14-20; 9:17; 13:1-4

laziness. Prov. 12:27; 18:9; 19:24; 21:25; Rom. 12:11; Heb. 6:12

leaven (type of sin). Matt. 16:6-12; 1 Cor. 5:6-8; Gal. 5:9

life from God. Gen. 2:7; Deut. 8:3; 30:20; Acts 17:25, 28; Rom. 4:17; James 4:15

Life, Book of. Ex. 32:32; Dan. 12:1; Luke 10:20; Phil. 4:3; Rev. 3:5; 13:8; 20:11-15

Light of Righteousness. Matt. 5:16; Acts 26:18; 1 Peter 2:9; 1 John 1:7

longevity. Ex. 20:12; Deut. 4:40; 22:7; Prov. 3:2, 16; 1 Peter 3:10-11

Lord's Day. Rev. 1:10; see John 20:1-25; Acts 20:7

Lord's Prayer for disciples. Matt. 6:9-13; Luke 11:2-4

Lord's Supper. 1 Cor. 10:16; 11:20, 27-32; See Acts 2:42; 20:7

love. 1 Cor. 13; Col. 1:8; 2:2; 1 Thes. 5:8; 1 Tim. 6:11; 1 John 4:7, 16-18

lukewarm. Rev. 3:2, 16; see Neh. 3:5; 13:11; Hag. 1:2-11

lust. Matt. 5:28; Mark 4:19; James 1:14-15; 2 Peter 2:18; 1 John 2:16-17

lying. Gen. 3:4; John 8:44; Acts 5:4; Titus 1:12; Rev. 21:8, 27

M

magi. Matt. 2:1-12

Magog. Gen. 10:2; 1 Chron. 1:5; Rev. 20:7-9

malice. Prov. 20:22; 24:17-18; Matt. 5:38-41; Rom. 12:19; 1 Cor. 14:20; Eph. 4:31; Col. 3:8

manna. Ex. 16:4, 15; Neh. 9:15; Ps. 78:25; 1 Cor. 10:3

marriage. Gen. 2:18, 20-24; Matt. 19:4-6; 1 Cor. 6:16; Eph. 5:31

martyrdom. Matt. 10:21-22, 39; 24:9; Luke 11:50; Rev. 6:9-11; 16:6

meditation. Josh. 1:8; Pss. 1:1-3; 63:5-6; 104:34; 119:11, 15-16; 143:5

meekness. Matt. 5:5; 11:29; Gal. 5:22-23; 6:1; Eph. 4:1-2; Phil. 2:3

Megiddo. Josh. 12:21; 17:11; Jud. 1:27; 5:19; Rev. 16:16

Melchizedek. Gen. 14:18-20; Ps. 110:4; Heb. 5:6-10; 6:20; 7:1-22

mercy seat. Ex. 25:17-22; Lev. 16:14-15; Isa. 37:16; Heb. 4:16

Messiah. Dan. 9:24-27; Luke 4:18-19; Acts 4:26-28; 10:38

Millennium. Rev. 20:1-15; see Matt. 25:34; Luke 12:32; Zech. 14:16-21

minister's duties. Acts 6:1-6; 20:28; Eph. 4:11-12; 2 Tim. 2:2; 4:5; Heb. 13:17

missions. Ps. 96:3, 10; Matt. 28:19-20; Mark 16:15; Luke 24:47-48; John 20:21

money. Matt. 6:19-33; Luke 16:1-13; James 1:9-11; 4:1-4; 5:1-6

mourning. 2 Sam. 18:33; Ecc. 7:2; Matt. 5:4; Luke 6:21

murder. Gen. 9:4-6; Ex. 21:14; Lev. 24:17; Deut. 19:11-13

murmuring. 1 Cor. 10:10; Phil. 2:14; James 5:9

mustard seed. Matt. 13:31-32; 17:20; Mark 4:31

mysteries. Deut. 29:29; Matt. 11:25; 13:11; John 3:5-12; 2 Thes. 2:7

N

new birth. John 1:12-13; 3:3, 5; 1 Cor. 4:15; Titus 3:5; 1 Peter 1:23; 2:2

O

obedience. 1 Sam. 15:22; Ps. 40:6-9; 2 Cor. 10:5; Col. 3:20; Heb. 10:8-9; 1 Peter 1:2

oil, sacred. Ex. 30:23-33; 31:11; 35:8, 15, 28; 1 Sam. 10:1

Olive tree (symbol). Zech. 4:2-14; Rom. 11:17-24; Rev. 11:4
only begotten. John 1:14, 18; 3:16, 18; Heb. 11:17; 1 John 4:9
ordain. Acts 6:5-6; 13:2-3; 14:23; 1 Tim. 4:14
overcome. Rom. 12:21; Rev. 2:7, 11, 17, 26; 3:5, 12, 21; 21:7

P

parents, duties of. Deut. 4:9-10; 6:7, 20-25; Eph. 6:4
parents, duties to. Ex. 20:12; Prov. 1:8; Eph. 6:1-3
Passover. Ex. 12:3-49; 23:15-18; Matt. 26:17-19; 1 Cor. 5:7
patience. Ps. 37:7-9; Rom. 5:3-5; Col. 3:12-13; 1 Thes. 5:14; James 5:7-8
peace from God. Isa. 45:7; 1 Cor. 14:33; Phil. 4:7-9
peace from Jesus. Matt. 11:29; John 14:27; 16:33; Col. 3:15
peace from Spirit. Rom. 14:17; Gal. 5:22
Pentecost. Lev. 23:15-21; Acts 2:1; 20:16; 1 Cor. 16:8
perdition. John 17:12; Phil. 1:28; 2 Thes. 2:3; 1 Tim. 6:9
perfection. Matt. 5:48; Phil. 3:15; Col. 1:21-22, 28; Heb. 10:14; 1 Peter 5:10
persecution. Matt. 20:22; 23:34-35; John 15:18-21; 2 Tim. 3:1-3, 12-13; 1 John 3:1
perseverance. 1 Thes. 5:21; 2 Thes. 2:15-17; 2 Tim. 2:1, 3; James 1:4; Titus 1:9
philosophy. 1 Cor. 1:17-22; 2:1-5, 14; Col. 2:8, 16-19; 1 Tim. 6:20
pit, the. Ps. 28:1; Rev. 9:1; 11:7; 17:8; 20:1-3
pleasure, worldly. Ecc. 2:1-13; 1 Tim. 5:6; 2 Tim. 3:4; Titus 3:3; 2 Peter 2:13
polygamy. Lev. 18:18; Deut. 17:17; Matt. 19:4-5; 1 Tim. 3:2, 12; Titus 1:6
power for saints. Acts 1:8; 6:8, 10; Eph. 1:19-20; 1 Thes. 1:5
praise. Eph. 5:19; Heb. 13:15; 1 Peter 2:9; 4:11; 5:11; Rev. 4—5; 19:1-7

prayer. Phil. 4:6; Col. 4:2; 1 Thes. 5:17-18; 1 Tim. 2:1-5; James 5:16-18
prayerlessness. Josh. 9:14; Ps. 53:4; Isa. 43:22
predestination. Acts 17:26; Rom. 8:28-30; 9:10-29; Gal. 1:15; Eph. 1:3-11
pride. Deut. 8:11-14, 17-20; Matt. 23:5-7; Rom. 12:3, 16; Phil. 2:3
procrastination. Matt. 8:21-22; Luke 9:59-61
promises. 1 Cor. 3:21-23; 2 Cor. 1:20; Heb. 6:12; James 2:5; 2 Peter 1:4
prosperity from God. Gen. 33:11; 49:24-26; Pss. 127:1; 128:1-2
providence. Ps. 104; Matt. 6:26-33; Acts 17:25-28
punishment, eternal. Isa. 34:8-10; Dan. 12:2; Matt. 25:41, 46; John 5:29; Rev. 20:11-15
purity. 1 Tim. 3:9; 4:12; 5:22; Titus 1:15; James 4:8

R

Rabbi, Jesus called. Matt. 23:8; John 3:2
railing. 1 Cor. 5:11; 1 Tim. 6:4; 1 Peter 3:9; 2 Peter 2:11; Jude 9
ransom. Isa. 35:10; 51:10; Matt. 20:28; 1 Tim. 2:6
rape. Deut. 22:25-27
Rapture. 1 Cor. 15:50-52; 1 Thes. 4:13-18
reconciliation. Lev. 8:15; Rom. 5:1, 10; 2 Cor. 5:18-21; Eph. 2:15-18
redemption. Rom. 3:24; Gal. 3:13; Eph. 1:7; 1 Peter 1:18-19
refinement of saints. Isa. 48:10; Prov. 17:3; Zech. 13:9; 1 Peter 1:6-7; 4:12-13
regeneration. John 1:12-13; 3:3-8; Titus 3:5; 1 Peter 1:23
remorse. Matt. 26:75; 27:3-5; Acts 9:6
rending of garments. Gen. 37:29, 34; 44:13; 2 Sam. 1:2, 11; 13:19; Acts 14:14

repentance. Mark 1:15; Acts 2:38; 3:19; 17:30; Rom. 2:4; Rev. 2:5, 16; 3:2-3, 19

reprobates. Jer. 6:30; Rom. 1:21-32; 2 Tim. 3:8

reproof. Matt. 18:15-17; Eph. 5:11; 1 Thes. 5:14; 2 Tim. 4:2; Titus 1:13

respect of persons. Prov. 24:23; 28:21; Titus 2:11; James 2:1-9

restitution. Ex. 21:30-36; 22:1-4; Lev. 6:2-5; Luke 19:8

Resurrection. Job 14:14-15; 19:25-27; Dan. 12:2-3; John 5:28-29; 1 Cor. 15; Rev. 20:1-15

revenge. Lev. 19:18; Rom. 12:17, 19; 1 Peter 3:9

reverence for God. Gen. 17:3; Ex. 19:16-24; Isa. 45:9; Heb. 12:28

rewards. Deut. 25:15; Eph. 6:1-3; Heb. 10:34; 2 John 8; Rev. 2:7, 10

riches. Prov. 30:8-9; Ecc. 5:10-12; Ezek. 7:19; 1 Tim. 6:9-11, 17; Rev. 3:17-18

rulers. Dan. 2:21; 4:35; Rom. 13:1-4

S

Sabbath. Gen. 2:2-3; Ex. 16:28-30; Matt. 12:1-13; John 7:21-24; Rom. 14:5-6; Col. 2:16

sabbatical year. Ex. 23:10-11; Lev. 25

sacrilege. Lev. 19:8; 1 Cor. 3:17; Titus 1:10-11

saint. Ps. 16:3; Acts 9:13; Rom. 1:7; 8:27; 1 Cor. 1:2; 2 Cor. 1:1; Eph. 1:18

salt of earth. Matt. 5:13; Mark 9:49-50; Luke 14:34; Col. 4:6

salvation. Acts 4:12; Phil. 2:12; 1 Thes. 5:8-10; Jude 3

sanctification. 1 Cor. 1:30; 6:11; Rom. 15:16; 1 Thes. 5:23; 2 Thes. 2:13; 1 Peter 1:2

Saviour. Luke 2:11; 1 Tim. 1:1; 2:3; 4:10; 2 Tim. 1:10; Titus 1:3-4

scapegoat. Lev. 16:8, 10, 26

AN ABBREVIATED TOPICAL CONCORDANCE / 235

scarlet, sin as. Isa. 1:18
scoffing. Prov. 1:22, 25; 9:12; Heb. 10:29; 2 Peter 3:3
scorners. Ps. 1:1; Prov. 9:12; 13:1; 14:6; 19:29
scourging. Matt. 27:26; Mark 15:15; Acts 16:23; 21:32; 2 Cor. 11:24-25
Second Coming. Matt. 24:36; John 14:3; Acts 3:20; 1 Tim. 6:14; Jude 14
second death. Rev. 20:14; 21:8
secrets, God knows. Deut. 31:21; 1 Sam. 16:7; Ps. 44:21; Heb. 4:12-13
seeking God. Deut. 4:29; Isa. 55:6; Jer. 29:13; Matt. 7:7
self-denial. Prov. 23:2; Matt. 5:29-30; 1 Cor. 9:24-27; Col. 3:5; 1 Peter 2:11-16
self-examination. Ps. 4:4; Hag. 1:7; 1 Cor. 11:28, 31; 2 Cor. 13:5
self-indulgence. Ecc. 2:10; Luke 12:16-20; 16:19
selfishness. Luke 6:32-34; Rom. 14:15; 15:1-3; 1 Cor. 10:24; Phil. 2:4
self-righteousness. Prov. 12:15; Matt. 9:10-13; Rom. 11:19-21; 2 Cor. 1:9; 10:17-18
self-will. Ps. 75:5; Prov. 1:24; Isa. 42:24; Jer. 5:3; 7:28; Acts 7:51; Heb. 3:7-12
seventy weeks (prophecy). Dan. 9:24-27
shadow of death. Job 12:22; 16:16; Pss. 23:4; 44:19; 107:10; Matt. 4:16
shame. Gen. 3:10; Mark 8:38; Luke 9:26; Heb. 12:2
10:1-16
sheep. Isa. 53:6-7; Jer. 13:20; Matt. 9:36; 10:6; 18:11-13; John 10:1-16
Shepherd, the. Ps. 23; Zech. 13:7; Matt. 26:31; John 10:1-16; Heb. 13:20; 1 Peter 2:25
shewbread. Lev. 24:5-9; 1 Sam. 21:6; Matt. 12:3-4; Heb. 9:2
sign. Matt. 12:38; 16:4; 24:30; John 2:11; 3:2; 4:48

sin. Gen. 3:6; Prov. 24:9; Hosea 6:7-8; Rom. 3:21—5:21; 14:23; 1 John 1:9

sincerity. Josh. 24:14; Rom. 12:9; 2 Cor. 8:8, 24; 1 Thes. 2:3-5; 1 Tim. 1:5; 1 Peter 1:22

sinlessness. Acts 24:16; Phil. 1:9-11; 1 Thes. 3:13; 5:23; 1 Peter 4:1-2; 1 John 1:8-10

slothfulness. Prov. 6:6-11; 10:4-5, 26; Rom. 12:11; 2 Thes. 3:10-12; Heb. 6:12

sober-mindedness. Rom. 12:3; 1 Tim. 3:2, 11; Titus 2:4-5; 1 Peter 1:13; 4:7; 5:8; 1 Thes. 5:6-8; Titus 1:8; 2:2, 6, 12

sodomy. Gen. 19:1-12; Deut. 23:17-18

sojourner. Ps. 39:12

sons of God. Acts 17:28; John 1:12; 1 John 3:10

sorcery. Lev. 19:26-28, 31; 20:6; Deut. 18:9-14; Acts 19:19

speaking, power of. Prov. 18:7, 21; 21:23; Matt. 12:36-37; James 1:19-20

spiritual gifts. Rom. 12:3-8; 1 Cor. 12—14; Eph. 4:11; 1 Peter 4:10

spiritual understanding. Matt. 13:23; Luke 10:21-22; John 7:16-17; Eph. 1:17-18

stability. Ps. 108:1; Matt. 24:13; 1 Cor. 7:20; 15:58; 2 Thes. 2:15; Heb. 10:23

steadfastness. Rom. 14:4; 1 Thes. 3:8; Col. 1:23; James 1:23-25; 1 Peter 5:9

strait gate. Matt. 7:13-14; Luke 13:24

strife. Prov. 26:20; Isa. 58:4; Hab. 1:3; Matt. 18:15-17; Phil. 2:3, 14; James 3:14-16

substitution of Christ. Isa. 53:4-6; 1 Cor. 5:7; 2 Cor. 5:21; Gal. 3:13; 1 Peter 2:24

suffering for Christ. Matt. 10:34-36; Rom. 8:17-18; Phil. 3:10

suicide. Matt. 27:1-5; Acts 16:27

sweet savor. Gen. 8:21; Lev. 1:9; 2 Cor. 2:14; Eph. 5:2

T

tabernacle. Ex. 25—38; Ps. 15:1; Heb. 8:2, 5; 9:1-12, 24
tact. Acts 16:2-3; 19:35-41; 1 Cor. 9:19-22; 2 Cor. 8:1-8; 9:1-5
tares. Matt. 13:25-30
tears. Ps. 56:8; Isa. 38:3-5; Rev. 7:17; 21:4
temperance. Rom. 13:14; 1 Cor. 9:24-27; Phil. 4:5; 1 Thes. 5:6-8; 2 Peter 1:5-7
temple of body. 1 Cor. 3:16; 2 Cor. 6:19-20
temple of church. Eph. 2:21
temptation. Matt. 6:13; 1 Cor. 7:5; 10:13; James 1:12; 1 Peter 5:7-9
Ten Commandments. Ex. 20:3-17; Deut. 5:7-21
testimony. Rom. 10:9-10; 2 Thes. 1:10; 2 Tim. 1:8; 1 Peter 3:15-16; 5:12
thankfulness. Deut. 12:17-18; Phil. 4:6; Col. 3:15; 1 Thes. 5:18; Heb. 13:15
theft. Ex. 20:15; Matt. 19:18; Rom. 13:9; Eph. 4:28; Titus 2:10; 1 Peter 4:15
theocracy. Ex. 19:8; 24:3, 7; 1 Sam. 8:7, 19; 12:12
thorn in flesh. 2 Cor. 12:7; see Num. 33:55; Josh. 23:13; Jud. 2:3
thoughts, importance of. Prov. 23:7; Rom. 2:15-16; 2 Cor. 10:3-5; Phil. 4:8
tithe. Gen. 14:20; 28:22; Lev. 27:30-33; Mal. 3:10; Matt. 23:23
tradition. Matt. 12:1-8; 15:3-20; 1 Cor. 11:2; 2 Thes. 2:15; 3:6
trance. Acts 22:17-21
transfiguration. Ex. 34:29-35; Matt. 17:1-9; 2 Peter 1:16-18
transgression. Prov. 17:19; Rom. 4:15
Tree of Life. Gen. 2:9; 3:22, 24; Rev. 22:2
Trinity. Gen. 1:26; Isa. 11:2; 42:1; Matt. 28:19; 2 Cor. 13:14; 1 John 5:6-7

truthfulness. Prov. 12:17, 19; Eph. 4:25; Col. 3:9

U

unbelief. Rom. 14:23; 2 Thes. 2:12; Heb. 11:6; 1 John 5:10
unfaithfulness. Ps. 5:9; Isa. 5:1-7; Hosea 9:1, 10; Mark 12:1-9; Luke 16:10
unfruitfulness. Matt. 7:19; 21:19-20; John 15:1-8
ungodly. Pss. 1:1-6; 73:12; Rom. 5:6; 2 Tim. 2:16; 2 Peter 3:7
unpardonable sin. Matt. 12:31-32; see 1 Sam. 3:14; 1 John 5:16
Urim and Thumim. Ex. 28:30; Lev. 8:8; Num. 27:21
usury. Ex. 22:25; Lev. 25:35-37; Prov. 28:8; Jer. 15:10

V

vagabond. Gen. 4:12, 14; Acts 19:13
vail, or veil. Ex. 34:33; 2 Cor. 3:13-16
vanity. Pss. 39:5, 11; 62:9; 94:11; Ecc. 1:2; 6:12; James 1:26
vengeance. Deut. 32:35; Ps. 94:1; Luke 18:7-8; Rom. 12:19; Rev. 6:10
Virgin Mary. Isa. 7:14; Matt. 1:23; Luke 1:27
voice of God. John 5:37; 12:28-30; Acts 7:31; 9:4, 7; 26:14-15
vows. Lev. 22:18-25; Num. 6:1-21; Ps. 61:5; Prov. 20:25; Acts 23:12-14

W

waiting upon God. Pss. 25:5; 104:27; Isa. 40:31; Jer. 14:22; Luke 24:49

walking with God. Deut. 5:33; Jer. 6:16; Rom. 6:4; Eph. 5:2; 1 John 1:7

washing (type). Ps. 51:7; 1 Cor. 6:11; Eph. 5:26; Titus 3:5

watchfulness. Ps. 39:1; Eph. 5:15; Col. 2:8; 1 Thes. 5:4; 1 Peter 5:8; 1 John 5:18
watchman. Ezek. 3:17; 33:3-6; Acts 20:26
water of bitterness. Num. 5:12-31
wealth. Deut. 8:18; Prov. 11:24; Matt. 19:24; Luke 16:19-31
weeping. John 11:35; 20:11; Acts 20:19; Rom. 12:15; Phil. 3:18
whirlwind. Jer. 23:19; 30:23; Hosea 8:7; Ezek. 1:4
whosoever. Deut. 18:19; John 8:34; Acts 10:43; 1 John 5:1; Rev. 22:17
widow. Acts 6:1-7; 1 Tim. 5:3-16; James 1:27
wisdom. Prov. 1:7; 3:13-26; 24:3-7; Rom. 16:19; Col. 3:16; James 1:5
witchcraft. Ex. 22:18; Lev. 19:31; 20:6-7; Micah 5:12
witnessing. Acts 1:8; 10:39; 22:15; 23:11; 1 Peter 3:15-16
works, good. Eph. 2:10; Col. 1:10; 1 Thes. 1:3, 7-8; James 1:22-27; 3:17-18
worldliness. John 15:19; Rom. 12:2; Titus 2:12; 3:3; 1 John 2:15-17
worship of God. Deut. 5:7-10; John 4:24; Acts 17:24-25; Heb. 10:25; Rev. 22:8
wrath of God. Deut. 9:7; Isa. 13:9; Rom. 1:18; Eph. 5:6

Z

zeal. Isa. 9:7; Rom. 10:2; 12:11; 1 Cor. 15:58; Tit. 2:14

www.ingramcontent.com/pod-product-compliance
Lightning Source LLC
Chambersburg PA
CBHW051046160426
43193CB00010B/1081